ETHNIC CONFLICT AND INTERNATIONAL RELATIONS

To Mary, Rachel and Sara

It is not some upheaval or uprising
Can lead us to the new life we desire
But open truth and magnanimity
And the storm within a soul afire.

(Boris Pasternak: After the Storm)

Ethnic Conflict and International Relations

Second Edition

STEPHEN RYAN
University of Ulster

Dartmouth

Aldershot • Brookfield USA • Singapore • Sydney

Published by
Dartmouth Publishing Company Limited
Gower House
Croft Road
Aldershot
Hants GU11 3HR
England

Dartmouth Publishing Company
Old Post Road
Brookfield
Vermont 05036
USA

British Library Cataloguing in Publication Data
Ryan, Stephen 1956-
   Ethnic conflict and international relations–2nd ed.
   1. Interethnic relations & race relations
   I. Title
   305.8

Library of Congress Cataloging-in-Publication Data
Ryan, Stephen, 1956-
   Ethnic conflict and international relations / Stephen Ryan.– 2nd ed.
      p.   cm.
   Includes bibliographical references.
   ISBN 1-85521-650-7 : $59.95 (est.)
   1. Ethnic relations. 2. International relations. 3. Conflict
management.   I. Title.
GN496.R93   1995
305.8–dc20   94-39415
                                                              CIP

ISBN 1 85521 650 7

Printed in Great Britain by Antony Rowe Ltd, Chippenham, Wiltshire

Contents

Part III: The United Nations and Ethnic Conflict

Preface to second edition

No writer that I know enjoys picking over the bones of his previously published work. Yet, when David Irwin of Dartmouth offered me that opportunity to write a second edition of this work I grasped the nettle for three reasons. The first was the changes that have taken place in international politics since 1989 and the impact this has had on the global awareness that ethnic conflicts are now one of the key problems for international society. The ethnic blindness that characterised a lot of post-war thinking about politics has now disappeared with a vengeance. The deep sigh of relief that followed the end of the cold war very quickly led to a sharp intake of breath as we all started to realise that the post cold-war system was more complicated and confusing than the one it replaced and, for many people, offered even less security. Der Derian (1992) captured this neatly when he stated that historical endings collapse into ambiguous beginnings. What is clear is that the cold war sustained some ethnic conflicts and restrained others. The end of this confrontation has therefore made it easier to resolve some conflicts that were previously thought of as intractable (South Africa, Palestine, Lebanon and Ethiopia) but it has released forces in other regions that have fuelled violent confrontation, most notably in the former Soviet Union and the former Yugoslavia. The way we refer to these two regions is itself symptomatic of the uncertain world we live in.

In the Sudan, Kashmir, Kurdistan, Angola, Northern Ireland, East

Timor, the Basque region of Spain conflicts have continued unresolved for a generation or more. The collapse of the Soviet Union has added new cases such as Georgia and Nagorno Karabakh to an already long list. In Sri Lanka a suicide bomber murdered President Premadasa in 1993 and the Tamil-Sinhalese violence has continued. In India the violence that erupted around the destruction of the Babri Masjid temple in Ayodhya caused the death of 1,700 people and demonstrated how fragile the Hindu-Moslem peace was in this country. Ethnic conflict has followed fast on the heels of the Soviet withdrawal from Afghanistan and violence has flared again in Burundi and Djibouti. There have been reports of ethnic cleansing not just in the former Yugoslavia, but also in the Shaba province of Zaire and in Azerbaijan. Political repression has continued in Burma, China, the Punjab, Bhutan and Kossovo. As a result of all of these conflicts millions have been killed or maimed or made homeless.

The second reason for this revised study is that it provided an incentive to come to terms with the large amount of excellent studies of ethnic conflict that have appeared since the original edition came out in 1990. In fact, the literature on ethnicity has proliferated at a such a rate that no one, I suspect, can now keep up with the new ideas and facts that are appearing daily. This work has not even attempted this impossible feat. Here I draw on published material (and some UN documents) that I consider especially important, but in the knowledge that there will be many significant books and articles that I have missed.

The third reason for embarking on this task is that it allowed me to correct many of the mistakes and faulty arguments of the first edition. Despite the faults of the first edition, it is my belief that its main conclusion, that the interstate system is poorly equipped to respond constructively and creatively to ethnic conflict, was a valid one. The events in Bosnia and Hercegovina would confirm this view. Indeed, it may be that international norms and institutions are now even more inadequate than they have ever been. The revisions offered here continue the attempt to suggest ways that the global system can improve its attempts to resolve ethnic conflicts.

In the past three years I have incurred more debts that should be acknowledged. The editorial staff at Dartmouth have been helpful and have prevented the author making several embarrassing mistakes. Many of the chapters offered here first saw the light of day as conference papers. I would especially like to thank the organisers and participants at the following gatherings: the ICON sessions at the International Peace Research Association conferences in Groningen and Kyoto; two workshops at International Alert's London headquarters; the conference on Ethnicity, Identity and Nationalism in South Africa at Rhodes University, Grahamstown; the meetings in Loccum and Ankara on the peaceful settlement of conflict organised by the Helsinki Citizens' Assembly; and the International Conference on Democracy and Minorities in Post-totalitarian states at the Institute of Ethnology and Anthropology of the Russian Academy of Sciences. Some of these original papers have been published elsewhere (Ryan 1992, 1993). The INCORE project at the University of Ulster, led by John Darby, has provided a fascinating chance to be informed about ethnic conflict. I would also like to express my thanks to John Vincent, and add my voice to all the others who, after his tragic death, acknowledged the contribution he made to both their own personal development and to the discipline of international relations.

Evniki was probably most responsible for stimulating my interest in ethnic conflict, and it was good to meet her and her two children, George and Maria, on a recent visit to Cyprus. Over the past three years I have taught a course at the University of Ulster on ethnic conflict. I once heard Ed Garcia say that the first responsibility of a teacher is to learn, and this course has provided me with a rich opportunity to do so. The more tedious moments in preparing this manuscript were lightened by friends who were able to drag me away from the word processor for coffee and conversation. But for them, and especially Sally and Jack, the book may have been finished sooner, but the journey would have been far less enjoyable.

ix

Preface to first edition

Even a brief glance at the newspaper headlines in the first two months of the new decade will reveal the continuing importance of ethnic conflict for politics both within and between states. The continuing violence in Beirut, Sri Lanka, Sudan and Kossovo; the intifadah on the West Bank and Gaza and the divisions within the Israeli government over the Egyptian peace plan; border clashes in Kashmir; talks between Hungary and Rumania on the fate of the Magyar minority in Transylvania; the breakdown and resumption of intercommunal talks in Cyprus; Eritrean rebels claiming military victories over the Ethiopian government and attacks on food convoys carrying food supplied by the international community; unrest in Azerbaijan and Tajikstan and moves towards independence in Latvia, Lithuania and Estonia; Chinese fears that such unrest in the USSR will spill over into China; terrorist attacks in Northern Ireland and England, Spain and the Punjab.

This study cannot hope to do justice to all the forms and instances of such conflict. Time and resources are limited. Language barriers exists. Access to accurate information is often impossible from a distance. Therefore, here we will limit ourselves to one aspect of ethnic conflict. This is the question of what can be done to reduce the dangers and the suffering associated with violent ethnic conflict, with particular attention being directed at the interface of domestic and international politics. Nevertheless, even with such a narrow focus it is necessary to be selective, for there are many such conflicts at present. Here, therefore, we will draw on information mainly from the conflicts in Cyprus, Lebanon, Palestine, Northern Ireland and Sri Lanka; though other cases will be introduced from time to time.

This book is not meant to be a series of case studies, however. Rather, we will examine specific ethnic conflicts in order to see what common processes exist in the areas of conflict escalation and conflict management and resolution, and we will use these processes to construct a model of ethnic conflict resolution which will allow us to throw light on the relative merits of certain types of third party involvement. Such an approach, inevitably, gives rise to an abstract and over-simplified analysis. But this study is not intended to provide a definitive account of third party involvement in ethnic conflict resolution. It is meant to stimulate debate about the chances of constructive involvement in such conflicts in response to the terrible dangers posed by violent ethnic conflict. What follows, therefore, is deliberately offered as a target, should others deem it worthy of taking pot shots at. If it contributes to the analysis of ethnic conflict resolution in any way, this author will be content. All that is possible here is to set out an open ended account of an ongoing project.

Acknowledgements

My thanks to the following individuals and organizations who contributed to this study.

For providing me with the finance to undertake research on specific areas dealt with in this book I am grateful to the ESRC for a grant that allowed me to spend nine weeks in the US (award number R00023 1101). Grants were also provided by the MaCrea Research Award and by the Research Sub-Committee, Faculty of Humanities, University of Ulster.

For granting me access to materials and for their assistance in my research efforts I thank the staff at the following libraries: the British Library of Political and Economic Science; the School of Oriental and African Studies; the Conflict Research Society Library (then at City University); the New York Central Library; the LIbrary of Congress; the UN Information Office (London); and the Dag Hammerskjold Library.

For contributing to the development of the ideas in this book I am grateful to numerous people who commented on various papers presented at several conferences and seminars. An early version of the arguments contained in chapters one and two of this book was published in the *Review of International Studies* in July, 1988. My thanks to the three anonymous referees and to Professor John Vincent, who commented on the first draft of that paper. I would also like to thank

Michael Banks, who, as my supervisor, started me on the road which has led a decade later to this book. At the UN I am especially grateful to Jurgen Dedring for ensuring that my visit to New York was a success. My thanks also to the various people who found time in their busy schedules to see me during that visit to Manhattan and Washington. They include Adamantia Pollis, J-C. Aimee, Alberto Charles, Tom Colossi, G. da Cunha, G. Feissel, M.L. Hanley, Hurst Hannum, Lois Jensen, James Jonah, Paul Martin, B.G. Ramcharan, Laura Reanda, and Tom Weiss.

Patricia Doherty helped type some of these pages and offered invaluable assistance on the word processor. Finally, my thanks to the staff and students of Magee College for creating a unique atmosphere in which to work, and, at times, to play. All errors and mistakes contained in these pages are, of course, my own responsibility.

Introduction

We need a new sense of political values. These times require a different order of thinking. We cannot expect to meet our problems with a few inherited ideas, uncriticised assumptions, a foggy vocabulary, and a machine philosophy. Our political thinking needs the infusion of contemporary insights. (Walter Lippmann, *A Preface to Politics*)

The new world order...died somewhere along the road from Vukovar to Sarajevo. (Jean, 1992, p. 18)

Introduction

Nowhere is the need for contemporary insights more urgent than in the study of ethnic conflict. Here, perhaps more than anywhere else, there is a feeling that inherited ways of thinking about politics are proving inadequate; the 'old vessels cannot be stretched to the present need' (Lippmann, 1962, p. 129). Just over a generation ago Hannah Arendt (1973, pp. 17-18) claimed that revolutionary war would replace interstate war as the dominant form of contemporary political violence. Clearly this has not been the case. Instead, if any one form of violence has been more prevalent than any other, it seems to be ethnic conflict.

1

Today, this occurs in three main types of situation. In the democratic west, sometimes called the first world, an 'ethnic revival' has taken place; a development characterised by a new found assertiveness among various minority ethnic groups. These include the Basques and Catalans in Spain, the Bretons and the Corsicans in France, and the Welsh and the Scots in the UK.

In the third world, states that inherited artificial frontiers that did not reflect pre-existing cultural divisions, have frequently experienced serious ethnic violence as they struggled to adjust to a post-colonial political process. This, of course, is not just a phenomenon found in the past generation. Over a million Hindus and Moslems were killed in the violence that accompanied the partition of the Indian sub-continent in the late 1940s. Up to 100,000 Karens were killed in Burma between 1948 and 1952. The problems between Arab and Jew in Palestine began during the British mandate period. However, such ethnic conflicts seem to have proliferated since 1960, when the process of decolonization reached its height. There have been bitter and protracted ethnic conflicts in the Congo, Nigeria, Bangladesh, Sudan, India (Kashmir and the Punjab, for example), Sri Lanka, Iraq, Ethiopia, Uganda, Lebanon, Liberia and a host of other states. Very few of these have been resolved in a satisfactory manner. In many the minority group, or groups, feel that they have been more badly treated since independence than before it, and have come to regard the dominant cultural group as new colonisers

Finally, with the liberalization of central and eastern Europe and the break-up of the Soviet Union, the second world has entered a period of renewed ethnic conflict. Central and eastern Europe was, of course, the main focus of concern about the damaging impact of ethnic conflict on interstate politics between the two world wars. However, with the imposition of Soviet hegemony over these states such conflicts were not allowed open expression, either within the Soviet Union itself, or within or between its eastern bloc satellites. The only exception to this has been Yugoslavia, which was outside Soviet hegemonic control and which experienced serious problems with its Albanian minority in Kossovo. Now all this seems to have changed, and we have recently seen a re-emergence of a whole host of ethnic conflicts that include the violent disintegration of Yugoslavia; the Bulgarian oppression of its Turkish minority; conflict between Rumania and Hungary about the fate of the Hungarian minority in Transylvania; and conflicts in Georgia, Azerbaijan, Moldova and other parts of the former USSR. So Vaclev Havel (Nato Review, April 1991, p. 33) was surely correct to state, in an address to the NATO Council in March 1991, that one of the most serious problems in Europe has arisen because the 'long suppressed desire of the peoples of Central and Eastern Europe for self-determination has suddenly made itself felt in all its unthought-of urgency, a number of times turning into nationalism, xenophobia and intolerance towards other minorities'.

Therefore, wherever one looks in the world there seems to be an unresolved ethnic conflict underway. It is clear, therefore, that the term nation-state is a misnomer in the vast majority of cases. In one study, for example, Connor (1972) found that of 132 states examined only twelve were 'essentially homogeneous from an ethnic viewpoint'. In another study by Nielsson (1985), it was found that out of 164 states studied only 45 could be described as single nation-group states. These are states where between 95 to 100 per cent of the population are from a single national group. Therefore, Nielsson (1985, p. 33) claimed that 'the conventional concept of the nation-state fits only one-quarter of the members of the global state system'.

It is inevitable that the problems experienced in a world where there is not a neat convergence between state frontiers and cultural boundaries will affect interstate relations, just as it is inevitable that the interstate system will affect how states are able to cope with the demands of a multicultural reality. However, before we can examine these issues it is necessary to look more closely at how ethnicity and nationalism have been defined.

Here we face a problem caused by a misuse of terms which has resulted in linguistic confusion. For as Connor (1978) has pointed out, the word nationalism has come to mean identification with the state, not loyalty to the nation. Thus we talk of the League of *Nations*, the United *Nations*, inter*national* law, the *national* interest, inter*national* politics, when we are really referring to states. Furthermore, this hijacking of the term nation by states has meant that true nations have to be described as something else; usually as sub-nations or as tribes. Connor (1990, p. 14) has also written about this 'Alice-in- Wonderland world in which nation usually means state, in which nation-state usually means multination state, in which nationalism usually means loyalty to the state and in which ethnicity, primordialism, pluralism, tribalism, regionalism, communalism, parochialism and sub-nationalism usually mean loyalty to the nation'. It would be nice to think that the use of the term nation could be reclaimed, however its present use seems so firmly fixed that this is unlikely. Perhaps one should bow to the inevitable in this matter and use terms like international politics when examining what should really be called interstate relations.

For the purpose of this study an ethnic group is taken to be a group of people who define themselves as distinct from other groups because of cultural differences. Gellner (1988, p. 274) has written that

Culture can be defined as the set of concepts in terms of which a given population thinks and acts. A concept is a shared way of grouping experiences and of acting and reacting, and usually has a name. A culture is a system, and not just a collection of concepts: the notions which constitute it are interrelated and interdependent in various complex ways, and it is plausible to suppose that they could not exist at all in isolation.

Raymond Williams (1989, p. 4) has attempted to define culture as follows:

> Culture is ordinary: that is the first fact. Every human society has its own shape, its own purposes, its own meanings. Every human society expresses these, in institutions, and in arts and learning... A culture has two aspects: the known meanings and directions, which its members are trained to; the new observations and meanings which are offered and tested... We use the word culture in these two senses: to mean a whole way of life - the common meanings; to mean the arts and learning - the special process of discovery and creative effort. Some writers reserve the word for one or other of these senses; I insist on both, and on the significance of their conjunction. The questions I ask about our culture are questions about our general and common purposes, yet also questions about deep personal meanings. Culture is ordinary, in every society and in every mind.

One obvious aspect of culture is well worth pointing out. That is that it is something valued by the majority of people who possess it even if the culture is not valued by outsiders. Therefore, serious threats to cultural continuity will usually be resisted. Cultures, as Williams has pointed out, are adaptive, creative and can be modified, but they tend to want to repel full frontal assaults on their core values.

Cultural differences can arise from a number of factors, but the most important seem to be language, religion, historical experience, geographical isolation, race and kinship. These can combine in a number of different ways so as to give rise to a unique set of beliefs, values, habits, customs and norms. Smith (1986a) has recently suggested that a distinctive shared culture is not the only component of an 'ethnie'. Other components are a collective name, a myth of common descent, a shared history, a sense of solidarity and an association with a specific territory which the group may, or may not, be in possession of. Nevertheless, a distinctive culture seems to be the most important component of an ethnic identity. As Stavenhagen (1990, p.2) has noted

when I speak of culture I mean the broad spectrum of hum..
activities, symbols, values, and artefacts that identify a human
group and distinguish it from others.... Ethnic groups, or ethnies,
then, may be thought of as collectivities that identify themselves
or are identified by others precisely in such cultural terms.

This study will not examine why an identification in terms of ethnicity
has become so important in contemporary politics, but we will note that
there is a strong tendency to organise political life according to cultural
boundaries. In the words of Horowitz (1985, p. 334), in many
multi-ethnic states ethnic identity tends to 'preempt the organizational
field' so as to 'crowd out parties founded on another basis'. When an
ethnic group organises itself politically and adopts a programme calling
for a separate state to coincide with cultural boundaries it can then be
termed a national group. For, according to Gellner (1983), the key to
national ideology is the claim 'one nation, one state'. This, in part, is
what Connor (1978, p. 388) seems to have meant when he referred to a
nation as a 'self aware ethnic group'.

However, very often ethnic groups will not demand outright
independence. In these circumstances the use of the term ethnic
minority may be more appropriate. (Though we should note that a
subordinate ethnic group can, in a few circumstances, also be in the
majority). The situation is often complicated because within a distinct
culture there will often be no agreement on the preferred constitutional
status of the group. Smooha (1989 and 1992) has provided a useful
classification of these different opinions in his study of Arab-Jewish
relations in Israel. He has referred to four distinct attitudes which he
has termed: accommodationist (accept the status quo); reservationist
(favouring 'critical' cooperation with the status quo); oppositionist
(radical change, but within existing state boundaries); and rejectionist
(which, as the name implies, rejects the legitimacy of the existing state).
In practise it will be extremely difficult to decide which of these groups
will be in the majority at any particular moment, and their relative
influence will change over time as individuals harden or soften their
attitudes. As one commentator on Sri Lanka has noted, Tamils tended to
be 'apolitical if left alone, nationalist if bothered, and accommodating if
it will do any good' (Kuruvaltampi as quoted in Whitaker, 1990, p.
151). It is, therefore, not always possible to determine if a subordinate
cultural group should be described as an ethnic or a national minority.
Here, since according to our definition, a national group is a special
type of ethnic group, the term ethnic conflict will usually be used in a
way that is meant to be applicable to both types of situation.

The impact of ethnic conflict on interstate politics

There has been a tendency in the international relations literature to ignore the issue of ethnic conflict. Whereas numerous works examined the 'minorities problem' in the inter-war period, ethnic issues were almost completely ignored by most, if not all, the standard texts on international politics between the second world war and the 1970s. Even for international relations specialists who wish to restrict the boundaries of their discipline to the study of interstate relations, this is surprising to this author, even if supporters of the narrow approach deny that there is anything odd about this (James, 1989a). For ethnic conflict can have a major impact on the interstate system in a number of ways. Some of these can now be examined.

(a) The problem of unstable multi-national states

Stanley Hoffmann has stated that the world is full of Austria-Hungaries. What he means by this, of course, is that there are many states in the world experiencing ethnic conflict where violence threatens to spill over into interstate relations. Urquhart (1987, p. 199) has referred to such states as 'detonators'. Azar (1990, p. 2) has pointed out there are over seventy identity related protracted conflicts in the world which present a serious challenge to the world community. For instability in certain states may tempt outside powers to intervene in these conflicts to pursue their own self-interest, so triggering a spiral of conflict escalation that can lead to a more general war. The instability in the Lebanon, for example, dragged in Israel and Syria, and there was always the worry that this could have involved the superpowers in a direct confrontation. The Cyprus conflict led to a major confrontation between Greece and Turkey that stopped just short of actual war, whilst in Bangladesh in 1971 an internal war of secession resulted in Indian intervention, and so in a wider conflict between Pakistan and India. There is a danger that many other ethnic conflicts could also result in regional or systemic instability.

(b) The problem of multi-state nations

This arises when an ethnic group is spread over more than one state. This 'ethnic overhang' can give rise to a number of different situations. One nation-state can be artificially divided into two by victorious powers after a war so that two new states are created. This is what happened to Germany and to Korea after the second world war. This artificial division meant that both states were, at various times, centre stage in the cold war. The issue of German reunification was the most

6

important item on the agenda of superpower politics in the immediate post cold war era, and the division of Korea remains an important item of the agenda of Asian regional politics.

Alternatively, an ethnic group may be divided up between several states, and will be a majority in none of them. This was the fate of the Kurds after the first world war, when they became a minority group in Turkey, Iran, Iraq and Syria. Similarly, the Azerbaijanis were, until recently, a minority in both the Soviet Union and Iran and the 100,000 South Ossetians are now fighting a war against Georgia in order to join with the 600,000 North Ossetians, who are located in Russia.

However, the most frequent scenario is where a dominant group in one state is separated from co-nationals, who make up a minority group in one or more other states. Such a situation can often give rise to irredentism, which is the desire to redraw the existing political boundaries in order to 'recover' these 'lost' co-nationals. The word itself is derived from the Italian for 'unredeemed'. Such movements have an obvious impact on interstate relations, especially when an aggressive and expansionist irredentist foreign policy results in war.

There have been several examples of militant irredentist movements giving rise to interstate war (Snyder, 1982b). The Greek government pursued such a policy, known as the *Megali Idea,* in the nineteenth and twentieth centuries. During this period they attempted to obtain or to take from the Ottoman Empire territories which contained a large Greek population (such as Crete, Anatolia, the Dodecanese). In post-war Europe Hitler's policy towards neighbouring states was inspired, in part, by the idea of the *volkgemeinnschaft,* the vision of a single German state that would contain Germans who were then living as minorities in states such as Poland and Czechoslovakia. Somalia has also pursued an irredentist policy in the Horn of Africa which led it into a major war with Ethiopia in the 1970s over the Ogaden region. Indeed, Neuberger (1986, p. 37) quotes a Somali proverb: 'how can an amputated man sleep comfortably at night'. Syria's irredentist claim over parts of Lebanon have been used to justify its intervention in this troubled country, whilst Pakistan's claim over Kashmir remains an irritant in this state's relations with India. The territory of Macedonia is claimed by Albania, Bulgaria and figures in the dreams of Greater Serbian nationalists. About 20 per cent of ethnic Magyars live outside Hungary, a statistic that leads some observers to predict the rise of Hungarian irredentism. This attitude is also on the rise in the former Soviet Union as groups question the inherited boundaries of the recently independent republics. Armenia is fighting a war against Azerbaijan, in order to reclaim the Armenians living in Nagorno-Karabakh.

Other, less militant, examples of irredentism exist. One example is

7

the claim over the territory of Northern Ireland set out in articles two and three of the Irish constitution of 1937. Article two claims that the national territory consists of the whole island of Ireland. Article three states that the actual practise of sovereignty is limited to the 26 counties of Ireland pending the reintegration of 'the national territory'. In this case, however, the government of Ireland has not been prepared to use physical force to make good the claim.

(c) Ethnic conflict and international terrorism

States have clearly had to respond to what Der Derian (1992, p. 105) has termed ethno-terrorism, which often operates across state boundaries. Frequently there has been little interest in explaining the origins of terrorist groups. Instead, the psychology of the individual is explored, or the terrorist is depicted as a member of a 'red network' (Rubenstein, 1987, p.51). The socio-enonomic and political environment that produces him or her is ignored. In other words, terrorism is seen as a disease in itself, rather than the symptom of a deeper problem. However, if we do explore the origins and motives of international terrorist groups we find that many international atrocities are carried out by people purporting to represent repressed ethnic groups and who see themselves as the vanguard of the struggle for national self-determination. For this reason Sikh terrorists planted a bomb on an Indian Boeing 747 that exploded off the coast of Ireland in 1985, killing 329 innocent people. The right to fight for self-determination seems to have been the justification for the bomb placed on the Pan Am jumbo that exploded over Lockerbie at Christmas 1988, causing the deaths of 270 people. It is the justification given by the Provisional IRA for their attacks outside and inside the UK and by the Armenian terrorist group (ASALA), who have carried out numerous attacks on Turkish diplomats. Jewish terrorist groups such as the Irgun and the Stern Gang felt justified in using violence to establish the state of Israel, and the PLO have used the argument to excuse their terrorist attacks on this Israeli state.

International terrorism has been seen to present a challenge to the international order for the reasons set out by Vincent (1986, pp. 2-3). These are that terrorism: interrupts the conduct of everyday international life; undermines the claim of states to enjoy the monopoly of the legitimate use of force; threatens the system of reciprocal restraints that exist between states (e.g. by triggering intervention); and has even been depicted as a threat to the security of the system as a whole. International responses to terrorism can take many forms. Extradition agreements can be signed between governments. The cooperation between state security services can be improved (e.g. the

TREVI process in the European Union). Anti-terrorist activities have even involved armed attacks against another sovereign state, as was the case with South African and Israeli attacks on their neighbouring states and the US bombing of Libya.

(d) The oppression of ethnic minorities

Terrorism, however, is a policy that can be pursued by governments as well as by members of dissatisfied ethnic groups. It is important to remember that victims of ethnic conflict are not just killed or maimed (either physically or psychologically) as a result of highly visible intercommunal clashes. This can frequently happen in state detention centres, or through the activities of death squads, or by deliberately depriving individuals of the basic requirements of life. Less dramatically, the oppression of ethnic groups can manifest itself in discrimination in employment, housing, access to education and disenfranchisement.

Even a cursory examination of the recent experience of multi-ethnic states will show how many governments have pursued policies that result in severe human rights abuses. Gurr (1989) has claimed that three-quarters of the 126 larger countries in the world have at least one minority at risk, and minorities are especially at risk in sub-Saharan Africa, eastern Europe and Asia. Amnesty International has expressed concern about these gross violations of human rights in ethnic conflict situations, including Somalia, Ethiopia, Sudan, Sri Lanka (both the treatment of Tamils and the state response to opposition from within the Sinhalese community), Punjab, Burma, East Timor, Northern Ireland, USSR, Kossovo, Tibet, Burundi, Mauritania, Chad, Kurdish regions of Turkey, Iran and Iraq, Bulgaria, Guatemala and the West Bank and Gaza (see e.g. Amnesty International 1992). In fact at their Yokohama Council meeting in 1991 the statute of this non-governmental organization (NGO) was amended to include explicit reference to discrimination by reason of ethnic origin, colour or religion. The precise nature of the ethnic oppression might vary, but such examples share a common destructive element which gives rise either to death or oppression. The worst human rights abuses seem to be associated with the following strategies.

(i) Forced Assimilation. Forced assimilation, sometimes termed cultural genocide or ethnocide or cultural colonialism, involves an attempt by a dominant ethnic group to destroy the culture of certain other ethnic groups and to force them to adopt the dominant culture. The use of a distinctive language, religion and specific customs will be banned and penalties imposed for expressions of the culture under

9

threat. The dominant culture will become the official culture and this will then be reflected in schooling, the media and public interaction. Sometimes the policy of forced assimilation will involve the flooding of areas of cultural difference with people belonging to the dominant ethnic group. Up to 400,000 Bengali settlers have been moved into tribal areas of Bangladesh (Chaudhuri, 1991, p. 141; Survival International, 1992, p. 3). The Chinese are supposed to have resorted to this tactic in the minority regions of their country, especially in Tibet after 1950, when China re-incorporated the region and subjected Tibetan culture to fierce assault (Heberer, 1989, p. 96-7). The Ethiopian government attempted to move Amhars into the Ogaden region, where the local culture is mainly Somali, and Javanese have been moved to East Timor by the Indonesian government.

One aspect of such assimilationist policies is that in a very real sense subordinate ethnic groups find that it is illegal for them to be 'themselves'. This is why a policy of forced assimilation is both inhuman and likely to be resisted. In Franco's Spain, for example, there was a ban on Basque books, journals, newspapers, street signs, sermons and even tombstones. Anyone caught speaking the Basque language, Eskedun, in public could be fined. The result was the growth of the Basque terrorist group (ETA) and strong nationalist sentiment in the region.

In communist Albania ethnic Greeks were not allowed to practise their Christian religion and Greek names were changed. In Turkey there was a long-standing policy which penalised the expression of Kurdish culture. According to a Helsinki Watch report as late as 1988 in Kurdish areas in the south east of the country the use of the Kurdish language was forbidden; village names had been changed; people were arrested for calling themselves Kurdish on census forms; and reference to the Kurds was prohibited by Turkish law (Helsinki Watch, 1988). As a result of such policies Turkey became involved in a protracted guerrilla war against Kurdish rebels.

In communist Bulgaria the Turkish minority, which makes up about ten per cent of the population, was subjected to a campaign to 'Bulgarize' them after 1984. This involved the enforced change of names; a ban on the Turkish language and dress (such as the traditional trousers, the *shalvari)*; the closure of Mosques and the prohibition of circumcision; a ban on the printing and importation of the Koran; the prohibition of the burial of the dead with Islamic rights; and the exclusion of a question on ethnic origin from the 1985 census. This, inevitably, led to resistance by the ethnic Turks, which in turn caused the Bulgarian government to confiscate land and to expel some of the Turkish leaders. The American human rights group, Helsinki Watch (1987), estimated that hundreds of Turks were killed resisting

10

government actions, which led to widespread international condemnation (the European Community postponed trade negotiations with Bulgaria in 1989) and severely strained Turkish-Bulgarian relations. By the end of 1989 it was estimated that up to one-quarter of Bulgarian Turks had left the country. Poulton (1991, p.156) estimates that 300,000 were ejected between June and August 1989 alone, though he also claims that many of these subsequently returned to Bulgaria. It may be that the post-Communist Bulgarian government will be able to stop these policies. Already, forced assimilation has ceased and original names have been restored. However, recent public demonstrations against a more humane treatment of Bulgarian Turks show that this will not be an easy policy to implement.

Another tactic of forced assimilation is the movement of ethnic minorities out of their traditional areas of residence. Stalin, for example, used forced internal transfer of peoples in his dealings with some of the minorities in the USSR. The government of Saddam Hussein has used it more recently against the Kurds. The latest phase of the forced relocation of the Kurds in Iraq began after the break-down of negotiations between Saddam Hussein and the Patriotic Union of Kurdistan in 1985. The policy involved moving Kurds from isolated towns and villages in the mountains to large, lowland housing complexes in the plains. This would cut them off from direct contact with neighbouring countries and allow them to be placed under more effective surveillance and control. To accomplish this thousands of the old towns and villages were destroyed, including schools and mosques. Up to 200,000 Kurds were relocated in this manner. These enforced movements were accompanied by mass killings and disappearances. Poisoned gas was also used against civilians in an effort to encourage the Kurds to make such a move (Gunter, 1993; Middle East Watch, 1990, ch. 5). According to one source at least 100,000 Kurdish civilians were murdered in 1988, when this operation was in its most intense phase (in Gunter, 1993, p. 88). This included the gassing of the town of Haabja, which killed over 5,000 Kurds.

Some recent reports from the Nuba Mountain region of the Sudan claim that Saddam-like policies are being implemented by the Arab dominated government against the Bantu speaking Nuba (*Independent*, 18 February, 1993). Nor should one forget that millions of black South Africans were relocated to homelands in the name of apartheid, though in this case the aim was to preserve difference, not eliminate it. In Malawi in 1975 President Banda ordered the country's Asian population to move to the cities of Blantyre, Lilongwe and Zomba, or face expulsion. He thought it would be easier to control them there.

(ii) Expulsion. The mention of the Moslem exodus from Bulgaria leads us on to our next objectionable strategy. Expulsion is the opposite of forced assimilation for instead of trying to eradicate ethnic differences through forcing different groups to abandon their culture, forced exclusion tries to remove these groups altogether from the state. Assimilation involves the rejection of cultural differences, expulsion involves the ejection of those who are culturally different. One of the best known cases in the UK was the expulsion of about 74,000 Asians from Uganda in 1972. Cases on a larger scale have also occurred in the twentieth century. They include the expulsion of Greeks from Anatolia after the Greek-Turkish war that followed the collapse of the Ottoman Empire and the expulsion of nine million Germans from Eastern Europe at the end of the Second World War. In the former case the Greek Government had sought to annex Anatolia after the Great War, when Turkey was weak and suffering from internal turmoil. The Greeks were inspired by the irredentist vision of the *Megali Idea*, the dream of a revived Hellenic-Christian state that would encompass all Greeks living in other states in the eastern Mediterranean. Unfortunately for the Greeks, they were defeated by the forces of Kemal Ataturk and there occurred instead a sort of *Megali Idea* in reverse, as over one million Greeks were expelled from Anatolia and moved to the existing Greek state. This expulsion was made legitimate by the Treaty of Lausanne in 1923, which euphemistically referred to the mass exodus from Anatolia as a population exchange. The mass expulsion of Germans from eastern Europe in 1945 was also endorsed by the great powers at the Potsdam meeting at the end of World War Two.

Forced expulsions are not just a thing of the past. They remain an issue in the politics of several states. In Western Europe neo-Fascist parties are growing in strength on a platform of forced 'repatriation' of immigrant workers (West Indians, Turks, Algerians etc.). In 1969-70 Ghana expelled about 155,000 foreign workers, many of whom had lived in this state for most of their lives. Thirteen years later the Nigerian government expelled up to two million foreign workers, who came mainly from Ghana. This action was undertaken despite a 1978 Organisation of African Unity Resolution condemning the arbitrary expulsion of national groups and Article 25 of the Draft African Charter of Human and Peoples' Rights, which was meant to prohibit mass expulsions.

Recently, in the former Yugoslavia, the policy of expulsion has been given the ominous name of ethnic cleansing. It is a phrase originating with the Serbs, but it is a tactic employed by all sides in this bitter war. According to figures produced by the UN High Commissioner for Refugees (UNHCR), this has resulted in the creation of at least 2.2

million refugees (*Independent on Sunday*, 19 July,1992).

(iii) Genocide. When forced assimilation has failed or is regarded as unpalatable, and when forced expulsions are impossible then a dominant group may attempt to eliminate a cultural group through mass murder. There is a strong link between ethnic discrimination and genocide (Fein, 1993, p. xiii), and two groups are especially thought to be at risk; those who are economically superfluous, such as the Red Indians of North America or the Amazonian Indians of South America, and those who have jobs that the dominant groups want - the so called middleman minorities such as the Jews in Germany or the Chinese in Indonesia. Kuper (1981) points out that groups pressing for self-determination are also vulnerable.

There was notable lack of interest in genocide in social science circles between the late 1940s and the early 1970s. This was the period when the assimilationist paradigm was dominant. Recently, however, there have been numerous studies of the phenomenon (e.g. Fein, 1992; Horowitz, 1980; Jonassohn and Chalk, 1987; Kuper, 1981 and 1985; and Porter, 1982). The term genocide was invented at the end of the second world war by the Polish academic Raphael Lemkin, whose family were murdered by the Nazis. He was one of three jurists consulted during the drafting of the original UN draft of the Genocide Convention by Emile Giraud. The first modern example of genocide was the massacre of 1.8 million Armenians by Turkish forces in 1915. Fein (1993, p. 2) points out how these mass killings were observed by German officers, and she also suggests that the lack of international reaction had an impact on Hitler, who in 1939 thought that Germany could get away with the mass murder of Jews because 'who, after all, speaks today, of the annihilation of the Armenians'.

The Holocaust is, of course, the most infamous case of genocide, but it is not the only one in living memory. Other twentieth century victims of genocide include the ethnic groups in the Soviet Union (such as the Balkars, Chechins and Tartars) who became the victims of Stalinism through mass starvation, murder and forced relocation (20 million deaths); the people of Tibet following a Chinese crack-down in 1959; the Bengalis killed by the West Pakistan army in Bangladesh in 1971 (1.2 to 3 million deaths); the Hutus murdered by Tutsis in Burundi in 1972 (up to 200,000 deaths); and the Ache Indians in Paraguay.[1]

At present much international attention is focused on the Indonesian treatment of the people of East Timor, who some claim, have been subjected to genocidal policies since the Indonesian invasion in December 1975. These policies have resulted in 200,000 deaths. After the invasion, undertaken using military equipment supplied by the West, the territory of East Timor was formally made the twenty seventh province of Indonesia in July 1976. Despite attempts by Jakarta to isolate this region, recent reports have indicated that the local people are still being subjected to great brutality. There are stories of disappearances, deliberate food shortages, forced labour, murders and torture during custody. In 1987 the UN Sub-commission for the Prevention of Discrimination and the Protection of Minorities called on Indonesia to facilitate, without restrictions, the work of humanitarian agencies in East Timor, but that request has so far been ignored. Meanwhile the bitter war between Indonesia and the East Timor resistance group Fretilin seems set to continue for some time (see e.g. Budiardjo and Liong, 1984). Yet western governments have turned a blind eye to human rights abuses because they value their relations with Indonesia, which is a strong regional ally and a rich source of materials and markets.

All these destructive responses to cultural difference often involve breaches of human rights standards as set out in the 1948 Universal Declaration of Human Rights and the two Human Rights Covenants of 1966, which unlike the 1948 Declaration, are legally binding on signatories). Gross violations of human rights are now considered by many to be the legitimate concern of the international community, and there is a growing international trend in support of economic and military intervention against states that do not live up to existing international standards or who fail to provide their citizens with the basic requirements of life. This is still a grey area in international law and there are many problems associated with humanitarian intervention, especially when it involves military action against a transgressor state. Yet the issue of military intervention for humanitarian reasons has become one of the key topics for debate within the field of international relations.[2]

(e) Refugees

In recent years there have been large scale population movements by ethnic groups in many parts of the world. Jean (1992, p. 121) estimated that at the start of the 1990s there were well over seventeen million refugees and twenty million displaced persons in their own countries. Many of these have fled ethnic unrest. They include ethnic Chinese fleeing from Vietnam; Palestinians, who moved to camps in Egypt, Jordan and Lebanon following the Arab-Israeli wars of 1948 and 1967; and Serbs, Croats and Moslems escaping the violence in the former Yugoslavia. It is estimated that up to 300,000 have fled from Burma into Bangladesh and Thailand and that 400,000 Tamils have left Sri Lanka for India and western states (Jean, 1992, p. 80). At the end of the 1980s there were also 400,000 Sudanese refugees in Egypt.

There is also the case of 'internal refugees', who have left their homes out of fear for their safety, and who have had to resettle in other parts of the same state. Four examples of this type of movement can be given. Firstly, the Greek and Turkish Cypriots who were displaced during the intercommunal problems of the 1960s and following the Turkish invasion of the island in 1974. It is estimated that half the Cypriot population have been displaced at least once. Secondly, the movement of 600,000 Ibo refugees from northern to eastern Nigeria was one of the causes of the Nigerian civil war in 1966. Thirdly, Protestants and Catholics in Northern Ireland were forced to move out of mixed population areas from 1969. Fourthly, in 1992 there were 573,000 displaced persons in Sri Lanka. Interestingly, the 1977 Additional Protocol dealing with non-international conflict makes no distinction between refugees and the internally displaced, and points out that displaced persons are in special need of protection during armed conflicts.

The international community has accepted that it has a responsibility for refugees. This is most fully expressed in the 1951 Geneva Convention Relating to the Status of Refugees, which is meant to give protection to individuals having a well-founded fear of being persecuted for reasons of race, religion, nationality, membership of a particular social group or political opinion (Article 1 paragraph 2). Article 33 of this Convention prohibits contracting states from returning a refugee to the frontiers of territories where his or her life or freedom would be threatened. The Convention is, however, limited in that it excludes refugees fleeing environmental or economic disasters and civil wars. It also has nothing to say about internally displaced persons. Another limitation was that until 1967 the Convention was only applicable in Europe.

International responsibility for the care of refugees also manifests itself in the work of the UN High Commissioner for Refugees and the United Nations Relief and Works Agency (UNWRA), established by the General Assembly in 1950 to provide basic services to registered Palestinian refugees living in the Middle East. Because the refugee issue has a cross-border dimension there has also been a growing tendency at the UN Security Council to define situations that produce large scale refugee flows out of areas of ethnic conflict as a threat to international peace and security. This has happened most notably to legitimise international intervention in Northern Iraq to protect Kurds from retaliation from Saddam Hussein after their failed uprising at the end of the Gulf War of 1991.

15

The neglect of ethnic conflict in mainstream international relations

For all the above reasons, therefore, the international community is affected by ethnic conflict and there are good grounds for arguing that the discipline of international relations cannot ignore ethnic conflict. J.H. Bagley (quoted in Sohn and Buergenthal,1973, p. 326) could write that

> The 'problem of minorities', with all its manifold implications, has troubled world peace and international goodwill for centuries. It has constituted a constant irritatory friction between states, an instrument of political design and aggression, a means of toppling state structures and a direct and indirect cause of local and general wars.

Yet after 1945 most international relations specialists preferred to leave the issue of ethnic conflict untouched. Part of the reason for this may be the academic lifestyle, which is cosmopolitan, transnational, middle class and rootless. But there are also deeper reasons for this neglect, and there seem to have been at least four main factors that have inhibited the development of an appropriate concern.

Firstly, the post-1945 world was dominated by the ideological battle between western liberalism and Soviet style Marxism. Neither of these systems of belief have shown much concern for ethnicity. Indeed, both have tended to be dismissive of ethnic sentiment. The liberal has been wary of viewing the world in terms of cultural groups because it seems to contradict his emphasis on the individual. Nationalism has been viewed as an irrational and dangerous sentiment. Group rights seem to be at odds with the idea of individual human rights. The Marxist has tended to see nationalism as nothing more than an unfortunate diversion on the road to a communist society. These ideological prejudices have, therefore, tended to inhibit a full appreciation of the importance of nationalism and ethnicity.

Secondly, a major assumption of western social science in the post-war decades was that ethnic conflict would disappear as nations modernised and minority groups were assimilated. Industrialization would lead to increased contact and communication between different groups. Urbanization would take place. Gradually this would result in something called acculturation, which would result in a transfer of loyalty from the ethnic group to the nation-state. This integrationist perspective led too easily to a belief that intercommunal problems would disappear with development. Indeed Smith (1971) has pointed to a long tradition in the social sciences from 'Durkheim to Deutsch' that has predicted the end of ethnicity; whereas Fishman (1980, p. 84) has referred to the sociological 'contempt for ethnicity'. Such beliefs were especially strong in the US, with its supposed 'melting pot' heritage. The idea of *e pluribus unum* was taken seriously there, though Gore Vidal once referred to it as the most sinister of all Latin tags.

Assimilationists had a particularly optimistic view of social and economic development in multi-ethnic states. This optimism was reflected in the crusading liberalism of the Eisenhower and Kennedy administrations. A good example of this is an editorial for the *Journal of International Affairs* (1962) which proclaimed that a 'new generation has emerged on the world scene dedicated to modernising its heretofore backward societies and truly building a nation which can achieve the aspirations of its people. No longer are disparate groups to be allowed to compromise the progress of the whole.' For as one article put it in the same issue, third world societies were emerging from an age of 'tribalism' into an age of 'nationalism'.

George Ball (1982), who has expressed disapproval for the hubris that was endemic in Washington at that time, has called the 1960s the 'golden age of development theorists', when US economics professors flew the world telling the natives how to build new Jerusalems with US aid. But this was a perspective not just confined to western academics. It should not be forgotten that traditional Marxists also had their own version of modernization theory based on the creation of a class consciousness through capitalist development (Warren, 1980). In fact, in the early 1970s the Central Committee of the Communist Party of the Soviet Union could praise a 'new historical collectivity of people - the Soviet people' based around 'common ownership of the means of production, unity of economic, socio-political and cultural life, Marxist-Leninist ideology, and the interests and communist ideals of the working class' (White, 1990, p. 124). And in the third world president Sekou Toure of Guinea, for example, could claim in the early 1960s that 'in Africa it is the state which constructs the nation' (quoted in Neuberger, 1986, p. 23). It has also been argued by the African writer Ayoade (quoted in Ronen and Thompson, 1985, p. 1) that a major reason for the failure of the Second Republic in Nigeria was that it underrated ethnic sentiment because of a belief that it was a middle class pathology that would be eliminated through modernization. However, all this nation building optimism was misplaced. For as Arthur Koestler (1976) once pointed out, there are more cauldrons than melting pots in the modern world.

It is interesting to note a renewed attempt to downplay nationalism in a recent book championing liberalism. This is Fukuyama's *The End of History and the Last Man* (1992); and in it the author makes several claims about the apparent prevalence of nationalist conflicts. One of these is that nationalism will become politically neutralized because of the force of economic factors which favour the breakdown of national barriers (p. 273). Thus, he predicts that nationalist passions will be confined to the historical non-liberal world, where they may even play a role in promoting democracy (p. 272). This prediction about the trajectory of nationalist belief is not implausible, but one is tempted to suggest caution, for it contains too many echoes of modernization theory's denial of the centrality of ethnicity. In fact the idea that modernization leads to acculturation is highly suspect, for it seems that nationalism is rooted in modernity and is a reaction to the isolation and uncertainty of modern societies (Giddens, 1990, p. 102).

Thirdly, reflecting this optimistic approach within the social sciences in general, the international relations discipline devoted much of its time to analysing integration between states. As Stanley Hoffmann (quoted in Mandelbaum, 1981, p. 80) put it, 'the whole perspective is one of solidarity, the dynamics of world economy, of world science, and technology is, for better (growth and welfare) or worse (population explosion, pollution, depletion, inflation and recession) a dynamics of integration'. In such writings the emphasis was on functionalism, federalism, transnationalism and interdependence (see e.g. Groom and Taylor, 1975; Haas, 1964; Mitrany, 1966). The realists, who resisted these ideas, were in turn wedded to a belief in the strength of the sovereign state and its durability as a form of political organization. Either way, little attention was given to the possibility that the state could break up from within because of ethnic particularism.

Fourthly, and finally, whilst some scholars in the international relations discipline, especially in the US, turned their attention to ideas of integration and interdependence, the so called 'English tradition' maintained an insistence that interstate behaviour should be the main focus of study. For this tradition the study of relations within states and the study of relations between states were really two quite separate disciplines, each with its own conceptual tool box (see Suganami, 1983). According to this viewpoint, promoted by writers such as Manning (1975), Bull (1977) and James (1973), students of international relations would study relations between sovereign states in an 'anarchical society', whereas relations within states, which rested on a different set of institutions, would be left to politics or government departments. The problem, however, is that many ethnic conflicts do not fit easily into either category and so defy neat systems of classification. Inter-ethnic conflicts are clearly not the same as interstate conflicts because they are not between sovereign states and therefore do not involve access by all parties to international 'institutions'. However, in severe and protracted ethnic conflict the legitimacy of a state is clearly being called into question by at least one distinct cultural group, and therefore such

18

conflicts are not like normal intrastate politics. For in many ways inter-ethnic conflicts do resemble interstate relations, and sometimes an ethnic group may consider itself entitled to its own state and will have its own army, its own system of enforcement and even its own 'government'. In fact Ramet (1992) has produced an interesting analysis of the conflict in Yugoslavia which draws heavily on Kaplan's famous typology of international systems and his analysis of the dynamics of each system.

A growing interest in ethnic conflict

Towards the end of the 1960s, however, the academic bias against ethnicity began to erode. This was due to changes in the real world and in the academic world. In the real world, in the words of Horowitz (1985, p. xi), 'ethnicity has fought and bled and burned its way into public and scholarly consciousness'. We have witnessed an 'ethnic revival' in western, developed societies and the emergence of bitter ethnic conflicts in the third world and the ex-Soviet bloc. Even in the US the melting pot hypothesis seemed increasingly inappropriate in a society faced with civil rights protests and urban riots.

In the academic world the international relations discipline came under attack because of its state-centric approach. The world society paradigm was developed (see Banks, 1984), which claimed that states were only one type of international actor among many others, including ethnic and national minorities. Furthermore, the development of subjects such as peace and conflict research not only produced critiques of the state-centric bias of realism, they were also interdisciplinary, and therefore more open to interesting developments in other branches of the social sciences, which included a growing interest in ethnicity. Conflict resolution specialists realised that a true understanding of many important conflicts was not possible from the state-centric perspective, and demanded that more attention should be given to 'identity groups', such as ethnic communities (Azar and Burton,1986; Azar and Marlin, 1987).

Of course, an individual will have more than one identity group. It is quite common to feel loyalty to one's immediate neighbourhood, one's town, one's region, one's state and even to a continent (e.g. a sense of being European or African). It is also possible to define oneself in terms of nation, state, class and gender all at the same time. However, there may well arise moments of truth when individuals have to define themselves more specifically than this. Glazer (1983, p. 244) has called this a terminal loyalty. In several parts of the world this will mean choosing between an ethnic and a state identity, and in such circumstances there is enough evidence to show that the primary or terminal loyalty of many people is to the ethnic group and not the state. This does not explain what factors determine the choice of a primary identity group and there seems to be no agreement on this issue in the literature. There is an on-going debate about the relative importance of class as both an alternative to ethnic identity and as a factor promoting ethnic identity (the so called cultural division of labour). We cannot explore this debate here, but readers are referred to books by Hechter (1975), Munck (1986), Nairn (1977), van den Burghe (1981a).

Third world writers also began to publish more frequently within the international relations discipline, and contributed to a greater sensitivity to the issue of ethnic conflict in the non-western world. So just as the assimilationists were coming under attack from ethnic relations specialists, so the study of international relations was becoming more receptive to analyses which included the serious study of non-state actors.

The neat division between international relations and politics proposed by the 'English tradition' has also been criticised in recent years. Postman (1989, p. 4) has referred to all such academic divisions as a 'hardening of the categories'. It is a theme taken up by Merle (1987, p. 7-8), who has condemned political science specialists for their neglect of the international environment. He writes that

> One nonetheless cannot fail to be surprised by the virtually systematic removal of the international dimension from the phenomena studied, as if the construction and functioning of a political society could be perceived and understood in isolation from the context and surroundings in which they began and where they are developing.

Giddens has made a similar attack from the opposite direction. He condemns the 'unfortunate and indefensible' (Giddens, 1985, p. 31) division between what goes on within states and what goes on between them, and argues that

> Theorists of international relations, relatively unconcerned with what goes on inside states, tend to underestimate the significance of internal struggles that influence external policies. Everyone acknowledges that to treat a state as an actor is a simplifying notion, designed to help make sense of the complexities of the relations between states. But what is only a theoretical model is all too often given a real significance, obscuring the fact that governments cannot be equated with states (as nation states) and that policy decisions within governments usually emanate from

highly contested arenas of social life. (Giddens, 1985, p. 288)

Some landmarks on the road to a greater awareness of ethnicity can be pointed out briefly. In 1969 the anthropologist Barth (1969) challenged the assimilationists by arguing that the empirical evidence showed that interaction need not lead to acculturation and that ethnic boundaries could remain stable despite inter-ethnic contact and interdependence. A year later the International Studies Association held its annual conference in Puerto Rico on the theme of 'Ethnicity in Nation Building: Regional Integration and International Conflict'. The papers presented at this conference were later published by Bell and Freeman (1974). Also in 1970 the International Sociological Association established a research committee on ethnic, racial and minority relations.

In 1971 the International Institute for Strategic Studies held a conference at Stressa on the theme of 'Civil Violence and the International System' and published the proceeds as two Adelphi Papers (1971). In 1972 Walker Connor published an important article in *World Politics* entitled 'Nation-building or nation destroying?'. It argued that it was wrong to treat ethnicity as an 'ephemeral nuisance' and warned against the optimism of the nation-builders. The article suggested that development would lead to ethnic conflict, not assimilation and that it was important not to underestimate the emotional power of nationalism or to overestimate the influence of materialism upon human affairs. It also argued that assimilation was not a unidirectional process and that the nation builders did not seem to realise that it was something that could be reversed.

The theme of the negative impact of modernization theory was also taken up by Cynthia Enloe in her 1973 study, *Ethnic Conflict and Political Development*. She points out how a 'basic nation-state bias' existed in political science that both relegated ethnic issues to the status of problems and implied that integration and assimilation were 'by definition' good. However, serious problems arise when societies attempt modernization which means that it is by no means clear that political development will have wholly beneficial results. In fact, the 'mobilization of ethnic groups may reflect the traumas of casting off tradition, but it may also portend innovative political forms for the future, beyond modernity' (Enloe, 1973, p. 274). Therefore, 'development does not automatically herald the demise of ethnicity' (Enloe, 1973, p. 34).

Throughout the 1970s new additions were made to the literature on ethnic relations from scholars within the field of international relations, and this can be seen as part of a more general revival of interest in this area of study during that decade.[3] This revival of interest is illustrated in a study of Library of Congress entries with the term 'ethnicity' in their titles. This found that from 1968-74 there were nine such entries. From 1975-80 there were 116 (Burton 1982, p. 29; 1983, p. 1). Another study has revealed that of all the doctoral theses written on ethnic themes between 1899 and 1972, a half appeared in the decade 1962-72, and the rate is accelerating (Walzer et al., 1982, p. v).

The aims of this study

Having traced the growing interest in the relationship between international relations and ethnicity, and having also attempted to justify it, it remains to set out how this relationship will be examined in this study. Anyone interested in ethnicity in general, and ethnic conflict in particular, needs to examine at least three questions. The first is: why is ethnicity of such continuing importance in a world that is becoming increasingly interdependent? This is not a question that this book will attempt to answer. Several excellent studies already exist on this topic (see, for example: Gellner, 1983; Horowitz, 1985; Rex and Mason, 1986; Smith, 1981 and 1986a; Stavenhagen, 1990). Here we will just take for granted that strong ethnic attachments do exist in the contemporary world and that there is a 'profound gulf between the concept of the state and the nation' (Smith, 1991, p. 15).

The second question is: why do ethnic differences lead so frequently to ethnic conflict and even to ethnic violence? Why, in other words, are multi-ethnic states often unable to preserve stability and order within a democratic system of government? We will attempt a partial answer of this question in part one, concentrating on international factors that contribute to the development of violent ethnic conflict. In chapter one we shall examine three models of ethnic relations within sovereign states. The first of these, what I call the incompatibility approach, is pessimistic about the chances of creating stable and democratic multi-ethnic states. This general approach includes several different theories, but the best known is the idea of the plural society. The pessimistic approach will then be contrasted with the alternative, and more optimistic, theories of consociational democracy and hegemonic exchange. We will argue that all three approaches are limited, however, because they omit an international dimension in their respective arguments. In chapter two we will develop this criticism and attempt to show that we must take notice of important systemic influences which will help determine whether a multi-ethnic state will become a plural society or a consociational democracy.

The third question that needs to be asked is: given that violent and protracted ethnic conflicts exist in many parts of the world which threaten international peace and security and create misery for the people caught up in them, what can be done to resolve such conflicts, or to reduce their severity? This will be the main focus of parts two and three of this book. A general proposition set out in chapter two is that it is usually a bad policy to internationalize an ethnic conflict if this means involving other sovereign states. However, certain types of third party involvement might be more constructive, such as crisis management or UN action. But to determine when such involvement is likely to be destructive or constructive we need to explore the structure of ethnic conflict. Chapters three, four and five will attempt to do this by developing a general model of ethnic conflict resolution which will set out the various processes that characterise violent ethnic conflicts and the different strategies that can contribute to their resolution. Too often conflict resolution is thought of as just a single process, whereas in fact it involves at least three distinct strategies that have been called peace-keeping, peace-making and peace-building. The differences between these will be explored and their interrelationships will be analysed. All three strategies can involve a high degree of third party participation, and special attention will be given to this particular area.

Part three will concentrate on the work of the United Nations (UN). Chapter six will examine the record of this organization as a peace-keeper, peace-maker and peace-builder. But these are all strategies that react to the outbreak of violence. There is also a need for a more proactive UN response to ethnic conflict. One area where the UN might be able to prevent conflict is by establishing an effective international regime to protect ethnic minorities within multi-ethnic states. Chapter seven will explore why the UN has been reluctant to establish such a system and why it has not been able to avoid the issue of minority protection altogether.

Before starting our analysis it is important to make two points. The first is that the term ethnic conflict should not be taken to mean that the ethnic differences that separate the groups are the cause of the conflict, any more than the term interstate conflict should be taken to imply that violence between sovereign states occurs because there are separate sovereign states. Rupesinghe (1987, p. 531) is correct to state that the 'mere existence of ethnicity is certainly no precondition for conflicts; it would be absurd to assume that there will be conflict merely because ethnic groups as such exist'.

The term ethnic conflict, therefore, refers to the form the conflict takes, and is not meant to suggest that ethnicity is the cause of the conflict. This is what Stavenhagen (1990, p. 119) seems to mean when he states that 'it might be argued that ethnic conflict as such does not exist. What does exist is social, political and economic conflict between groups of people who identify each other in ethnic terms'. The actual causes of such conflicts may vary from case to case and can include exclusion from political power, a sense of injustice because of the way resources are distributed within a national or international division of labour, fears that an identity is under threat and so on (see e.g. Esman, 1990; Tagil, 1984; Zariski, 1989).

The second point is that ethnic conflicts can be enormously difficult to resolve and tend to drag on across generations. Miall has calculated that since 1945 only three out of the twenty eight conflicts involving minorities that he has studied have been peacefully resolved. Therefore, it appears as if the 'international dispute settlement system is better at coping with conflict over "interests" between states than with conflicts over values and relationships involving non-state actors' (Miall, 1992, p. 185). There is no single reason for this. Rather, the difficulty of resolution can be attributed to a cluster of factors. One is the difficulty of resolution through separation. Secession is a rare phenomenon in international relations and so ethnic groups have to continue to live in close contact within a single sovereign state. Unlike conflicts between states, ethnic conflicts cannot be resolved by withdrawal to clearly defined international boundaries (Darby, 1986). Another problem is that as many ethnic conflicts are conflicts over control of territory, they are zero sum games which are not open to easy resolution. The asymmetric nature of many ethnic conflicts, where one party will be a sovereign state whilst other groups will lack any international legitimacy, complicates the search for peaceful settlements, as does the impact of external interventions. Finally, because of a history of close contact, there may well exist a strong legacy of past hatred and antagonistic folk memories. For all of these reasons ethnic conflicts can be very difficult to resolve and to manage.[4] To make matters even worse, even when the parties to ethnic conflicts can be persuaded to sign peace accords they can prove difficult to implement or sustain (de Silva and Samarasinghe, 1993). However, it is hoped that this book can at least contribute to the discussion about how these difficulties can be overcome.

Notes

1. Experts do not always agree on the exact numbers killed in most cases of genocide. The figures used here are taken from Haff (1988).
2. See, for example, de Waal and Omaar (1993), Mayall (1991), Roberts (1993).
3. See especially Bertelsen (1977); Neuman (1976); Said and Simmons (1976); Suhrke and Noble (1977). More recent examples include Midlarski (1992) and Schechterman and Slann (1993). See also the important study of nationalism and international relations by Mayall (1990). Several journals have now published special issues on ethnic conflict. Some examples include *Bulletin of Peace Proposals* (1988) on ethnic conflict and human rights and *Survival* (1993) on ethnic conflict and international security. Also of interest is Ryan (1988) and Carment(1993)
4. There is a good discussion on this in Mitchell (1992).

Part I
General Issues

1 Approaches to ethnic conflict

> With blithe lightness of mind, we assumed that the world was moving irrevocably beyond nationalism, beyond tribalism, beyond the provincial confines of the identities inscribed on our passports, towards a global market culture which was to be our new home. In retrospect, we were whistling in the dark. The repressed has returned, and its name is nationalism. (Ignatieff, 1993, p. 2)

Introduction

As long as the nation-building illusion dominated the thinking about multi-ethnic societies it was possible for social scientists to relegate the phenomenon of ethnicity to the status of a problem that would soon be solved. Because of its integrationist assumptions this view had little, if anything, to say about how to establish stable and democratic multi-ethnic states. As a result, the vast bulk of writings on multi-ethnic societies which emerged from the nation-building approach is of little help to us today in our search for constructive ways to respond to ethnic conflict.

However, by the end of the 1960s the optimistic assumptions of assimilationist theory were coming under increasing attack. As the experience of multi-ethnic states in both the rich and poor worlds pointed out the flaws in nation-building theory a new pessimism seemed to spread through the academic literature on ethnicity. One of the main consequences of this was a growing interest in the theory of the plural society, which posited that multi-ethnic societies could not remain both stable and democratic. Although this theory was developed by the British economist J.S. Furnival and was then modified by the West Indian anthropologist M.G. Smith, these writers were not the first to adopt such a pessimistic evaluation of multi-ethnic states. There is, in fact, quite a long tradition of such thinking. It is interesting to note that the Grand Design of the Duke of Sully, written in 1638, included a warning that when territory was redistributed

> Care must be taken to respect the natural dispositions and peculiar characteristics of peoples and races and thus guard against the folly of trying to unite in any one state...men whose differences of temperament or diversity of language, law and tradition are so great as to be incompatible (Russell, 1972, p. 172).

For nationalist writers, of course, the very existence of a national group living in a multi-national state was enough to legitimise the calls for political independence that might emerge from such a group: 'one nation, one state'. But many liberal writers also presented pessimistic assessments of the viability of multi-national states. The best known of the liberal incompatibility theorists is J.S. Mill (1972, p.361), who argued that

> Among a people without fellow-feeling, especially if they read and speak different languages, the united public opinion, necessary to the working of representative government, cannot exist. The influences which form opinions and decide political acts, are different in the different sections of the country.

Mill goes on to pay particular attention to armies in such societies and claims that they will be unable to form a link with all the people they are meant to serve since many of these people will be 'foreigners' living under a single government. In such cases, it is suggested, the army will identify not with the people but with the government and their only public duty will be obedience to orders. Such armies, Mill claims, have been the 'executioners of liberty through the whole duration of modern history'. Few modern writers on ethnicity have followed up Mill's interest in the role of the military, though there have been a handful of important studies (e.g. Enloe, 1980; Horowitz, 1985, p. 443f.). These tend to confirm that the police and military frequently exacerbate rather than resolve conflict in multi-ethnic societies.

Another liberal who championed the separation of nations living within multi-ethnic states was the US president Woodrow Wilson. At the Versailles Peace Conference of 1919 he championed a policy of national self-determination and claimed that thwarted nationalities deprived of their own state would be a major threat to world peace. Others have shared a similar view of the instability of multi-ethnic states. Ernest Baker (Janowsky, 1945, p. 28), for example, declared that 'a democratic state which is multinational will fall asunder into as many democracies as there are nationalities, dissolved by the very fact of will which should be the basis of its life'.

One of America's leading liberal philosophers has recently restated this incompatibility argument. Walzer (1982, p. 6), has written that 'it must be said that politics follows nationality, wherever politics is free. Pluralism in the strong sense - one state, many peoples - is possible only under tyrannical regimes'. Walzer argues that there is only one exception to this; the US. This, however, is due to a set of circumstances that may never be repeated. Fukuyama, another champion of liberalism, has also questioned whether it is possible to have democratic and stable multi-ethnic states. He writes

> Democracy is also not particularly good at resolving disputes between different ethnic or national groups. The question of national sovereignty is inherently uncompromisable.... The Soviet Union could not become democratic and at the same time remain unitary, for there was no consensus among the Soviet Union's nationalities that they shared a common citizenship and identity. Democracy would only emerge on the basis of the country's breakup into smaller national entities. (Fukuyama, 1992, p. 119)

Schermerhorn (1978, p. 68), has argued that studies of ethnicity, both historical and anthropological, show that the 'probability is overwhelming' that contacts between cultural groups will lead to domination and subordination and inequality of power. Claude has echoed these arguments, claiming that

> generally speaking human beings have seldom been able to accommodate themselves to the fact of human diversity; in most socio-political settings, differences of one sort or another ...have been so seriously regarded as to give rise to politically significant problems (Claude, 1969, p. 1).

All of the arguments discussed so far against the viability of the

31

multi-ethnic state are general ones. However, in actual conflict situations it may be that participants or commentators who favour separation do not state their case on such abstract grounds. Instead they will probably argue that there is something about the specific situation they are in that makes it impossible for different ethnic groups to live together in the same state. In the case of Cyprus, for example, Harry Luke argued that although Greeks could live under Turkish rule, Turks could not live under Greek rule (in Georghallides, 1979, p. 137). Israeli (1980) has claimed that no Islamic group can accept minority status in a non-Islamic state. Banac (1993, p. 140), in an examination of the Yugoslavia situation, has argued that although multi-national states are not always incompatible with democratic government, there is something about the nature of South Slavic national ideologies in general and Serb nationalism in particular, that, in this case, makes it impossible for the two ideas to coexist.

The Plural Society Theory

The most systematic version of the incompatibility approach is, however, the theory of the plural society. According to Furnival plural societies exist where different sections of the 'community' live side by side, but separately, within the same political unit. Whereas Mill placed particular emphasis on the relationship between the military and society, Furnival, writing in the inter-war and immediate post-war periods, stressed economic competition between the different cultural groups. Believing that in plural societies inter-communal relations were confined to the market place, he argued that there could be no common will or over-arching loyalty that would transcend the cultural differences and therefore no mutual respect for legal and moral rules meant to restrain ethnic interaction. This results in unrestrained competition which is not moderated by any form of social cohesion. Therefore, such societies are doomed to fall apart unless an external force for unity was exerted from outside. So Furnival (1986, p. 459) claimed that

> In a plural society, then, the community tends to be organised for production rather than for social life; social demand is sectionalized, and within each society of the community the social demand becomes disorganised and ineffective, so that in each section the members are debarred from leading the full life of a citizen in a homogeneous community. Finally, the reaction against these abnormal conditions, taking in each society the form of a nationalism, sets one community against the other so

as to emphasise the plural character of the society and aggravate its instability, (thereby enhancing the need for it to be held together from outside).

Furnival believed that this opposite force was provided by colonialism. Even though he does concede that some inter-communal problems might be resolved by reason, in the absence of any internalised restraining force conflicts are much more likely to become battles of will. For, he says, there can be no more than a formal legality when the only duty is not to be found out. Or, as he also put it, in a sarcastic tone, within multi-ethnic states the rules of 'international morality' apply (Furnival, 1986, p. 450).

Smith refined and altered the plural society theory, placing more emphasis on culture than economics. He also extended the scope of the theory from the colonial tropical societies like the Dutch East Indies that particularly interested Furnival to all multi-ethnic states. Smith (1986, p. 183), has defined a plural society very broadly as a society 'whose members are divided into categories or groups on the basis of such factors as language, race, ethnicity, community of provenance or descent, religion, distinctive social institutions, or culture'.

Although Smith does accept that there are various ways in which different cultural groups can be incorporated into multi-ethnic states, he is, nevertheless, pessimistic about the chances of creating stable and democratic societies. The first type of incorporation which Smith examines is termed uniform. This is when individuals are incorporated as 'citizens into the public domain on formally identical conditions of civic and political status' irrespective of culture (Smith, 1971, p. 434). He acknowledges that such regimes are inherently assimilative in 'orientation and effect' (*ibid*).

The second type of incorporation is called equivalent, and exists where a 'number of institutionally diverse collectivities may be united in a single society as corporate units holding equivalent or complementary rights and status in the public domain' (1971, p. 446). Such societies have been termed, even by Smith himself, as consociational democracies, and we shall explore this theory in more detail later in the chapter. There are some writers on ethnicity who see consociationalism as the great hope for multi-ethnic states, but Smith does not share their optimism. He has serious doubts about the durability of such states. They are, he claims, an 'imperfect and conditional basis for union' because formal equality between the ethnic groups can be consistent with real inequality. For

Almost always, the components of a consociation are unequal in numbers, territory, and economic potential....Under such conditions, real or perceived segmental disparities may evoke segmental protests and policies designed to alter or to maintain current conditions of union and current distributions of power and influence. Autarchic segmental identities are correspondingly reinforced by such inter-segmental conflicts; and unless these are effectively restrained or reduced, they may subvert and destroy the consociation by transforming its internal political order into a system of external relations between mutually hostile segments (Smith, 1971, p. 442-3).

Smith has tried to reinforce this argument through an empirical analysis of a selection of consociational democracies. His list is, perhaps, somewhat idiosyncratic, and includes states such as the U.S.A., Australia, and the Central African Federation as well as states such as Switzerland and Belgium, which are more usually defined as consociations. He acknowledges that consociationalism is the state structure 'probably most favourable for segmental pluralities', but would claim that they can guarantee neither internal order nor political development (Smith, 1986, p. 262). His overall assessment is that the record of such states does not inspire confidence in their ability to provide stable and orderly government.

So, according to Smith, consociations are rarely a satisfactory long term solution to the problems posed by multi-ethnic states. Either they will move towards a more perfect union, which resembles Smith's first category of uniform incorporation, or the differences will give rise to a situation of differential incorporation, which is Smith's third category. In this sort of state the dominant group will try to ensure its position by excluding from real power the other ethnic groups, who will then become second class citizens in their own state.

Smith offers a rather bleak vision of multi-ethnic states. This is reflected in the assessment by Rabushka and Shepsle (1972) that stable democracy is impossible in plural societies.[1] If this is correct then it is extremely unlikely that ethnic groups will be able to work out a mutually acceptable system of government since some groups are bound to resent the lack of democratic participation. Because both uniform and differential incorporation deny that ethnic differences should be respected by governments, it is likely that both types of states will be prone to inter-ethnic violence. It is hardly surprising, therefore, that Kuper (1985, p. 201), has argued that 'social processes in plural societies have many distinctive qualities....However, these processes share in common a tendency to destructive violence'. He has also written that one important characteristic of the plural society is that there is 'often a history of conflict' and that issues of conflict 'tend to coincide with the plural divisions' (Kuper,1990, p. 22). However, he also rejects a determinist stance and argues that violence is not inevitable in plural societies and the decision to resort to violence rests with specific actors (Kuper, 1988, p. 168).

The policy implications of the pessimistic approach

The two main prescriptions about multi-ethnic states that emerge from the pessimistic perspective are both problematic. One is control by the dominant group, which is what Smith predicts. The other is Mill's preference for political separation. However, serious doubts exists about each of these alternatives.

The obvious problem with structural dominance is that it rests on the repression of subordinate groups. This idea of control has been developed both by Benvenisti and by Lustick in analyses of Israeli society (Smooha, 1990). Benvenisti, for example, has argued that the Jews and Palestinians in Israel and the Occupied Territories are locked into a confrontation that cannot, under the existing circumstances, be solved by occupation, annexation or power sharing. All that is available to the Israeli's is a policy of permanent control. As a result of similar analysis Lustick (1979) has developed a 'control model' as a way of solving the problem of disorder in multi-ethnic states. This, he accepts, is not as desirable as consociational democracy but is preferable to the realistic alternatives that exist such as civil war, genocide or expulsion (McRae, 1989, p. 100). Yet, such societies are characterised by exploitation, manipulation, an absence of true democracy and a biased administration.

This is why structural dominance or control models are not a viable long term solution to conflict in multi-ethnic states. For, as well as moral objections to this approach, it has to be suggested that such policies are likely to reinforce intercommunal antagonisms and to deepen conflict. Such structural dominance also seems to offer little opportunity for genuine reform and progress since it is firmly wedded to the discriminatory status quo and to majority (or at times even minority) rule. For 'the idea of domination and supremacy excludes the principle of equal rights and as long as this idea survives the majority and minority become polarized' (Deletant, 1992, p. 53). The result is, in Raymond Aron's phrase, a peace of empire not a peace of law. We only have to consider the case of Northern Ireland to see how the control approach can lead to intercommunal violence.

The 1921 partition of Ireland gave rise to a civil war in the south and civil unrest, leading to repressive policies, in the North. Here unionists loyal to the United Kingdom, who were in the majority, took action to ensure the continuing oppression of Catholics, who were deemed to be a threat to their survival.[2] In the words of Lord Craigavon, Northern Ireland was to have a Protestant Parliament for a Protestant people. So the Northern Ireland government introduced a Special Powers Act in 1922 which allowed it to suspend the normal process of law. The same year internment was introduced and proportional representation, which was meant to protect the Catholic minority, was abolished in local elections in favour of the first past the post Westminster model. A restricted franchise was used and gerrymandering was also adopted, especially in the city of Londonderry where a Protestant minority controlled the city. In this way the electoral domination of unionists was assured. There was also widespread economic discrimination against Catholics. The whole discriminatory structure was reinforced through the Protestant Orange Order, founded in 1795 to uphold the constitution and the Protestant religion (Lyons, 1979, p. 135). Eventually, of course, in the 1960s the Catholics began a civil rights campaign against this discriminatory government. This lead to intercommunal violence which has lasted for 25 years.

There are other examples which point to the poor record of control and structural dominance in ensuring stable government. Ramet (1992a, p. 35) has noted how repression did not work in Yugoslavia. For 'neither the repressive Serbian centralism of the inter-war period nor the hegemonistic unitarism of the postwar period (1946-66) succeeded in producing the modicum of stability essential for the orderly functioning of Yugoslav society'. In a study of 'hegemonic' regimes in Africa, Rothchild (1991, p. 210) points out how such states tend toward 'military solutions to the ethnic and regional challenges, leading to intractable conflicts between determined adversaries'. Therefore, he concludes, hegemonic regimes are reasonable effective at blocking low-intensity conflict but are 'more likely to face rebellions than are the open and more responsive regime types' (*ibid*).

The separation argument, which involves secession and partition (or if this hasn't worked well, re-partition), is set out clearly in chapter sixteen of John Stuart Mill's *Considerations On Representative Government*. Here he argues that multi-national states cannot be stable and democratic at the same time. Therefore, 'it is in general a necessary condition of free institutions, that the boundaries of governments should coincide in the main with those of nationalities'. This analysis was modified in the case of 'backward nations', where it was better, Mill thought, for peoples such as the Bretons and the Basques to be brought into 'the current of the ideas and feelings of a highly civilised and cultivated people...than to sulk on (their) own rocks, the half savage relic of past times, revolving in (their) own little mental orbit, without participation or interest in the general movement of the world' (Mill, 1972, p. 363). In the supposed cultural egalitarianism of the late twentieth century it has become less acceptable to denigrate other cultures in such a way and calls for the separation of ethnic groups often go unqualified by any reference to civilization.

Van Dyke (1985, p. 13) also supports the separation approach in theory (he doubts whether it can be implemented in practice), and argues that in plural societies 'self determination may well be vital, for in such societies...the tendency is for one of the peoples to establish its political dominance'. Such a solution should not be dismissed lightly. Lijphart (1977, p. 44-7), for example, has argued that the obvious costs involved in such a move have to be weighed against the possible greater costs in forcing some ethnic groups to live together. The case of the 'velvet divorce' in the Czech and Slovak Federative Republic (as Czechoslovakia was called after March 1990), by which this state split into two separate sovereign states on January 1, 1993, shows that a quick and peaceful separation of ethnic groups is possible. Nevertheless, in most cases there are formidable difficulties to be overcome in implementing this approach and secession 'remains an option very likely to produce violence' (McGarry and O'Leary, 1993, p. 14).

The first of these problems is the inability to obtain a clean break. It is not usually possible for ethnic groups to split apart without leaving residual problems of disputed territory and trapped minorities. For the population distribution may not make for an easy separation of cultures (the so called ethnic fruit-cakes) or disputed territories will remain (e.g. the Crimea, which is claimed by Ukraine and Russia). The partition of the Indian sub-continent after British withdrawal, for example, left 100 million Moslems in the state of India and a territorial dispute over Kashmir that has poisoned relations between New Delhi and Islamabad ever since. The fate of the large Russian minority that was stranded in Estonia after this Baltic state obtained its independence in 1991 has deeply troubled some observers and has been an important factor in relations between Tallinn and Moscow. Eleven million Russians live in the Ukraine, a proportion of the 65 million people of the former USSR who now live outside their republic of origin (Jean, 1992, p. 12). The problem of the clean break has also bedevilled the successor states in the former Yugoslavia and has led to violent conflict between the governments of both Croatia and Bosnia and Hercegovina and their Serbian minorities.

A second problem was identified by George Orwell (1970, p. 282), who once observed that when group B was being oppressed by group A, a sensible solution was to allow group B to determine its own future. However, there always seemed to be a group C, which claimed that it was being oppressed by group B and also wanted its independence. This can result in what Morgenthau described as the A-B-C paradox, where nation B invokes the principle of self-determination against nation A, but denies it to nation C (see Snyder, 1990, p. 1). This observation does seem to be supported by the experience of those states that have achieved independence. So the Bengalis in Bangladesh fought a bitter war against Pakistan for their own state, but are now suppressing calls for autonomy from the Chittagong Hill Tribes within the territory under their control. These tribes, which total about 600,000 people of Chinese-Tibetan descent, are Buddhist, not Moslem, and even though they had enjoyed special status under British rule, this was taken away from them in 1963. Following the successful secession attempt of Bangladesh in 1971, there were calls from the tribes to reinstate this special status. This has been resisted by Dacca, however, and increasing unrest has been met with increased repression. Chaudhuri (1991) notes that an International Commission found that the army of Bangladesh was responsible for forced relocations, murder, rape, and the desecration of Buddhist temples and Christian churches in the tribal areas.

There has also been concern expressed about the treatment of the Biharis in Bangladesh (Whitaker et al., 1982). Many of these Urdu speaking Moslems emigrated to East Pakistan, as it was then called, following the partition of the subcontinent, and today they are found dispersed throughout Bangladesh. In the late 1960s they supported a united Pakistan, and so were treated with suspicion by Bengalis, and there were attacks on them both before and after the independence of Bangladesh in 1971. Since then they have become an oppressed minority, sometimes deprived of their former jobs, often living in ghettos around cities where they are subjected to harassment.

A third problem with separation is that there still appears to be resistance to this approach within the international community, and in the present international system a state will rarely accept the loss of part of its territory without resistance. There are special cases where a peaceful separation has occurred: the secession of Norway (1905) and Finland (1917) from Sweden, Singapore from Malaysia (1965), and the Vatican from Italy (1929). But these are very much the exception. Secessionist attempts invariably lead to increased violence. This was the case during the Nigerian Civil War, the war in Bangladesh, the Ethiopian-Eritrean conflict and the war between Katanga and the central government of the newly independent Congo (see Heraclides, 1990). It remains the case in Iraq and Turkey (Kurds), India (Sikhs) and Sri Lanka (Tamils). Outside states are also reluctant to help secessionist movements because of the fear of a chain reaction or 'epidemic' effect. Since most states contain dissatisfied ethnic groups they have a vested interest in not encouraging minority demands for separation. Thus, Smith (1982, p. 35) has pointed out that 'the unfavourable international climate is undoubtedly the main reason for the relative lack of success of outright separatism since 1945, and it tends to favour instead autonomist or communalist solutions'. The inter-state system, then, prefers the separate bedroom arrangement over outright divorce.

Perhaps this is why, whatever the inherent merits of a particular secession claim, between 1945 and the end of the Cold War only Bangladesh (de jure) and the Turkish Republic of Northern Cyprus (de facto) succeeded in severing links with an existing state when this was opposed by the dominant group within the state. One of the most obvious features of the 'new world order' appears to be a growing tolerance for secessionist claims. The inter-state system was willing, after some hesitation, to recognise the new states of Slovenia, Croatia, Bosnia and Hercegovina and Macedonia despite opposition to their secession from the government of Yugoslavia. Yet there is little evidence that this new-found openness to the claims of secessionist territories will be extended to other cases. In Iraq for example, the inter-state system has been careful not to recognise Kurdish claims for a separate state. As yet, therefore, there is little evidence of an emerging international norm in favour of the secession of oppressed groups (see Mayall, 1991).

There are other problems with secession. It can lead to the creation of an 'unviable' or 'infirm' state; or it can result in a 'stranded majority' if the secession is by the most prosperous economic area (Buckheit, 1978). Then there is the whole issue of who should be consulted about secession Is the future of Northern Ireland to be determined by the people of Northern Ireland, the people of the island of Ireland, the people of the United Kingdom, or all of these? Similarly is it the people of the Crimea or the Ukraine or Russia who should decide the fate of the Crimea? For these, and other reasons, claims for separation often result in conflict escalation.

Doubts about the incompatibility approach

All the examples discussed in the previous section would tend to support the view that pessimistic 'solutions' to conflict in multi-ethnic states tend to reinforce instability and violence in the long term. If Gandhi was correct to argue that a society should be judged according to how it treats its minorities, then many clearly fail the test comprehensively, including those in the Indian subcontinent during Gandhi's own lifetime. Yet despite the apparently dismal record of stable democratic life in such societies doubts have been expressed about approaches based on the incompatibility view of ethnic relations within a single sovereign state.

Firstly, critics have argued that approaches such as the plural society theory overstate the extent to which culture creates permanent, polarised and watertight boundaries (Horowitz, 1985, p.74; Rothchild, 1970). Such an approach ignores the possible existence of cross-cutting cleavages between ethnic groups, which allow the formation of what Horowitz has called slender threads of consensus. Critics argue that the incompatibility theorists ignore the fluid and changing nature of ethnic identification. In other words, the plural society theory seems to adopt a primordial view of ethnicity which would argue that ethnic identity is an unalterable constant around which politics is organised. Opposed to this view is the rational choice approach which takes as the constant the individual pursuit of self-interest within certain structural constraints, which will then determine the identity that is adopted (Banton, 1977; Cross, 1978; Hechter, 1988; Lawler, 1976; Wu, 1982). From this perspective ethnic identity and group loyalty is more flexible than the incompatibility approach would have us believe.

Secondly, the incompatibility theorists tend to believe that societies need some kind of general will, or at least be united in the pursuit of common goals, to hold them together. Furnival thought that states that are culturally homogeneous possessed such a will, whereas states which are culturally heterogeneous did not; and this was enough to explain the unstable nature of plural societies. So although plural society writers emphasise conflict, they do so from an underlying functionalist belief that good societies need to be based on agreement about basic goals and values. However, such a viewpoint has been challenged by a 'conflict' view of society which claims that all societies are to some extent malintegrated and involve conflicts of interests, sectional divisions, and coercion (Cohen 1968; McFarlane, 1974; Nardin, 1983). According to this view societies owe a peaceful and ordered existence, not to the presence of a general will, but to the creation of formal rules of mutual accommodation. Crick (1964, p. 141), for example, has written that 'most technologically advanced societies are divided societies, are pluralistic and not monolithic'. Giddens (1976, p. 21), has also attacked the functionalist approach because of its failure to 'make conceptually central the *negotiated* character of norms, as open to divergent and conflicting "interpret-ations" in relation to divergent and conflicting *interests*'. Oakshott also made an important distinction between purposive association, based on shared ends, and practical association, based on mutually acceptable procedures and rules. In complex societies it is the importance of these common rules which is crucial, not the absence of shared purposes.

If one accepts this approach to social order then the emphasis of writers like Furnival on common interests and goals becomes irrelevant, because no modern society rests on this foundation. So if we were to accept Furnival's argument we would have to believe that all modern societies must fall apart, since they all lack a general will, irrespective of their ethnic composition. This is clearly not the case. For stability in complex modern societies rests not on common interests, but the successful accommodation of conflicting interests. Therefore a theory that rests on the division of states into unitary (peaceful and ordered) and heterogeneous (probably doomed) should be rejected in favour of one that sees ethnic differences as one case (perhaps an exceptionally difficult case) of conflicting values and interests that exist in all societies (Cross, 1977; van den Berghe, 1971). As van den Burghe has noted

> I do not believe that pluralism is inevitably associated with either democracy or despotism. The relationship is much more complex. Some moderately pluralistic societies have been relatively democratic, but so have many highly homogeneous ones. Conversely, many pluralistic societies have been quite despotic, but so have a number of homogeneous countries (Van den Burghe, 1971, p. 74).

Thirdly, there is some dispute as to whether the plural society approach is a theory with predictive power, or a system of classification. Smith, himself, seems to use it as both; others have tried to strip it of some of its analytical power. Jenkins (1988, p.181), for example, has claimed that the 'best which can be said is that it is merely profoundly descriptive, going no further than the extensive cataloguing of concrete situations by reference to a classificatory scheme of ideal-typical plural societies'. This, however, is not a totally accurate account of Smith's position. For the real difficulty for Smith is that if the plural society wants to be a theory which wants to predict that multi-ethnic societies are condemned to violence and/or authoritarian rule it can be disproved by pointing to democratic and stable states that contain more than one ethnic group. However, to the extent that it is acknowledged by plural society thinkers that multi-ethnic states are not doomed, then the approach does become more of a system of classification, and loses predictive power.[3]

Kuper (1974b, p. 23), has tried to defend Smith from the charge that he is too deterministic in his approach to ethnic relations. He argues that Smith's approach to the plural society does not claim that 'the mere presence of ethnic differences creates a plural society and that ethnicity is, in and of itself, a sufficient cause of conflict'. He is right to warn us about underestimating the sophistication of Smith's views, but it cannot be denied that even if he is not a cultural determinist, he is a determined pessimist about the possibility of constructive inter-communal relations in multi-ethnic states. In one of his recent studies, for example, Smith (1988, p. 224) writes that

> Whether or not some African countries institutionalise conditions to fulfil their constitutional declarations of freedom and equality for all citizens before the law, given the tensions inherent in their plural compositions and in the actual conditions of collective life, unless some centrally coordinated unit has such preponderant power as to discourage challenge, they are unlikely to escape the disruptive effects of the contradiction between the structures of their societies and the conditions of universalism intrinsic to the state. It is this fundamental contradiction...that generates the social unrest and internal violence from which they suffer, and the political instability that commonly involves military coups, changes of constitution, government and regime.

Lastly, it has been questioned whether an explanation of particular conflicts as inevitable can really be considered a satisfactory analysis. In looking at the Cyprus case, for example, Loizos (1976, p. 14), has stated that it is a facile view which sees the Cyprus problem as the simple result of the inability of the Greek and Turkish Cypriots to live together. What is being argued here is that to explain away an ethnic conflict as a tragedy of necessity is to neglect the complex interplay of factors out of which it arose. It undervalues history and context and shows a disrespect for the 'importance of political variables' (Horowitz, 1985, p. 139). Furthermore, it may be that an examination of specific cases of ethnic conflict will reveal that the hardening of cultural boundaries and a deepening of segregation was not the cause of the conflict, but a result of inter-ethnic problems that can arise for a number of reasons that are not inevitable, but contingent on decisions made in the political, social and economic spheres.

As a reaction to the plural society's pessimism there have arisen at least two alternative approaches to the issue of stability and democracy in multi-ethnic states. The best known of these is the consociational democracy model developed by Arendt Lijphart, which argues that although it may be difficult to maintain stable and democratic government in multi-ethnic states, it is not impossible to do so. For how can the incompatibility theorists explain the success of Switzerland, Canada, Malaya and Belgium? The other approach is known as hegemonic exchange, and is usually associated with the name of Donald Rothchild. Such writers lend support to the claim by Horowitz (1985, p. 684) that 'there is no case to be made for the futility of democracy or the inevitability of uncontrolled conflict. Even in the most severely divided society, ties of blood do not lead ineluctably to rivers of blood'.

Consociational democracy, hegemonic exchange and ethnic democracy

Lijphart's influential work on consociationalism, *Democracy in Plural Societies* (1977), sets out the conditions under which stable and democratic multi-ethnic states are possible. He derives these conditions from a study of four classic cases of consociational democracy: Belgium, Holland, Austria and the Netherlands, and from states such as Canada, which contain consociational elements. The book is meant to be a 'challenge to democratic pessimists' (Lijphart, 1977, p. 1). For Lijphart is not just concerned to present an empirical study of political stability in multi-ethnic states, he is setting out a normative ideal. This comes out quite clearly in a passage where he states that the message of the book to political elites is 'to encourage them to engage in a form of political engineering; if they wish to establish or strengthen democratic institutions in their countries, they must become consociational engineers' (Lijphart, 1977, p. 223). This normative approach has recently been applied to South Africa, where Lijphart (1989a, p. 23) has proposed consociational engineering, claiming that 'we do not need to deny ethnicity in order to be realistic advocates of democracy'. He has also challenged analyses that claim that there is no solution to the Northern Ireland problem, claiming that such a perspective is 'as provocative as it is wrong' (McGarry and O'Leary, 1990, p. vi).

Lijphart claims that the idea of consociationalism can be traced back to Johannes Althuser's *Politica Methodice Digesta* of 1603, even though the term was first used by David Apter in a 1961 study, *The Political Kingdom in Uganda*. It proposes a democratic system of government that differs from the traditional Westminster majoritarian model. In its pure form the Westminster model is characterised by one-party cabinets, a two-party system, a first past the post electoral system, a unitary and centralised government and an unwritten constitution. Consociational democracies, on the other hand, involve multi-party cabinets, a multi-party system, proportional representation, political decentralisation (e.g. federalism), and written constitutions which recognise certain rights of minority groups (Lijphart, 1984).

There are, according to Lijphart, four main characteristics of consociationalism, one of primary importance and three of secondary importance. The primary characteristic is the grand coalition of political leaders that represent all the significant communities. This elite cooperation is, for Lijphart, the central feature of consociational democracy. The secondary characteristics are the existence of a veto power for all communities on legislation that affects their vital interests; a system of proportionality in parliament, the civil service and other government agencies; and a high degree of segmental autonomy so that each community has a considerable degree of freedom to run its own internal affairs.

The nine conditions that support such elite co-operation are then set out, though Lijphart is keen to emphasise that the presence or absence of these conditions are not decisive and are 'neither indispensable nor sufficient in and of themselves to account for the success of consociational democracy' (Lijphart, 1977, p. 54). These factors, then, cannot be said to cause an overarching loyalty, which raises the question what does? Lijphart leaves this unanswered, perhaps because of the strong voluntaristic element in his work. Nevertheless, Lijphart considers the following factors to be significant. The existence of a balance of power between the various groups so that none of the groups can form a majority on their own. The existence of a multi-party system. The small size of a state, which means that elites are more likely to know each other personally and interact more. Though why this should encourage peace and democracy is unclear to this reader. Lijphart also qualifies his argument about the small size of a state being a supporting condition when he argues that one of the reasons for the failure of consociationalism in Northern Ireland is that it is too small to supply enough people with political talent (Lijphart, 1977, p. 139). Cross-cutting cleavages will have a moderating effect, as will a patriotic feeling or a common religion that transcends the specific cultures. The existence of clear boundaries reduce the chances of dangerous contacts, though this seems to contradict the claim that cross-cutting cleavages are to be encouraged; and a tradition of elite cooperation will encourage an overarching loyalty. But the two most important conditions are the absence of an ethnic group that is a clear majority of the total population and the absence of large socio-economic differences (Lijphart, 1989b, p. 497).

The approach to multi-ethnic states favoured by Lijphart is also advanced by Nordlinger in his influential book, *Conflict Regulation in Divided Societies* (1972). He also rejects the majoritarian model and stresses elite cooperation. Indeed Nordlinger (1972, p.87), claims that 'structured elite predominance is a necessary conflict regulating condition'. Certain conditions motivate elites to attempt conflict regulation. These are: a desire to fend off an external threat; a sizable commercial class dedicated to the pursuit of economic values; the inability of any one group to obtain political office without support from other groups; and the threat of serious civil strife in the absence of elite co-operation. In pursuing a strategy of co-operation there are six main conflict regulating practices: the stable coalition, the proportionality principle, de-politicization, the mutual veto, mutual compromise, and concessions. Unlike Lijphart, Nordlinger does not believe that cross-cutting pressures and segmental isolation are likely to have a very positive impact. He argues that there is little evidence that cross-cutting cleavages do reduce violence, and questions whether ties across cultural boundaries are as salient as cultural identity. If they are not, they are likely to fall victim to ethnic conflict rather than be a force which moderates it. Here it should be pointed out that Lijphart (1977, p. 87) also claims that the evidence that cross-cutting cleavages are conducive to consociational democracy is often weak and ambiguous. Nordlinger, unlike Lijphart, claims that geographic isolation can increase conflict by increasing unequal development and by encouraging calls for greater autonomy, which can raise the stakes of the conflict. He cites six examples of successful conflict regulation through the measures he describes. They are Belgium from 1830-1958; Holland from 1890-1917; Austria from 1945-1965; Switzerland; Malaysia; and the Lebanon.

The consociational democracy approach has, of course, attracted its critics. Some of the arguments made against it were also applied to the plural society approach. These include the claim that the theory places too much emphasis on the permanence of ethnic boundaries, exaggerates ethnic cleavages and undervalues the existence of cross-cutting cleavages. There are also more specific points that need to be looked at. The first is that consociationalism tends to freeze ethnic relations, by making cultural divisions the basis of political life and constitutional structures. Therefore it may actually enhance cultural divisions and makes political activity more uncompromising and inflexible. Conflicts over constitutional provisions could be encouraged, instead of allowing the sides to debate and negotiate over interests and needs. Or perhaps, more accurately, the rigid adherence to constitutional provisions become defined as the most important group interest. This results in the 'frozen quota pitfall' (Horowitz, 1985), an unwillingness to adapt to changing circumstances which will then encourage conflict rather than efforts to manage or resolve it. The Christians in the Lebanon clearly fell victims to this pitfall when they insisted on retaining the majority position allocated to them by the 1944 National Pact (a clear example of consociational engineering) even when the Moslem groups became the majority population, probably sometime in the 1970s. A willingness to bargain with, and make concessions to, the Moslem groups might have better served the long term interests of the Christian communities.

Another problem with the consociational analysis is its apparent tautological claim that elites will be able to work across ethnic boundaries when there is a tradition of elite coexistence. Other criticisms are that consociationalism offers an inferior form of democracy, that minority veto provisions can replace the tyranny of the majority with the tyranny of the minority and that it gives rise to inefficient government based on slow decisions and segmentation. Lijphart (1977, p. 47f) has persuasively answered these criticisms by arguing that such disadvantages are mild when compared to the benefits that consociational engineering could bring. The inefficiencies that arise from a complex decision making process, for example, have to be weighed against the inefficiencies that arise out of the bitter conflict that can arise if this approach is not adopted. He also argues that there is nothing in consociational democracy to stop states moving to a more conventional democratic system which remains plural but which is more adversarial in form.

Critical observations on the consociational democracy theory have also appeared in an analysis of Switzerland by Church (1989). He claims that this theory is really a 'screen which is not needed to explain the real workings of Swiss politics' (p. 52). Indeed, it may even be a 'barrier to understanding' (p. 36). The attempt to explain the stability of Switzerland in terms of consociationalism is flawed because it undervalues the role of cross-cutting cleavages in Switzerland; concentrates too much on the elite level; ignores the extent to which the mutual veto coexists with a form of majoritarian rule through the referendum; neglects the importance of economic prosperity and neutrality; and does not emphasise enough a political culture that is specific to this country.

The issue of political culture is an interesting one, especially because nearly every successful case of consociational democracy is found in the developed West. This has led even some sympathetic writers to question its effectiveness when applied to third world states. Even in the few cases of success in the third world the states concerned seem to possess qualities more often found in the rich world. Singapore, for example, which is often put forward as a successful case of ethnic conflict management, is relatively democratic, economically prosperous, is quite small, lacks a large number of different ethnic groups, and exists in a relatively secure and non-threatening regional environment (Clammer, 1986).

The apparent failure of consociationalism in the third world has encouraged some theorists to develop a modified approach which is a mixture of consociational democracy thinking and control and dominance theory. This mixture of strategies is reflected in the name these theorists have applied to their model - hegemonic exchange. Such regimes, although not democratic in the western sense, are characterised by a greater openness to ethnic demands than is found in plural societies, and this flexibility will result in open or tacit bargaining with representatives of various ethno-regional interests. The hegemonic exchange approach is most clearly associated with Donald Rothchild, who has applied it in his writings to states in Africa (Rothchild 1986a, 1986b; Rothchild and Chazan, 1988; see also Mozaffar, 1986). These states, he claims, cannot impose solutions on all ethnic groups because they lack the capability to do so. In Rothchild's terminology they are 'soft' states. Enloe (1972, p. 92) pointed to this phenomenon when she claimed that

> The problem nagging at multi-ethnic, underdeveloped nations is this: underdevelopment in the modern era creates a need for centralized authority to offset communal fragmentation; yet centralization effective enough to control disintegrative forces requires resources beyond the reach of underdeveloped systems. When the dilemma is acute - that is, when intergroup animosity is strong and central authority is weak - countries are mired in apparently endless civil war.

Rothchild suggests a way out of this problem, and it involves governments engaging in a process of exchange with ethnic groups. However, the state is not so soft that it cannot impose a certain degree of hegemony that, for example, prohibits open partisan competition. So:

> As an ideal type, hegemonic exchange is a form of state-facilitated co-ordination in which a somewhat autonomous central-state actor and a number of considerably less autonomous ethno-regional interests engage, on the basis of commonly accepted procedural norms, rules, or understandings, in a process of mutual accommodation. (Rothchild, 1986b, p. 72)

Government at the centre, then, is undertaken by a hegemonic coalition of representatives of the various ethnic groups and regions and informal routines are established which promote balanced coalitions based on widespread participation by ethno-regional representatives. These can then devise methods to ensure an acceptable distribution of scarce resources and jobs. The result is a somewhat inefficient, but pragmatic, response to problems of multi-ethnic states in Africa. Such an approach, unlike that of the plural society, does not see ethnic relations as a primordial clash of exclusive identities. Rather it posits that ethnic groups have tangible interests that can be pursued in a rational, utility maximising manner. Therefore, trade-offs and bargaining are possible, and ethnic violence can be ended by changes in the way that power and wealth are distributed According to this model the state acts not as oppressor, but as a mediator and facilitator; and in order to play this role it must reject an exclusivist approach to access to power in favour of an inclusive strategy based on ethnic balancing. An example of hegemonic exchange in action was the unity agreement signed in Zimbabwe at the end of 1987. Following the creation of an independent Zimbabwe in 1979 there was serious tension between the Shona dominated Zanu party led by Prime Minister Robert Mugabe and the Zapu party of Joshua Nkomo, whose power base was in Metebeleland. On December 1987 Mugabe became the state's first president, but as part of a deal to ease ethnic tensions Nkomo became one of two vice-presidents and two other Zapu members also obtained cabinet seats. Furthermore, in December 1989, after two years of negotiations, Zanu and Zapu delegates met for a five day unity conference in Harare. Examples of hegemonic exchange cited by Rothchild include post-civil war Nigeria, Mauritius, Togo, Ivory Coast, Zambia and Kenya.

A final theoretical answer to the question of whether stable and democratic multi-ethnic states can be established is found in the recent writings of Smooha. In his analysis of the state of Israel (ie excluding the Occupied Territories), which is based on extensive attitude surveys, he has identified some positive developments in Jewish-Arab relations. He believes that Jewish attitudes have moved slightly from control to an emphasis on equality and integration (Smooha, 1992, p. 260). He also claims that Arab-Jewish relations can best be understood in terms of increasing Jewish accessibility and increased Arab politicization, which is itself indicative of a growing willingness to work within the state of Israel when fighting for better treatment rather than rejecting the legitimacy of this state outright.

Such a situation, however, cannot be characterised as either a conventional or a consociational democracy because the Israeli Arabs are still clearly in a subordinate position. But they also enjoy civil and political rights and are able to exercise these rights vigorously. As no model exists to account for this state of affairs, Smooha has used the term 'ethnic democracy'. The term is meant to be applied to a 'low rate' democracy, inferior to consociationalism, where there is no equality between the ethnic groups, but where there are low levels of violence, a large measure of stability and a degree of democracy.

Conclusions

There is something to be learnt from all the approaches to ethnic relations presented in this chapter. The plural society and control theories remind us of the deep problems that exist when trying to create stable and democratic multi-ethnic states. Consociationalism, on the other hand, is surely right to question the almost undiluted pessimism of this approach by pointing out the existence of successful multi-ethnic states and by offering an analysis of how ethnic groups can manage their conflict within stable democracies. It shows us a way that these groups can be offered a stake in a political system in a way which may stop them wanting to destroy that system. However, the hegemonic exchange model serves to warn us of over-optimism by pointing out the features of third world states that make it unlikely that consociational engineering will be a viable strategy. Indeed, there have been notable failures for the consociational approach in Cyprus, Lebanon and Fiji. Nevertheless, this model also takes issue with the pessimism of the plural society writers, and offers a form of modified consociationalism as an alternative to exclusive control by a dominant group. Smooha's recent analysis of Israeli society also reminds us that a more imperfect form of democracy can provide the starting point of intercommunal accommodation in divided states. To believe that multi-ethnic societies are doomed to conflict or oppression may, therefore, be labelling a tragedy of possibility as a tragedy of inevitability.

There are plural societies, consociations and states based on hegemonic exchange and ethnic democracy, and we can learn from studying them all. We should probably think of a continuum of possible forms with the plural society at one end and a fully democratic state at the other, with multi-ethnic states being located at various points along it. It would be possible, even likely, that states could move along this continuum in either direction as a result of decisions made by the key actors. For this reason any attempt by one of the approaches to claim universal significance should be rejected. The existence of alternatives to the plural society model is, at least, a source of some optimism about the viability of multi-ethnic states. It is easy to dismiss the consociational democracy approach. However, one should remember the arguments of McGarry and O'Leary (1990, p. 295) in their normative conclusion that consociationalism is the best means of stabilizing the Northern Ireland conflict. They point to its advantages. It emphasises agreement rather than coercion. The theory believes that the parties themselves, not outside powers, must regulate their conflict. It is compatible with democratic legitimacy, and it has a partially successful track record. McGarry and O'Leary don't believe that the conditions are yet ripe in Northern Ireland to apply the consociational model, but this does not lead them to abandon it for less attractive models. Instead they believe that policies should be adopted that can promote the consociational alternative. Wilson (1988 , p. 16) has also argued that if the elites in Sri Lanka had adopted consociationalism they 'could have prevented the frictions and bitterness that lay ahead'.

The importance of establishing alternatives to pessimistic analysis is important, because it has implications for the policies which will be adopted in response the conflicts within multi-ethnic states. In the former Yugoslavia many observers already seem to have abandoned the idea of a viable, stable and democratic multi-ethnic state. This has led to considerable international feeling that the best way to deal with the conflict is through separation, and this was reflected in the case of Bosnia and Hercegovina in the Vance-Owen cantonization plan of January 1993.[4] The problems with this 'solution' are that it writes off a long-established multi-ethnic society, rewards aggression and means total surrender to the arguments of extreme nationalists.

Despite their obvious differences, however, all the theories discussed here share two assumptions which may be a source of weakness for each of them. The first of these is the emphasis each places on elite interaction and the neglect of popular opinions and non-elite attitudes that follows from this. Lijphart (1977, p. 53), for example, has claimed that what he calls the 'mass public' tends to be 'rather passive and apolitical almost everywhere'. he believes this to be a good thing since this means that there is unlikely to be opposition from this group to elite cooperation. He neglects, however, the possibility of building peace from below in multi-ethnic states by creating a constituency for peace at the grass roots level. Lijphart believes and hopes that the mass public will remain passive and ignores 'popular sentiment and opinion' (Church, 1989, p. 41). The role of grass-roots action will be examined in chapters four and five, where it will be pointed out that in the process of conflict resolution the attitudes and wishes of followers are ignored by elites and by outside mediators at their own peril.

The second weakness is the way that these theories ignore the international setting within which attitudes of elites and non-elites are formed. This appears to this author to be a serious omission, and it is the topic which will be analysed in the next chapter. For the international influences within which multi-ethnic states operate may, ultimately, have a crucial role in determining whether such societies end up as plural societies, consociations, or hegemonic exchange states. It is to these influences that we can now turn.

Notes

1. There is also a brief discussion of Rabushka and Shepsle's views in Lijphart (1977,p. 232).
2. See, for example, Farrell (1980) and O'Leary and Arthur (1990).
3. The use of the plural society as a system of classification comes out most strongly in Smith, 1986. An interesting development in Smith (1988) is the distinction he makes between race and ethnicity. Racial distinctions are, he states, biological and therefore immutable. He seems to go on to make the prediction that societies that have racial divisions are more likely to experience differential incorporation (Smith, 1988).
4. Under the Vance-Owen plan Bosnia and Herzogovina would be divided into ten autonomous provinces in which the Moslems, who make up 43.6 per cent of the population, would receive 27 per cent of the territory.

2 The international dimension of ethnic conflict

The modern state is intrinsically, not just contingently, a nation state, existing in a world of other nation states. (Giddens, 1984, p. 198)

We want to know if Lebanon is a sovereign state or a whorehouse. (Camille Chamoun, 1978)

Introduction

In the first chapter we have examined some of the common patterns of ethnic relations and noted the frequency with which these relations become destructive. There are, of course, several reasons why this should be the case, but in this chapter, in accordance with the theme of our study, we will concentrate on the ways in which the interstate system influence the development of ethnic relations within states. We are not claiming that this is the only important variable in explaining ethnic violence, but it is an important aspect that is frequently over-looked. As we have already noted a major weakness that both the plural society and consociational democracy approaches to ethnic relations share is that they restrict their analysis to the single states and ignore the wider interstate setting of facts and values within which individual states have to function. As C.W. Mills might have put it, the 'sociological imagination' has not been extended far enough. Too often in analysing ethnic conflict it remains restrained within the boundaries of a single sovereign state.

Because the plural society theory tends to regard the development of either structural dominance or violence as inevitable in multi-ethnic socieites, in seeking explanations for inter-ethnic tensions it has no need to look any further than the multi-national nature of the state. Outside influences might make such conflicts more complicated, but these influences will be restricted on the whole to the dynamics of the conflict rather than its causes. The consociational democracy approach also adopts this narrow viewpoint and also tends to regard external influences as secondary. Often the interstate setting is dismissed in a few paragraphs which show how an outside threat might be a cohesive force in multi-ethnic states the way that the fear of the Soviet Union is supposed to have maintained a stable state in Yugoslavia. In specific cases consociationalists do seem to be aware of the powerful influences of outside forces. Lijphart (1980, p. 27), for example, has stated that the explanation for the failure of consociational democracy in the Lebanon was not the inherent weaknesses of that society, but the 'extraordinary external pressure of the Middle East conflict and the increasingly heavy burden of the pressure of large numbers of Palestinian refugees and guerrillas on Lebanese soil'. Nevertheless Lijphart has not as yet incorporated such insights into his more general theory; preferring at this level to continue to regard the influences of the international environment as secondary. His discussion of this environment's impact on consociational engineering is, as a consequence, rather limited. In his discussion of conditions which favour the consociational approach, for example, he limits the discussion of external factors to the security of small states threatened by big powers, the restricted role of small states in international affairs which may limit internal cleavage, and the impact of external threats on elite solidarity (Lijphart, 1977, p. 66-70).

Two aspects of the interstate system will be studied. The first factor we will consider is the way in which national self-determination has become one of the key legitimising principles in international relations. The second is the decentralised distribution of power in the system which, on the whole, makes interstate relations more like a state of nature than domestic relations. It will be suggested that both these influences adversely affect the chances of creating a democratic and stable multi-ethnic society as proposed by the consociational democracy theory.

National self-determination

The importance of the principle of national self-determination has been acknowledged many times in declarations and policy statements. Reference to it can be found in the 1941 Atlantic Charter; in Articles 1(2) and 55 of the UN Charter; in the 1966 Human Rights Covenants; and in Article 8 of the Helsinki Final Act. Many General Assembly Resolutions also contain a reference to the principle.[1] The best known of these is the 1960 Declaration on the Granting of Independence to Colonial Countries and Peoples of 1960. But there have been numerous declarations since then, most notable with reference to Palestine, Namibia and South Africa.[2]

It is certainly true that states have attempted to qualify their support for national self-determination in a number of ways and that neither international law nor international practice allows for an unqualified right for any national group to secede from an existing state. Even though it may be understandable why states should fear the potential destabilising effects of an unrestricted right of self-determination the fact remains that ethnic groups who are victims of internal oppression and who have a highly developed sense of their own distinctiveness will claim for themselves such an unrestricted right. This is the case with Sinn Fein, the PLO, the Tamil Tigers, the Turkish Cypriots, and many other ethnic groups. The Turkish Cypriot leader, Denktash, for example, has referred to the 'inalienable right of national self-determination' to justify the creation of the Turkish Republic of Northern Cyprus in November 1983 (Ertekun, 1981, p. 127). Arafat has also talked repeatedly about the sacred right of Palestinian self-determination.

This important principle of national self-determination seems to have two major effects, one on the ethnic group challenging the state and the other on the state itself. For the ethnic group seeking greater autonomy it will provide an increased sense of legitimacy and encouragement. In other words it will make it more likely that an ethnic minority will become a national minority. For the state the principle creates a real problem. For so widespread is the idea that national self-determination is a legitimate right that it cannot be dismissed out of hand. Indeed, even the South African government felt it necessary to establish the Black homelands. This, however, was not regarded as a legitimate policy by the international community because it was not an example of self-determination by black South Africans, but was a case of 'other determination' undertaken by a government representing the minority white community. But to accept the principle of national self-determination wholeheartedly would threaten to undercut the legitimacy of the the multi-national state. For as Young (1985) has pointed out this

54

will give rise to a conflict between the normative idea of the nation-state and cultural and political realities.

Ruling elites will seek different ways out of this dilemma and most of them will involve some degree of self-delusion. Sometimes an attempt will be made to deny that a state has any problems with its ethnic minorities. On occasions this tactic will be taken to extremes and it will be denied that an ethnic minority exists at all. Turkish governments, for example, for many years officially referred to the Kurdish people in their state as 'mountain Turks' or 'separatist bandits' and references to the Kurds in atlases and books were deleted. Ironically, the Turkish minority in Bulgaria has recently suffered a similar fate when the Bulgarian government pursued a policy of forced assimilation claiming that this minority was really composed of ethnic Bulgarians who had adopted a foreign culture (Helsinki Watch, 1987). Meanwhile, both the Bulgarian and Greek authorities refuse to accept that there is a Macedonian minority in their country. In a similar vein many Israelis deny that the Palestinians are really a distinct ethnic group and could easily be accommodated within existing Arab states. David Ben Gurion (1970, p. 118), in his memoirs, argues that 'Palestinian nationalism is highly artificial' and talks about the lack of true nationalist feeling among Palestinians. This is a sentiment reflected in Golda Meir's statement that there is 'no such thing as a Palestinian...it was not as though there was a Palestinian people in Palestine considering itself as a Palestinian people' (Christision, 1987).

Even when a government recognises that it has an ethnic minority and that there are problems associated with these cultural differences the response may be to claim that the unrest is created by an unrepresentative minority or by outside forces. This is a tactic used frequently by governments. In April 1988, during the Armenian unrest in Nagorno-Karabakh, for example, Pravda accused Western radio stations of inciting unrest and instigating trouble (Guardian, 5 April, 1989). For many years the official position of the government of the Republic of South Africa to the violence of the ANC was that it was carried out by a handful of extremists who were linked to an outside communist threat. Tully and Jacob (1985, p. 208) have pointed out how in India there arose a strong belief that the unrest in the Punjab is due, in large part, to the involvement of Pakistan.

That the principle of national self-determination might have this troublesome impact was recognised by Lord Acton. He stated

> The greatest adversary of the rights of nationality is the modern theory of nationality. By making the state and the nation commensurate with each other in theory, it reduces practically to a subject condition all other nationalities that may be within the

boundary. It cannot admit them to equality with the ruling nation which constitutes the state because the state would then cease to be national, which would be a contradiction of the principle of its existence. According, therefore, to the degree of humanity and civilisation in that dominant body which claims all the rights of the community, the inferior races are exterminated, or reduced to servitude, or outlawed, or put in a condition of dependence (Dalberg-Acton, 1907, pp. 297-8).

This vital warning about the dangers of nationalist doctrine in a world where a neat division of ethnic groups along territorial lines is impossible has been echoed by later writers. Claude (1969, p. 42) has made a similar point. So has Van den Burghe (1981b, p. 347), who has stated that 'any recognition by the state of ethnic sub-groups with a special relationship to the state...would be inconsistent with the idea of popular sovereignty'.[3]

It is not difficult to find historical examples to vindicate Acton's warning. From the French Revolution, through the Hungarian, German and Turkish national 'revolutions' to contemporary nationalist movements, strong nationalist sentiment has often coincided with the persecution of ethnic minorities and the attempt to deny the validity of competing national claims. Coulon (1978), for example , has traced the neglect of the ethnic issue in French political science to the Jacobin tradition of being 'indifferent toward differences'. In the early years of the French Revolution this was typified by Barere, who declared in 1794 that 'the language of a free people ought to be the language of all' (in Janowsky, 1945, pp. 15-16). The 1822 Greek Constitution, drafted against the background of a national uprising against Ottoman rule, effectively excluded Moslems and Jews from suffrage and office. When Jeremy Bentham was asked to comment on the draft of this constitution he wrote that

It places the Turks under the Greeks [as] the Helots were in under the Spartans, in the situation that the Protestants in France were in under the Catholics, in Ireland the Catholics under the Protestants, in the Anglo-American United States the Blacks under the Whites. In no country can any such schism have a place but in point of morality and felicity both races are, in however different shapes, sufferers by it: the oppressors as well as the oppressed (quoted in Rosen, 1992, p. 85).

Paul (1985) has analysed the attitude of the Magyars to their Slovak minority following the Hungarian national 'revolution'. Here a policy of enforced 'Magyarization' included censorship of the press, the closure of Slovak cultural institutions and support for anti-Slovak organisations (Anderson, 1983, pp. 96-100). During this period the radical nationalist poet Petofi described minorities as 'ulcers on the body of the motherland'. Niederhauser (1993) has pointed out how the liberal reformers in the new Hungarian government believed that equal treatment before the law on the basis of civil rights would satisfy non-Magyars. In fact the Serbian, Croatian, Rumanian and Slovakian minorities all organised some form of military action in support of their claims to special recognition.

In Germany, Trietschke complained that the people of Alsace-Lorraine had been misguided for too long in wishing to be part of France and it was up to the Germans to 'restore them to their true selves against their will', claiming that the Germans who knew both France and Germany knew better than the inhabitants of this area what was good for them (in MacArtney, 1934, p. 100). Whilst in Turkey, according to Chaliand (1980, pp. 65-6), a minister for justice is reported to have proclaimed in the 1930s that groups not of Turkic stock had only one right - the right to be slaves. The Turkish attitude to the Armenian people during the First World War is also well documented, despite Turkish claims that the evidence is fabricated. The Turkish refusal to face up to the multi-cultural nature of the state is best exemplified in Article 89 of Turkish Law. This stated that

> No political party may concern itself with the defence, development, or diffusion of any non-Turkish language or culture; nor may they seek to create minorities within our frontiers or to destroy our national unity (in Hannum, 1990, pp. 188-9).

There was a revival of Polish nationalism in the 1920s following the establishment again of an independent Polish state after the First World war. This gave rise to a 'Polonization' campaign which resulted in discrimination against the Ukrainian, Byelorussian, Jewish and German minorities. The Poles themselves had been victimised during the period of Bismark's *kulturkampf*. But now they were in the position of top dogs many supported the National Democratic Party of Roman Dmowski, with its 'Poland for the Poles' attitude. Many Poles refused to accept that there was a distinct Ukrainian people in their state, preferring to call them 'Ruthenian' (Korzec, 1991, p. 197).

Irish nationalism, which has tended to stress a Gaelic, Catholic identity, is reflected in the 1937 Constitution. It introduced the compulsory study of Irish in the schools and gave a special position to the Catholic Church. Catholicism also influenced, and continues to influence, the government's attitude to issues such as divorce and contraception (see Lyons, 1979, ch. 6). Morality in the Republic of Ireland, it appears to many Protestants, means Catholic morality. Furthermore, Irish nationalists have trouble in recognising the distinct Protestant, Loyalist identity that predominates in the north-east of the island of Ireland. One way out of the problems posed by the existence of this identity is for Irish nationalists to argue that Protestants have rejected their Irishness and have become the dupes of either a Unionist ruling class or British imperialism (Smyth, 1991, p. 137). Many commentators seem to casually dismiss the authenticity of Protestant values. Michael Collins, for example, one of the founders of the Irish state, once compared Northern Ireland to 'real Ireland' (Boyce, 1991, p. 21). This rather patronising approach makes many Ulster Unionists even more suspicious of the motives and actions of Irish Catholics.

Chinese minorities suffered greatly during the Cultural Revolution in China. Heberer (1989) has revealed how this Han-dominated movement made extensive revisions to policies towards cultural minorities. It was denied that China was a multicultural state. Special economic policies and special financing arrangements to minority territories were ended. Expressions of local culture became prime targets for 'smashing'. The use of minority written scripts was restricted and schools for minorities were closed.

More contemporary examples can also be uncovered. Rabbi Moshe Levinger of the Gush Emunim movement in Israel has stated that

> We invite the Arabs to live everywhere. But we don't believe they have the right to change the idea, the purpose of the state. For that reason, I believe that they shouldn't be able to vote in national elections for the Knesset, because if they could they would vote to change the purpose, the Jewish nature, of the state (in Reich, 1985, p. 18).

Another leading Gush Emunim writer, quoted by Lustick (1987, p. 124), put his attitude to the Palestinians even more brutally. They could, he stated, 'fight, flee or accept Jewish rule'.

In post colonial Africa a policy of 'Africanization' in some states led to discriminatory policies against Asian groups; most notably in Uganda where there was a wholesale expulsion of Asians in 1971. In Burundi, Lemarchand (1990, p. 104) has referred to the 'politics of ethnic amnesia' which allows the dominant Tutsi's to claim that there are no ethnic divisions in their country. He goes on to observe that

> Proceeding from the axiom that ethnic labels and stereotypes belong to the dustbin of colonial historiography, the official attitude of the Burundi authorities is that ethnic references are at

best a figment of the colonial imagination and at worst part of a neo-colonial stratagem....What is involved here is the creation of myth intended to mask the realities of a coercive state apparatus and, at the same time, to ensure its own survival through the spread of "false consciousness" among the subordinate Hutu masses (Lemarchand, 1990, p. 104).

Again, in Sri Lanka, a resurgence of Sinhalese nationalism has, in the words of one observer, 'excluded the Tamils in a final way and made the Tamils yearn for the lost Tamil Ilam of their forefathers' (Rajanayagam-Hellmann, 1986, p. 138). Particularly after the advent to power of the Bandaranaike government in 1956 the Tamils began to feel themselves increasingly threatened by demands of 'Ceylon for the Sinhalese'. This pro-Sinhalese policy of Sri Lankan governments was followed by Bandaranaike's successors. President Jayawardene, for example, established a special department of Buddhist affairs and incorporated the Buddhist wheel of righteousness in his presidential flag. In Burma the post-independence ideal of 'unity in diversity' has been abandoned for what appears to many to be a policy of 'Burmanisation of the minorities' (M. Smith, 1991, p. 34).

More recently, we have witnessed the impact of nationalist euphoria on dominant groups in Croatia and Estonia. Following independence Serbs were sacked by the new Croat state as the government of President Tudjman made ethnicity a factor in government employment practices (Glenny, 1992, p. 13). Serbs in Croatia were also appalled to see the newly independent state adopting symbols and policies which only alienated them further. In Estonia Russian speakers were disenfranchised and severe residency qualifications were applied before they could become citizens.

Therefore, there seems to be abundant evidence to give support to Claude's claim (1969, p. 42) that, 'within the frame of reference set up by the ideology of nationalism, national states and national minorities are incompatible'. For this reason, as van den Burghe (1990, p.6) has observed, the 'fiction of the nation-state is seldom innocuous', and tends to push the state into policies of minority suppression, forced assimilation or genocide.

Realism and the threat of ethnicity

Interstate relations take place in a decentralised power structure which results in a competitive self-help system in which, to use Meinecke's phrase, no state trusts another around the corner. In such a system, far more than in intrastate relations, serious violence is an ever present danger or possibility. The result is that a state 'is so constituted that it is apt for war; it is in one of its basic aspects a war making machine' (Calvocoressi 1981, p. 138). This has a significant impact on ethnic relations. For as Kant pointed out in his writings on peace, the form of domestic society is linked to interstate anarchy, which results in a permanent sense of insecurity and requires states to be in a constant state of war preparation. Therefore, as Kant observed in his seventh proposition in the *Idea for a Universal History with a Common Purpose*, 'the problem of establishing a perfect civil constitution is subordinate to the problem of a law-governed external relationship with other states, and cannot be solved unless the latter is also solved' (Reiss, 1991, p. 47). So, Kant believed, the creation of a good civil constitution within a state cannot be separated from the problem of the external relations of states (Hurrell, 1990, p. 187).

As long as interstate politics promotes a general atmosphere of anxiety minorities will be more feared and distrusted than might otherwise be the case and ethnic groups may be seen as a threat to state security: a Trojan horse serving the interests of outside powers. As a result dominant groups will be less tolerant of ethnic minorities, for in the words of Simmel 'groups in any sort of war situation are not tolerant. They cannot afford individual deviation from the unity of the coordinating principle beyond a definitely limited degree' (in Coser, 1956, p. 95). In modern states, of course, nationalism is often the major 'coordinating principle' and cultural difference is a threat to it.

In addition to this states fear internal dissension because a divided state will be weaker than a united rival. Sterling (1979, p. 414) has made this point, arguing that 'just as soon as separatist discontent surfaces an affected state becomes relatively weaker than surrounding states whose internal unity is intact. In all cases and in all stages separation affects state power'. One might want to take issue with Sterling's absolute tone. It could be suggested that a state might become stronger by allowing an ethnic movement a right to cultural expression or even secession so as to create a less conflict ridden entity more able to compete with its rivals. Realism could therefore lead to an acceptance of separation rather than a resistance to it. But states rarely adopt this viewpoint, and when ethnic groups are regarded as a source of internal weakness they are often more likely to be persecuted than accommodated.

Many examples can be provided to show how the view that an ethnic minority is a threat will lead to increased oppression of these groups. The stab in the back theory applied to Jews in Nazi Germany is a good example of this. The Israeli fear of the Palestinians in the West Bank and Gaza is another. The British suppression of the 1916 Easter rising in Dublin involved similar feelings. Occurring during the Great War, the British knew of secret contacts between Irish republicans and Germany and this coloured their ill-fated reaction to the rebels. Other cases would include the Vietnamese treatment of the Chinese minority; the Khmer Rouge persecution of the Vietnamese minority in Kampuchea; the Sandinistas treatment of the Meskito Indians in Nicaragua; and Yugoslavia's treatment of the Albanians in Kossovo after Albania had joined the Soviet led Cominform campaign against Tito in the late 1940s. In 1952 the Rumanian constitution provided for an autonomous region for ethnic Hungarians in Transylvania, but this policy was changed to one of assimilation after the 1956 uprising in Hungary because Bucharest feared a spill-over of unrest into Rumania (Enloe, 1973, p. 141).

Another example is the American treatment of its Japanese population following Pearl Harbour (Hirabayashi and Hirabayashi, 1984). What is interesting here is that the United States was not only one of the most liberal states of the period, but was also one of the most invulnerable. Yet it still decided in early 1942, on a wave of anti-Japanese hysteria, to transport about 80 per cent of Japanese-Americans to internment camps in desolate areas of the country. Furthermore, Ziedler (1984) has reminded us that this is an event unique in American history only because of the severity of the measures taken and because it linked into a long history of American racist attitudes to Orientals. He points out that during World War One there was at least one lynching of a German-American and many cases of less serious assault. German books were burnt and Wagner's and Mendelssohn's marches were removed from wedding ceremonies.

Conflict between the Walloons and the Flemish in Belgium was exacerbated by the experiences of two world wars. This is because of the collaboration of many Flemings with Germany in both of these wars. In the first world war, in particular, Germany presented itself as the ally of Flemish nationalism in Belgium, and indeed, in 1917, partly as a result of such encouragement Raad van Vlaanderen proclaimed an independent Flemish state. After the Second World War thousands of Flemings were put on trial for collaboration with the Germans.

This pattern of often exaggerated distrust of ethnic minorities is so common that Horowitz (1985, p. 179) is surely correct to point out that such fear cannot be dismissed simply as aberrant psychology, because in the existing state system such worries are based on an ever present possibility. It is also a point made by Ceadal (1987, p.189), who writes that 'political cultures and strategic situations tend to be found in predictable combinations: the degree of liberalism normally correlates with the degree of security'.

Of course it would be a gross exaggeration to claim that ruling elites at all times have this exaggerated fear of ethnic minorities. Attitudes will tend to fluctuate from mild suspicion to outright hostility depending on both the internal and external situations. The attitude of the Grand Vizir of Sultan Hamid, Kibrili Kamil Pasha, to minorities in the Ottoman empire is therefore the exception rather than the rule. He wrote in 1877, against the background of presumed Armenian support for a Russian invasion, that 'in Asia Minor...it is incumbent upon us as a state to wipe out any subject race which is suspect. For our future security, we should exterminate therefore the Armenian nation so that no trace and memory is left of her'.[4] This turned out to be an horrific prediction of what the attitude of some Turkish nationalists to the Armenians was to be in the Great War.

For wartime situations not only increase insecurity, they also provide ample opportunities to link the outside threat with an 'internal menace'. In such critical situations, to use Dervla Murphy's telling phrase, it is possible to 'disguise bigotry as patriotism' (Murphy, 1979, p. 64). One only has to think of the 360,000 Palestinians expelled from Kuwait after the end of the Gulf War because they were thought to have been sympathetic to Saddam Hussein. Some of these were subjected to arbitrary arrest and torture. There were also cases of deaths during custody. However, fears and resentments arising out of the experience of invasion is only one way in which an often exaggerated fear of an ethnic minority might develop. Feelings of insecurity will also be especially strong in in 'double minority' situations, where one group may be the majority within a particular state but is the minority group in the region as a whole. Such is the case of the Israelis in the Middle East, the Loyalists in Northern Ireland, the Greek Cypriots in Cyprus and the Sinhalese in the Indian sub-continent. Ethiopia, ruled by Christians, saw itself surrounded by Moslems and viewed its civil war with Eritrea in this context.

There is an extra twist to some of these double minority situations. For there are some places, such as Northern Ireland, where the minority may become the majority and the dominant group will then be a minority both within the area it traditionally dominates and within the region as well. Fear of this is a major reason why Israel has not annexed the West Bank and Gaza - for it would then have to include within the Israeli state many more Palestinians. The Christians in Lebanon have already reached this situation. For although at the time of the founding of the state they were the largest group, their relative population has declined when compared with the Moslems, and they now feel more insecure than ever about their destiny.

So far we have examined how the legitimising principle of national self-determination and the anxieties associated with a self-help system have influenced ethnic relations within single sovereign states. To complete the picture it is essential to look at how these two features of contemporary interstate society affect the attitudes of outside states to specific ethnic problems. Many writers have pointed out how states are supposed to operate in the interstate system in accordance with the norm of non-intervention (see, e.g. Bull, 1984; Vincent, 1974.) In practice, however, this norm is often flouted, and two reasons for this are effective links with a group fighting for national self- determination and the logic of the self-help system already examined above.

States that have close effective links with ethnic groups in another state will often not remain indifferent to the fate of these groups. Connor (1980, p. 172) is surely right to state that many governments hold transborder causes in more esteem than the traditions of international law. Such governments will often regard it as their right and their duty to involve themselves in the ethnic problems of other states. They will often justify this in a way suggested by Mackey (1975, p. 352), who writes that 'the principle of non-interference in the internal affairs of sovereign states, while protecting them from the use of force from without, simply sanctifies the role of force from within. Sometimes not only will states feel sympathy for their kin group in a neighbouring state, there might also exist an irredentist claim over part or whole of that state. For not only will the principle of national self-determination tend to disrupt multi-ethnic states, multi-state nations will also use it to legitimise calls for possession of 'lost territory'.[5]

Rarely though will effective concerns prompt forceful action without the existence of fears about security and loss of geopolitical advantage. Even the desire to redeem 'lost' territory and people will be tempered by practical and prudential considerations, and frequently instrumental calculations negate ethno-political affiliations. So, in an analysis of irredentism in Africa, Neuberger (1990, p. 107) concluded that

> Because "enthusiasm for 'redemption' of all but the most fervid ethno-secessionists is affected by cost/benefit expectations" and because "governments will always make these calculations and take their decisions in the context of a prevailing interstate systemic environment as well as in the context of domestic political pressures, opportunities and risks," irredentism in Africa is relatively rare. Even in cases where the state would like irredentism to succeed, instrumental calculations will usually override ethnofraternal emotions and prevent the state from

active involvement and commitment.

The constitution of the Republic of Ireland, to take another example, claims sovereignty over the whole of the island of Ireland. Yet, as one specialist on Irish politics has admitted, 'to judge from the past 15 years the South's concern is selfish, not altruistic, focused less on what might happen in Northern Ireland if unification becomes a reality and more on what could happen in the South if unification provokes a violent Loyalist reaction' (O'Malley, 1983, p. 84). In this case rational calculations have tempered the sympathy many Irish citizens feel for their fellow Catholics in Northern Ireland.

Regard for the realities of power balances and concern about the spill over of a conflict into one's own territory may be inhibiting factors stopping active intervention in ethnic conflict. Yet there are also several practical considerations that might promote rather than impede such a course of action. This may be because the loss of influence over a strategically located piece of territory would tip the balance of advantage in favour of a rival. Or an opportunity might arise to embarrass or harm a rival. Or a prior commitment will have to be honoured to maintain credibility. Or a supply of an important raw material will have to be guaranteed. But whatever the reason states cannot remain indifferent to conflicts going on in regions that border them; nor can they assume that things will work out for the best. As Hoffmann (1981, p. 23) has noted, international politics is the 'domain in which, far more than domestic politics, one pays a price for behaving decently'. He has developed this point by claiming that a key variable in explaining intervention is the nature of the interstate system in which there is no single principle of legitimacy and an abundance of targets of opportunity (Hoffmann, 1984).

Most direct interventions in the internal affairs of sovereign states experiencing ethnic conflict will therefore reflect a mixture of affective and instrumental factors. The help from Arab states such as Saudi Arabia and Kuwait for the Eritrean rebels in Ethiopia, for example, was partly due to an affective link with fellow Moslems fighting a Christian government. But it also stopped the self-proclaimed Marxist government of Ethiopia, and their allies the Soviet Union, obtaining a secure coastal area bordering the Red Sea. The Turkish invasion of Cyprus in 1974 was an attempt to protect Turkish Cypriots from forced annexation with Greece, but it was also due to a desire to deprive Greece of a strategically located island near the Turkish mainland.

Whilst not wishing to argue that external involvement by other states will always have a negative influence on ethnic conflict, there seems to be considerable evidence that such intervention is more likely to escalate rather than de-escalate conflict. For if a state intervenes for mainly instrumental reasons the conflict will be seen as something to be exploited rather than resolved. As a result there will often be a lack of sensitivity to the local issues, sides may be taken and new issues will be introduced into the conflict. If, on the other hand, affective reasons for intervention are important then such intervention will be be biased and will merely reinforce one side. Of course, if biased intervention on one side is great enough a conflict may well be brought to an end quickly through outright victory. This is what happened as a result of the Indian intervention in the war between Bangladesh and East Pakistan in 1971. However, such decisive intervention is rare, and external involvement frequently produces counter-intervention. This danger has been noted by Northedge and Donelan (1971, p. 131), who write

> As we have seen, intervention always tends to lead to counter-intervention of some sort, if there is time and opportunity for it. When this happens, the effect of intervening is often that the intervening state wins nothing; that both the intervener and the counter-intervener incur great costs; and that the dispute itself is simply protracted and raised to a higher level of violence.

This has happened in several of the most protracted and severe ethnic conflicts. In Lebanon, for example, the inter-communal wars have been greatly complicated by the involvement of Israel and Syria. After several years of uneasy peace in Cyprus we saw an attempt by the Greek Colonels to overthrow President Makarios in 1974, which provoked a Turkish invasion and the de facto partitioning of the state. In the Angolan Civil war the conflict was made more intractable by the South African intervention which provoked a Cuban involvement on the side of the Marxist government. This pattern of intervention and counter-intervention has also been repeated in the civil war in Chad.

Systemic threats to stable and democratic multi-ethnic states

All of this has important implications for the optimistic approaches to multi-ethnic states and attempts to create stable and democratic societies. It appears that the two factors discussed here operate within the state system in such a way as to work against such societies. As a result the attempt to escape from nationalist pride and prejudice through institutional devices within a single state can fail because this state has to operate in an interstate system where realist fears are greater and where the idea of national self-determination is a major legitimising principle.

The simplifying, ruthless idea of national self-determination and the affective national sentiments it both promotes and reflects tends to emphasise an exclusive identity rather than a compromise with other national groups. Smith (1986b, p. 48) pointed this out when he argued that since nationalism is about defining 'us' it must, in order to have a test of membership, start excluding others - 'them'. The principle also means that a nation without a state may feel a sense of what Edward Said has called national incompleteness and will have to tolerate, in Ernest Gellner's phrase, the 'psychic humiliation' of belonging to a state that does not reflect its culture.

But as well as this, the decentralised self-help system encourages realist fears which emphasise conflict and competition over power rather than reasoned mutual co-operation. So even if elites within societies may be able to move beyond the Hobbesian state of nature within individual states, this single state will operate in a Hobbesian interstate system, which can then reintroduce security fears into ethnic relations. Here it is significant that two of the major cases of successful multi-ethnic states, Canada and Switzerland, have been relatively isolated from mainstream international politics. Canada has been able to do this because of its geographical position; Switzerland because of its geographic position and its foreign policy based on strict neutrality. This has even stopped Switzerland joining the United Nations, a policy reaffirmed in various referenda, the last one in 1986. Also, one of the factors which has contributed to the success of the Aland Island experiment in Finland, with its Swedish population, is the neutralization and demilitarization of the island. In a similar way it has been argued that the relative success until recently of Yugoslavia in establishing a relatively stable, if less democratic, state was due, in part to its policy of non-alignment and a rejection of close identification with either superpower bloc in Europe. This is because of the issue of the cultural differences between the Croatians, who use a Latin script and are Catholic; and the Serbs, who use a Cyrillic script and belong to the eastern orthodox tradition. As a result the Croatians tend to see themselves as West European, the Serbs as East European. Therefore, any attempt to identify with either of the superpower blocs would have raised anxieties about cultural identity. The collapse of Yugoslavia, however, warns us that non-alignment and neutrality in itself is no guarantee of ethnic peace; and the isolationist policies of Burma and Albania have not stopped ethnic conflicts emerging. On the other hand, these states were not democratic societies and in these cases isolationism seems to have strengthened authoritarian tendencies and popular unrest.

On the other hand, two of the greatest failures of the politics of democratic accommodation are Lebanon and Cyprus and in both cases there has been an extensive degree of external involvement.

Interestingly, even in the successful consociational democracies, greater involvement in interstate politics has resulted in increased intercommunal tension. In Canada the decision by the government in 1917 to introduce conscription to help Britain during the Great War provoked violence in Quebec even though Britain and France were allies in that war (Flowers, 1984). So one can imagine what strains might have been induced in Switzerland had it been dragged into either of the two world wars.

Very few states are blessed with a geographical position that allows them to adopt a successful policy of neutrality or to remain relatively isolated from a potentially dangerous interstate system. However, despite this it is possible that the adoption of certain courses of action might result in a form of limited disengagement from this system. Marlin and Azar (1981) suggest as much when they argue that any successful conflict resolution process in the Lebanon has to involve reduced dependency on outside actors. However, perhaps not all external actors should be excluded. The United Nations, after all, is able to provide a degree of insulation from international relations through the dispatch of peace-keeping forces. As we shall see in chapter six, one of the main functions of such a force is to provide a barrier, more moral than physical, against outside intervention by states. Unfortunately the UN is an imperfect instrument and may be unable to fulfil this role properly. In both the Lebanon and Cyprus it was unable to stop external interventions by Israel and Syria and Greece and Turkey. However, in both of these instances these interventions pointed out the dangers that the UN presence was meant to address. For on each occasion the Eastern Mediterranean was brought to the brink of a more general war. In a perverse sort of way, therefore, although the authority of the UN was undermined the reasons put forward for its presence were vindicated.

The need to de-internationalize ethnic conflict?

Of course it would be wrong to suggest that external involvement by states in ethnic conflict will always be destructive. But clear examples of success are not easy to find. This would lead us to support those writers who claim that non-intervention usually creates conditions of peace. We can, however, look briefly at some arguments that might cause us to modify this general rule. But first we can examine an interesting argument that fails to convince.

Suhrke and Noble (1977), in their comparative study of ethnic conflict and international relations have argued that it is not always the case that outside involvement will lead to escalated conflict.[6] These two authors are, in fact, not concerned directly with issue of whether the interstate system causes or escalates ethnic violence. Rather they are examining what they term the 'Wilsonian postulate', proposed by the US president at the end of the first world war. This states that ethnic conflict will be a cause of interstate violence.

To use the famous system of classification introduced by Waltz (1959), Suhrke and Noble are interested in the second image as a cause of interstate war. Waltz uses this term to categorise those theories that try to explain war in terms of the nature of certain states (in this case states experiencing ethnic conflict) rather than in terms of the nature of individuals (the first image) or the nature of the state system itself (the third image). In this book we are not really concerned with this, but it might be said that we are interested in what has been termed the second image reversed; which attempts to determine the extent to which the interstate system creates conflict within states? So although the concerns of Suhrke and Noble are not directly the same as this book they share a common interest, even though they approach it from opposite directions. The findings of these authors are therefore of interest.

On the basis of a comparative study of several ethnic conflicts by different authors they conclude that the Wilsonian postulate is incorrect and instead they argue that situations of outside intervention in ethnic conflict can be classified along two simple dimensions. The first of these is the scope of the external involvement - is there a large (complex) or small (simple) number of external actors. The second dimension is the nature of the relationship between the various parties - is it co-operative or conflicting. These two different dimensions allow the authors to describe four possible ideal types of external involvement. These are complex conflict expansion, simple conflict expansion, complex conflict containment and simple conflict containment.

The fact that Suhrke and Noble can argue that internationalizing a problem can result in conflict containment as well as conflict escalation at first sight might lead us to question our earlier observations about the destructive impact of the interstate system. However three points can be made about Suhrke and Noble's claims. Firstly, it is not the intention of this study to take a deterministic stance on the questions considered. It is not being suggested that internationalizing a problem will always lead to more, not less conflict. It is suggested, however, that this will be a common result.

The second aspect of Suhrke and Noble's argument that needs to be addressed is that they talk only of containing, not resolving ethnic conflict. Containment is a rather ambiguous state of affairs that may mean that the parties to the conflict are relatively happy with the way the situation is developing or it may mean that one or more party is being forced to tolerate a state of affairs it does not regard as legitimate.

If the latter is the case, and Suhrke and Noble do not really distinguish the two types of situation, it is by no means certain that short term containment will not lead to a long term deterioration of the situation, rather like trying to keep the lid on a pressure cooker for too long. In the Lebanon, for example, Syria has been able to play the role of 'container', in the short term, but its interventions only served to increase fear and distrust among the Christian population who are opposed to greater links with Moslem states in general, and Syria in particular. In this way Syrian intervention deepened the conflict, supporting the argument that external intervention in ethnic conflict will probably increase the insecurity of at least one of the parties to the conflict.

The third point to be made is that a closer examination of Suhrke and Noble's study reveals that little evidence is available to support the argument that 'internationalization' can lead to either simple or complex conflict containment. The authors can find plenty of examples of complex (Cyprus, Lebanon, Eritrea) and simple (Kurds, Kazahks) conflict expansion. But they have to admit that 'none of the cases' studied in their volume can be categorised as complex conflict containment; though UN peace-keeping is suggested as a possible example. This suggestion will be examined in the rest of this book. Here it can be pointed out that UN peace-keeping operations can be seen as a deliberate attempt to de-internationalize a conflict because one of reasons for sending such missions is to deter interventions by other states. In the one case of simple conflict containment analysed (the Thai Moslems) the authors have to state that the success of this was due to both the 'low level of the local conflict' and to the decision of the main interested outside party (Malaysia) to declare a policy of strict non-intervention. Once again this would reinforce the case for de-internationalizing ethnic conflicts.

It can be argued, therefore, that Suhrke and Noble's study need not force us to revise greatly our arguments for trying to divorce ethnic conflicts from what Lawrence Durrell once called the stock-market of international affairs. Indeed, the study seems to be in the embarrassing position of establishing two categories of conflict containment that would support their hypothesis, and is then unable to find examples of cases to include there. There are, however, two other arguments about the impact of the inter-state system which we have to address.

The first of these has arisen, *inter alia*, in the Northern Ireland conflict, and in particular the decision by the British government to include the Irish Republic in the search for peace in Northern Ireland through the Anglo-Irish Agreement of November 1985. This international treaty has created an Intergovernmental Conference which allows the Irish government to put forward views and proposals on political, security and legal matters and on the promotion of cross border co-operation. In this case the internationalizing of the dispute has been widely applauded and is seen by many as the best way to break the political deadlock in Northern Ireland. (see e.g. Arthur and Jeffery, 1988). It has undoubtedly forced all sides to reassess their positions, and to this extent has had some positive benefits. However, this co-operation between the governments of Ireland and Britain, the result of a negotiation process going back to May 1980, has not yet spilled over into relations between the Protestant and Catholic communities in Northern Ireland. On the contrary. In the short term, at least, violence and intimidation has increased and the siege mentality of the Protestant community may have been reinforced. It should also be pointed out that this 'internationalizing' of the dispute has been made with the mutual consent of the governments, has been approved by both Irish and British parliaments, is embodied in an international treaty and has the support of one of the major political parties in the North (the SDLP).

Furthermore, both governments have committed themselves to respect the wishes of the majority of the population about the status of Northern Ireland (Article 1 of the Agreement). Such reasonable attitudes are usually not found when states intervene in ethnic conflicts and in this case success may be due to the unique historic relationship between Britain and Ireland, which Robert Kee once said was full of 'confusing contradictions'. Other interesting examples where states have supported inter-ethnic accommodation through bilateral action are the South Tyrol (Austria and Italy) and the Aland islands (Sweden and Finland).[7] These examples would, therefore, cautiously force us to modify our de-internationalization rule, but not to revise it fundamentally. They show that thoughtful international management of ethnic conflict by states is possible.

The second challenge to this rule comes from those who argue that the external involvement of international organisations might do more to promote peace than interventions by other states. This involvement can take several forms, including peace-keeping forces, mediation attempts, assistance for intercommunal projects of a functional nature, and what Farley (1986, p. 50) calls 'election management' - that is the international supervision of elections or plebiscites to ensure they are conducted in a fair and free manner. This qualification of our de-internationalization rule we will accept, and in part three we shall examine in more detail what the United Nations in particular can do to manage or resolve ethnic conflicts.

Conclusions

Several writers have expressed dissatisfaction with the existing interstate system and the way it appears to be unable to respond to ethnic conflicts so as to ensure international peace and security whilst paying proper regard for the legitimate claims of the warring communities. The alternatives proposed tend to fall into two categories. The first, examined in chapter seven, is the suggestion that an effective system of minority protection should be created based not on states but an international organization. Such a regime would do two things. It would guarantee the rights of ethnic groups and also remove the grievances that might give rise to violent conflicts. The second suggestion, which will be the main focus of part two, is that more thought should be given to improving the techniques of conflict resolution so that a more constructive response can be made to violent ethnic conflicts when they occur. As we shall look at each of these approaches in later chapters, here we can simply note that both involve some move away from the state-centric approach to international problems which invariably give rise to statist solutions whatever the merits of the case.

Several writers have argued for such a shift in perception. Walzer (1977) has challenged the dominant legalist/statist attitude to secession from a social contract perspective. He concedes that he does not deal with the problem of national minorities directly. These he describes as a group who have not joined at all, or only in part, in the social contract of the nation (state?). However, in his discussion of the rule of non-intervention in interstate affairs in the light of secession movements he does comment on this issue. Here, he seems to agree with Mill that intervention to support a national group fighting for their freedom is morally permissible if the group in question has proved their own desire for their own nation through 'arduous struggle' and if the government of the state concerned is 'morally', if not 'legally', foreign. Walzer goes on to argue, however, that although it would be a virtuous act to support the secession of such groups it may not always be prudent to do so. He is, therefore willing in some cases to accept the argument of writers such as Vincent (1974), who claim that the principle of non-intervention is important for world order and Walzer would therefore argue that a virtuous act to promote secession may have to be tempered by prudence. However, he neglects to examine whether prudence would sometimes lead us to support intervention to allow secession in order to partition an unstable multi-ethnic state that threatens regional stability.

Buckheit (1978) puts forward an argument that is similar to Walzer's, except that he does not view the issue as one of justice versus prudence, but as a clash of two principles of justice. He accepts that according to the social contract principle any oppressed national group should be allowed to create their own state. But he qualifies this with a utilitarian concern about the disruptive effects of secession on the interstate system and the rump state. He does not, however, offer much guidance on how to measure this disruptive effect, which seems to this author to be an impossible task. He may also be underestimating the capacity of the international political system to adapt to change. The granting of independence to Bangladesh, for example, did not bring about the collapse of international order.

Smith (1986c), approaching the question from the perspective of ethnic conflict resolution, also comes down in favour of an attitude that allows for greater sensitivity to each case of ethnic conflict seen in its context rather than one that wants to always impose a statist solution. The need to move away from a state-centric interpretation of many conflicts in favour of a greater emphasis on 'identity groups' has been pointed out by many writers, including Azar (1990) and Burton (1979).

There is, of course, no guarantee that any of these suggestions will be adopted. However, serious ethnic conflicts seem likely to remain an important feature of the interstate system for some time. As long as they exist they will continue to be a threat to international peace and security and to existing standards of conduct which try to restrict arbitrary killing and unnecessary suffering. We have argued in this chapter that when explaining the prevalence of ethnic conflict factors external to individual states need to be taken into consideration. Furthermore, this needs to be done in a way which does not just see external influences in terms of intervention, but takes into account the deeper structural influences of the interstate system. If this view is the correct then it seems to follow that actions directed at resolving or managing ethnic conflicts should take this into consideration, not as an afterthought but as an important part of any initiative. This is to support the claim of Guelke (1990, p. 194), that external factors have a paramount influence on the nature of many ethnic conflicts. Therefore, it 'would be futile...to attempt to work out lasting mechanisms for conflict resolution without taking external factors into consideration' (Hansen, 1987, p. 4). To emphasise this point we can end by quoting a specialist on the Lebanese conflict. In criticising the attempts to deal with the problems of Lebanon that do not take into account outside factors, Khalidi (1979, p. 101) writes that

For the fundamental weakness of the 'federal model'...lies precisely in its concentration on the contents of the Lebanese box...In their assessment of the viability and future of the society under consideration, watchers are put on notice to scrutinise the regional environment of the box no less than the contents of the box itself.

Notes

1. Every year the General Assembly passes a resolution on 'The importance of the universal realisation of the right of peoples to self-determination and of the speedy granting of independence to colonial countries and peoples for the effective guarantee and observance of human rights'. See UN Docs 37/43 (1982), 38/17 (1983), 39/17 (1984), 40/25(1985), 41/101 (1986), 42/95 (1987).
2. The UN has even established a Committee on the Inalienable Right of the Palestinian People to Self-determination. This has published a set of Security Council and General Assembly resolutions on Palestinian self-determination for the period 1980-88. See UN Doc. A/AC. 18L/L.2/Add. 1-8.
3. See also van den Burghe (1990).
4. Quoted in a prepared statement given by Professor Dadrian to the House of representatives Sub-Committee on Future Foreign Policy Research and Development: Hearings on Investigation of Certain Past Instances of Genocide and Exploration of Policy Options in the Future, US Government Printing Office, 1976, p. 12.
5 See the introduction for a discussion of irredentism.
6. This view has recently been supported by Shiels (1984).
7. See, for example, Alcock (1986).

Part II
Ethnic Conflict Resolution:
A Model

3 'The voice of sanity getting hoarse': The dynamics of ethnic conflict

That is what the war is doing to us, reducing us to one dimension: the Nation. The trouble with this nationhood, however, is that whereas before, I was defined by my education, my job, my ideas, my character - and yes, my nationality too - now I feel stripped of all that. I am nobody because I am not a person any more. I am one of 4.5 million Croats. (Drakulic, 1993, p. 51)

I have been lucky, Through all this trouble I have been able to remain aloof. I was not required to avenge anything or anybody. But if my mother or father or sister or brother had been killed in that riot, I would have had no choice but to avenge them. That is the way we live in Asia. (A Tamil quoted in McGowan, 1992, p. 105)

Introduction

The purpose of this chapter is to explore what happens to ethnic communities when they engage in violent ethnic conflict with each other. This concern with the dynamics of such conflicts is prompted by a view, which is quite commonly held, that the experience of violent intercommunal conflict will 'bring the sides to their senses'. In fact, what often seems to happen is quite the opposite. The more violence that occurs the more bitter and protracted the conflict becomes. This seems to be the case because the experience of violence triggers certain destructive processes which then feed back into the conflict situation. In fact, the shift to violence in intercommunal relations crosses an important boundary. Curle (in Woodhouse, 1991, p. 50) has pointed out that 'when quarrels rise to a certain pitch of violence the difficulty of reaching a peaceful settlement seems to increase sharply'.

The existence of this destructive dynamic has been recognised in several theoretical studies of conflict. Kuper (1977), for example, in an important analysis of plural societies, has examined the processes which result in the aggregation of the parties into hostile groups. Wedge (1990), in an article on how psychoanalysis can contribute to thinking about peace and conflict, has identified the importance of group processes such as the diabolical enemy image, the virile self-image, selective inattention, the absence of empathy and military overconfidence. Wehr (1979) has also identified several such processes under a general heading of conflict dynamics: the movement from specific to general issues, the distortion of information, reciprocal causation, and the emergence of extremist leadership.

Mitchell (1981a) has produced a slightly different list of these processes (tunnel vision, premature closing of options, misattribution of motives, stereotyping, bolstering and polarization) whilst Agnew (1989, p. 50-51) identifies four sources of intractability in ethnic conflicts: the production of new material stakes in conflict, the creation of new symbolic issues, an enhanced ethnocentrism, and the power of sacrifice. Pruitt and Rubin (1986) have developed a structural change model of conflict escalation to explain how conflicts escalate, which argues that the tactics used to pursue conflict result in 'residues', in the form of changes in the parties. Such theoretical analyses have been supported by empirical studies of specific conflicts. Studies of Catholic communities in Northern Ireland have confirmed many of the destructive processes identified in the peace and conflict studies literature. In a study of the Bogside in Derry, for example, Apter (1990, p. 150) has claimed that violence 'generates its own objects' and 'creates its own ordering discourse'. Whilst Burton (1978, p. 36) has referred to the 'radical gemeinschaft' he encountered in an anthropological study of a Catholic community in Belfast, which produced a level of 'mediated reality'.

These processes interact with one another in a complex way, but for analytical purposes they can be separated out into separate processes, all of which inhibit peace-making work and help establish an uncompromising *weltanschauung* within communities at war. In this chapter the processes examined are: militarization; an exaggerated ethno-centrism; physical separation and the sharpening of territorial boundaries; the various processes associated with psychological distancing (stereotyping, dehumanization etc); sanctification and demonization; entrapment and over-commitment; economic under-development; and a sense of cynicism and powerlessness. These are found in different intensities in each specific situation, but they all seem to exist whenever ethnic groups engage in violent conflict. What is more, they can spring up in areas where there is no history of severe grass roots antagonism. One of most poignant aspects of accounts of the war in the former Yugoslavia is how the different communities in cities like Vukovar and Sarajevo could not believe that extreme violence would visit them because inter-ethnic relations were so good (Glenny, 1992). Destructive processes then can exert a powerful force and we can now look at each in turn. In so doing we may be able to glimpse how ordinary people, so often excluded from discussions of ethnic conflict, react and adapt to violent situations. It was Lippmann (1962) who pointed out how the lack of emphasis on the dynamics of social processes in politics led to the study of human problems by excluding humanity.

Militarization and the creation of garrison communities

The existence of a violent conflict creates a demand for the specialists in violence to protect their own communities and exact revenge on the enemy side. As Pruitt and Rubin (1986, p. 107) point out, groups 'usually choose as their leaders people who resonate with the dominant sentiments of the members'. So if conflict involves heavy contentious activity 'leadership is more likely to fall into the hands of militants, who can mirror the anger of the membership and build a fighting force' (ibid.). Laswell (1964) produced a pioneering study of the spread of militaristic values in wartime and coined the phrase 'garrison state', which has here been transformed into the phrase garrison communities.

The more militarised communities become, the less tolerant they seem to be of moderate opinion. One only has to think of the despair of Gandhi in the last years of his life, unable to stop the vicious intercommunal violence that accompanied the partition of the Indian sub-continent. As Kuper (1974a, p. 266-7) points out

> There can be little doubt that liberals are not viable in extreme racial conflicts. They have no mass following, they have no power, they have no skill, nor inclination for violence. In consequence they are easily emasculated by governmental repression, or liquidated by extremists on both sides. The mediating position becomes a no-man's land...when combat is

once engaged, and the groups begin to polarise, the appeals for conciliation, moderation and humanity become strangely insipid and meaningless.

Or to put it another way, whereas it may be easy to sit on the fence in peace-time, it is a lot harder to straddle a barricade in time of war. The growing influence of the military, paramilitaries and vigilantes can have two important results.

Firstly, self-perpetuating war machines can be created in the opposing communities that can then feed of each other to legitimize their own existence. The most effective way of justifying the existence of a military capability in one's own community is the existence of a military capability on the other side. Secondly, the more influential the war machine becomes, the more likely it is that militaristic values will spread through the community. As a result there is likely to be a reduced toleration of dissent, greater pressure to conform, a reduction of open and free debate, a glorification of violence and the spread of ideologies of violence.

Eckhardt (in Krull, 1990, p. 54) has pointed out how militarism tends to be correlated with a rigid cognitive process, dogmatism, intolerance of ambiguity, lack of creativity and an emphasis on law and order. In such an atmosphere the middle ground is squeezed and moderates are marginalized. As Kuper (1977, p. 220) put it after looking at the civil war in Algeria, where liberals where called 'half breeds' by the French settlers, 'there is no room for discourse between visceral commitment and reasoned argument'. O'Malley (1990,p. 154-5) has quoted a Northern Ireland Catholic community leader, Paddy Devlin, who writes about his own impressions of what happened in Belfast during the 1981 Hunger Strike

> In the ghettos, not to display a picture of a hunger striker or fly a black flag was to draw suspicion on yourself; not to respond in the middle of the night by turning on your lights to the rattling of the dustbins and the blowing of whistles that announced the death of a hunger striker was to invite a brick through the window; not to heed the demand of the placards held up by activists manning the white line pickets to toot your horn in support of the hunger strikers put you in danger of having your car window smashed.

Therefore, according to Devlin, 'decent' people kept their doors locked as crowds paraded around their streets and 'moderation fell silent, sullenness became a substitute for passiveness'. Often the war machine will turn against dissenting voices within its own community, and voices of moderation will be warned to keep quiet or may even be eliminated.

Hannum (1990, p. 306) has pointed out how in Sri Lanka, the 'moderates on both sides were among the earliest casualties of the escalating violence'. And as a man in Belfast observed, in a divided society to 'fire questions in your own community takes far more courage than to fire a bullet in somebody else's' (Belfrage, 1988, p. 385). The attraction of the war machine is that it seems to offer security for its own community. However, by inhibiting the emergence of moderate opinion and by increasing the sense of fear in the other communities in the conflict it may actually contribute to the continuation of insecurity.

Increased ethnocentrism

The rise of militarism is closely associated with the exaggerated ethnocentrism that tends to flourish in situations of violent ethnic conflict. Agnew (1989, p. 51) has noted how 'ethnic conflicts produce an enhanced ethnocentrism that is manifested linguistically in what is best characterized as "war talk".' Morton Deutsch (1991, p. 34) has argued that one of the 'reasonably well established propositions relating to the occurrence and intensity of ethnocentrism' is that 'the more intense the competition between groups, the greater the tendencies towards ethnocentrism in their relations; the more intense the cooperation between groups, the less the ethnocentrism'. Hobsbawm (1990, p.167-8), in a recent study of nationalism, quotes George Simmel, who once stated that

> Groups, and especially minorities, which live in conflict... often reject approaches or tolerance from the other side. The closed nature of their opposition, without which they cannot fight on, would be blurred...Within certain groups, it may even be a piece of political wisdom to see to it that there be some enemies in order for the unity of the members to be effective and for the group to remain conscious of this unity as its vital interest.

Northrup (1989, p. 74) mentions an hypothesis by Brown and Ross that 'the level of in-group bias and the intensity of feelings of hostility toward the out-group will increase in proportion to the degree of threat to identity that is perceived to originate from the out-group'. Since it is difficult to imagine a more intense form of competition than protracted violent conflict it seems reasonable to assume that such conflict will give rise to an exaggerated ethnocentrism as calls are made by leaders to show unity in the face of outside threat and as dissenters are accused of giving explicit or implicit support to the enemy. Glenny (1992, p. 85), in his study of the disintegration of Yugoslavia, has written that the most striking manifestation of the collapse of rational politics in this former state was 'the homogenization of consciousness among Croats and later among Serbs' which was 'fascinating to observe, if ultimately incomprehensible and distressing'.

Smooha (1992, pp. 140-43) has tried to quantify ethnocentrism in Israel. His findings are revealing. He determined that 29.7 per cent of Jews surveyed in 1985 thought that Arabs were 'primitive', whilst 64.9 per cent of Arabs believe that Jews do not care about self-respect and honour. In 1988 65.2 per cent of Arabs agreed that it was impossible to trust most Jews in Israel, and 60 per cent of Jews agreed that it is impossible to trust most Arabs. Jewish unwillingness for inter-ethnic contact was revealed by findings that 48 per cent rejected Arabs as co-workers, 65 per cent as schoolmates and 75 per cent as neighbours. Similar figures for Arabs showed a greater willingness for contact. Ninety-seven per cent of Jews and 92.5 per cent of Arabs showed an unwillingness to have their daughter marry a man from the other community. Sixty-eight per cent of Jews are not prepared to accept an Arab in a superior job. He concludes that 'Arab and Jewish ethnocentrism is substantial', but he also discovered that leaders exhibit much less ethnocentrism than the public at large. The depth that this ethnocentric identification can reach is revealed by Volkan (1990, p. 32). He recounts how Armenian victims of the severe earthquake that hit their region refused blood transfusions that had come from Azerbaijani donors.

In Sri Lanka the increased ethnocentrism has been noted by McGowan (1992, p. 278), who points out the impact it had on the university campuses. He claims

> By 1988 any instructor or lecturer who dared to challenge the Sinhala Buddhist consensus could be sure of at least a hectoring, if not a physical assault, a profound phenomenon in a culture where almost all teachers were usually accorded Confucian-like deference. As a result, most of the Westernized intellectuals, already driven out of the mainstream of academia, hardly set foot on campuses, fearing a hostile, if not violent reception for their politically incorrect opinions.

This echoes the claims of Dragan Klaic (Guardian, 17 January 1992), formerly professor of theatre studies in Belgrade, who argues that in what used to be Yugoslavia 'each ethnic group's intellectuals and artists are caught up in the web of provincialism. They are made subservient to nationalist ideology. They risk being branded as traitors by the authoritarian elites who have come to power everywhere in Yugoslavia in the first multi-party elections'.

This exaggerated awareness and concern about cultural difference tends to translate into greater hostility towards outsiders and a greater intolerance of insiders who question these exaggerated attitudes. In the atmosphere engendered by such intolerance and hostility, amid what George Bernard Shaw once called the 'rhetoric of the barricade', it becomes extremely difficult to stand against the pressures to conform. The case of Sarajevo television is of interest here. In 1989 it obtained editorial freedom and a degree of financial autonomy. Under editor-in-chief, Nenad Panic, it tried to adopt an independent position in the face of the Serb-Croat-Moslem hostility and resisted suggestions that the station be divided into three national sections. Panic resisted this because of the effect it would have on accurate journalism. He stated

> During the civil war in Croatia, Croatian TV would give news about a Catholic priest who had been beaten up by the Serbian forces, and on the same day, absolutely the same story would be reported by Serbian TV, but about an Orthodox priest who had been beaten up by the Croatian forces. The point is that both stories are true, but the important thing is that Serbian TV did not broadcast the story about the Catholic priest and Croatian TV did not broadcast the story about the Orthodox priest. We broadcast both stories...But if you try to be professional during a war you will not have success with either side. You are a traitor to both. (Index on Censorship, 1992, no. 6, p. 8)

As a result, Panic himself heard that he had been put on both Serbian and Croat death lists; journalists were physically assaulted and their homes were bombed; offices were attacked. This is not an isolated attack on an independent media.

When Milosevic came to power in Serbia he almost immediately purged both the main newspaper in Yugoslavia, *Politika*, and radio Television Belgrade (Glenny, 1992, p. 44). During the war in Croatia Yutel, the federal television station of Yugoslavia was forced off the air in both Croatia and Serbia for trying to remain impartial. Nor is the media the only target. Moderate opposition parties, anti-war groups and individual activists have all been subjected to attempted intimidation in Serbia and Croatia. As a report in the Guardian put it, Serbs in Belgrade 'bold enough to dissent from the black-and-white view of the war are also branded Ustashe and risk being gaoled, sent to the front, or having their homes and offices attacked by dapper, young, club-wielding thugs' (Guardian, 28 November, 1991).

The best account of the pressures to conform in the former

Yugoslavia is found in the writings of Slavenka Drakulic (1993). She recounts numerous examples of attempts to resist what one of her friends called the 'one dimension only, that of the nation'. Such people were invariably branded traitors. An unwillingness to be 'pinned to the wall of nationhood' inevitably led to persecution. Drakulic (1993, p. 52) noted how in 'the new state of Croatia, no one is allowed not to be a Croat'. Even though Drakulic resents the 'cruel, self-perpetuating game' she is forced to play and the way that 'the war devours us from the inside, eating away like acid' she also finds it difficult to resist the pressures to conform.

These pressures make it more difficult to think creatively. Thus

> It becomes increasingly difficult to consider new events in an objective and flexible way. The scope of perception of reality diminishes. If the true situation is more complex, more varied, one must ignore the complexity, this diversity. One's position gradually no longer fits the facts; the facts must be tailored to fit one's position (Warren, 1987, p. 31).

Elshtain (1989, p. 120) makes a similar point when she states that during crises there is a tendency

> for our spines to stiffen collectively and our voices to speak as one. When we perceive a threat to our honour, our security, or our way of life, most of us prefer not to hear discordance, and all too many among us construe dissent as disloyalty.

Physical separation and the sharpening of territorial boundaries

A common feature of violent intercommunal conflict is the movement of populations out of mixed areas to places where their own community is dominant. This movement can be forced ('ethnic cleansing') or 'voluntary' to the extent that the move is prompted more by a general fear than by a direct threat. In Cyprus several waves of population movements have led to the almost total separation of Greek and Turkish Cypriots who now live on different parts of the island. In Northern Ireland Darby and Morris (Darby, 1986) estimated that between 30-60,000 people living in the Belfast area evacuated their homes between August 1969 and February 1973. Many of these moved to mono-cultural areas. The separation in Northern Ireland, however, has never reached Cypriot proportions. Whyte (1990, p. 33f) quotes studies which show that in the mid-1980s about 38 per cent of the population in

Northern Ireland lived in areas where their own community made up 95 per cent or more of the total population. Segregation tends to be highest in urban working class areas in cities such as Belfast and Derry. However, a recent study, based on 1991 census data, seems to demonstrate that polarization has increased in the past few years (*Independent on Sunday*, 21 March 1993). It claims that 50 per cent of the population now lives in areas more than 90 per cent Protestant or Catholic and fewer than 110,000 out of a total population of 1.5 million live in areas with roughly equal numbers of Protestants and Catholics. In the past 20 years the number of predominantly Catholic wards has increased from 43 to 120, and the number of predominantly Protestant wards has increased from 56 to 115.

Similar population movements have occurred in Palestine and Sri Lanka, and it is happening today as an accompaniment to the violent break up of Yugoslavia. Here hundreds of thousands of Croats, Serbs and Moslems have fled mixed areas in Serbia, Croatia and Bosnia and Hercegovina. Furthermore, in a recent study of the nationalities question in the USSR Smith (1990, pp. 151-7) estimated that 200,000 refugees had fled to areas of comparative safety as a result of the Armenian-Azerbaijan fighting over Nagorno-Karabakh.

By reducing inter-communal contact in volatile situations the physical separation of warring communities may help conflict management in the short term and may help to create, in Galtung's terminology, a 'negative peace' or peace through dissociation. This is why the separation is often 'legitimised' through the establishment of Green Lines in places like Beirut, Nicosia and Palestine and by the building of a peace line in Belfast. These may make people feel more secure. Conroy (1988, p. 113) recounts how a proposal in Belfast to demolish part of the 'peace line' that separates Protestants and Catholics to build a landscaped park was opposed by both communities who lived in that area, who argued both that this would simply give the other side a clearer shot and that the park would become a battleground for stone-throwing youths. In fact, just recently residents of a West Belfast Catholic area which had been the sight of several murder attempts by Unionist paramilitaries threatened to take legal action against the Northern Ireland Office for refusing to build a 'peace wall' to protect them (*Irish News*, 22 September, 1992). This exaggerated sense of territoriality manifests itself in Northern Ireland in graffiti on walls, which mark out areas as belonging to one or other community, and in movement patterns that reveal how people avoid the areas identified with the other side (Pringle, 1990).

On the other hand the 'good fences make good neighbours' approach has its drawbacks because, in the longer term, physical separation creates serious obstacles for those wanting to build a long term 'positive peace', or peace through association. Bonds of friendship and common interest that transcend community divisions are shattered and new contacts between the communities are inhibited. Also the separated groups often become more attached to their own 'territory' and the places where these territories meet creates an interface between communities that can become 'shatter zones' (Bell, 1990, p. 155). Poole has also found that there was a high correlation between the extent of residential segregation in urban areas of Northern Ireland and the level of violence in these areas (Hamilton et al. 1990, p. 6).

Galtung (1985) is clearly doubtful that separation will produce peace, and has argued that

> No peace story ends with dissociation...It is too negative, too uncooperative, non-integrative - even if there may also be harmony in dissociation. The goal lies beyond negative peace, hence the necessity of a positive peace concept in addition.

Darby (1986, p. 164), is less sure about this, but points out that

> It is at least plausible that greater segregation has reduced the level of violence and made people feel more secure. More speculative is the concern that, while reducing the number of local incidents, polarisation has facilitated more serious confrontations in the future, by ensuring that the protagonists will be numerous, more homogeneous and more determined.

Allport (1954, p. 19) has also recognised the limitations of the peace-through-separation approach. He writes

> People who stay apart have few channels of communication. They easily exaggerate the degrees of difference between groups, and readily misunderstand the grounds for it. And, perhaps most important of all, the separateness may lead to genuine conflict of interest, as well as to many imaginary conflicts.

Allport's warning about physical separation would tend to confirm the idea that distance tends to dull the hearing and dim the sight. Thus segregation is not just a consequence of violence, in Northern Ireland at least there is evidence that it also contributes to it (Pringle, 1990).

Psychological distancing and the deepening of the 'enemy image'

Several writers have noticed the development of an 'enemy image' within groups in conflict (e.g. Horowitz, 1985, ch. 4). Spillmann and Spillmann (1991, p. 71) have written that such images are 'always the result of an escalation going hand in hand with a step-by-step regression and dissolution of the differentiated cognitive and emotional patterns of perception and behaviour'. This syndrome, they believe, can become pathological. Each writer will have a different list of what contributes to the creation of the enemy image, but there seems some consensus on the main factors involved. First, there is stereotyping, which is a term derived from French printers who applied it to a method of mass producing an image. According to Allport (1954, p. 191) a stereotype is an 'exaggerated belief associated with a category'. All members of that category are then assumed to share a set of traits and are assumed to be similar to each other and different from other groups. So stereotypes allow people to 'see what they want to see, and often oversee what they wish to ignore' (Hewstone, 1988, p. 78). In this way the world is divided into crude categories, something which Horowitz (1985, p. 144) calls 'cleave and compare'. As a result of this black and white thinking 'deindividualization' takes place, a collectivist ethic emerges and polarization becomes easier (Loizos, 1989). In fact, situations can be created where people are murdered simply because they belong to the 'wrong' community and are in the wrong place at the wrong time. Thus Sikhs have dragged Hindus off buses in the Punjab at random and have killed them on the spot, whilst Christian gunmen in Lebanon have selected Moslems at random at roadblocks and have stabbed them to death (Fisk, 1990, p. 485). Deng and Zartman (1991, p. 389) have also touched on the creation of over-generalised images of the enemy. They write

> Violence causes key changes in conflict. Actors begin to form what Rothchild called "essentialist" perceptions of their adversaries: to see opponents as possessing a character that precludes compromise and to believe that such a character is ingrained and unchanging...Survival stakes then drive the actors to believe that any settlement will be tactical on the opponent's part, a lull in which the enemy still plans their elimination.

In a 1985 study of Haifa, a city with a mixed population, Cohen found that the four words that Jewish primary children most associated with Arabs were kidnapper, murder, terrorist and criminal (*Times*, 3 November, 1985). In a more general study of Jewish-Arab attitudes

Smooha (1987) discovered that two-thirds of Jews thought they could not trust Arabs and two-thirds of Arabs thought they could not trust Jews. Stereotyping can give rise to some amusing anecdotes. Belfrage (1988) reports on a Belfast man who thought he had trained his dog to bite 'Fenians'. But this should not blind us to the destructive behaviour it gives rise to, for, along with the other aspects of the enemy image, it desensitizes one community to the suffering of adversary groups, facilitates selective perception and deprives people of their individuality.[2]

A second aspect of the enemy image is dehumanization, which is a direct attack on the humanity and dignity of the victims. This occurs when members of other groups are regarded as sub-human, either because they are no better than 'animals' or because they are crazy and irrational. Dehumanization is most obvious in the derogatory labels attached to different cultural groups. Such labelling not only makes acts of aggression more acceptable, it is itself an act of aggression meant to injure and insult (Allen, 1983). Conroy (1988, p. 14), for example, quotes a Protestant in Belfast who told him that 'I treat them (Catholics) like animals because that is what they are'. Sometimes the label of 'terrorist' can be used to dehumanize if it is meant to imply that such people are mindless deviants. Fisk (1990, p. 127), in his excellent study of Lebanon, certainly argues that the term can inhibit accurate perception and he shows how local actors would argue that, 'terrorists were animals. Animals had to be put down'. Thus the Israelis could justify brutal actions in Lebanon because they were fighting 'terrorists'. Villages, towns and cities had to be 'cleansed' of them. Begin could talk about rooting out 'the evil weed of the PLO', who were a 'cancer' or were 'cockroaches'. In Belfast a Unionist councillor could talk about 'evil gunmen who have crawled out of the ghettos of West Belfast, evil human pus and part of the Republican poison in this city' (Belfrage, 1988, p. 295). On the other side of the barricade, pro-IRA graffiti in Northern Ireland could proclaim that the explosive 'semtex kills more germs than vortex' (a toilet cleaner). In the former Yugoslavia the label 'fascist' seems to play a similar dehumanising role. The process of dehumanization is also explicit in the term ethnic *cleansing*.

Thirdly, there is scapegoating. This is the attempt to put responsibility for the conflict on to another party. Sometimes this will be the 'other side', but frequently blame will be placed on a third force who is believed to be secretly manipulating the conflict for their own ends. This has been labelled as the 'hidden hand' or 'malevolent ghost' theory. Mitchell (1981a, p. 107) has called it the 'puppet enemy image'. It tries to blame unwelcome developments on evil manipulators (e.g. international conspiracies by the Devil, Jews, capitalists, communists or Freemasons). Fisk (1990, p. 523) , in his study of Lebanon, has also noticed this type of thinking. He calls it The Plot. But as Karl Popper (1992, p. 180) points out the phenomenon of scapegoating goes back at least as far as Homer, where it was the gods who were blamed for bad occurrences such as wars.

Psychological processes such as these lead to a decline in empathy for 'the other side' and create negative anticipation in the minds of community members. Acts committed by the other side are attributed to motives that are different to the motives attributed to similar acts committed by one's own side. Hewstone (1988, p. 49-50) has explored this phenomenon, and quotes findings by Taylor and Jaggi that Hindus would explain socially desirable acts by other Hindus on the basis of internal (dispositional) attributions and undesirable acts by Hindus on the basis of external (situational) attributions. Whereas Hindus would explain undesirable acts by Moslems according to internal attributions and desirable acts according to external attributions. In other words, crudely put, Hindus behaved well because they were good people, Moslems behaved well because they were forced to do so. Hindus behaved badly because they were forced to do so, Moslems behaved badly because they were bad people. Oberg (1990) has also noted how the attachment to the enemy image causes denial of contradictory information and results in the re-definition of peaceful overtures to confirm this image.

Demonization and Sanctification

These terms have been introduced into the study of genocidal societies by Kuper (1989). He would distinguish these processes from dehumanization because they draw on deeper levels of the unconscious mind. There seem to be similarities here with Cohn's idea of messianic deliverance, and the connection between this and genocidal activity motivated by apocalyptic fantasies promising social salvation (Fein, 1993, p. 49-50). In such situations the enemy group becomes the embodiment of evil.

Sanctification and demonization occur when conflicts come to be seen as Holy Wars where one side is upholding the forces of light against the forces of darkness. They can give rise to fantasies of 'unspeakable horror and ineffable bliss'. In his article Kuper refers to the Reverend Ian Paisley, the Free Presbyterian leader and Member of Parliament, who has described the Northern Ireland conflict as one between the Lamb of God and the Whore of Babylon. He has also called on his congregation to attack the people who represent the 'anti-Christ in our midst' (Murphy, 1978 p. 158). Morrow (1991) has shown how sanctification accompanies this demonization. In writing about Paisley's church he quotes a minister who proclaimed that 'we have a God given responsibility. We are ambassadors for Christ. That is why we take such a strong stand against modernism, liberalism, ecumenism and romanism'. Another example of demonization is a statement by Margaret Thatcher in a Christmas address to the British people in 1982, in which she said that the United Kingdom was 'fighting the forces of darkness in Northern Ireland' (Conroy, 1988, p. 217).

In Lebanon Islamic Jihad have defined their battle as a holy war against the Great Satan. Hamas, a Palestinian fundamentalist group, have defined their own conflict with Israel in Gaza and the West Bank in similar terms. There are those in Nagorno-Karabakh who see the Armenian-Azerbaijani conflict as a Holy war between Christianity and Islam, whilst in Sri Lanka some groups see their intercommunal conflict as a battle to preserve Buddhism in the face of a threat from the Hindu 'demon people from the North', an attitude reinforced by contemporary readings of ancient Buddhist texts that identify the Sinhalese as the people chosen to protect Buddhism.

It would be comforting to believe that the tendency to think in such a way is confined to a small group of religious fanatics. However, it seems that demonization is something we may all be prone to in differing degrees. Moses (1990, p. 52) points out how it is 'rampant particularly at times of hostilities and wars', partly because 'the more the enemy is the demon, the more pure we become ourselves'. This then makes it harder to be self-critical.

Entrapment

Entrapment happens when decision makers or their followers become over-committed to a particular course of action. They then find it difficult to renounce this action or change policy without a loss of face or prestige or damage to their credibility (Teger, 1980). Conflicts can therefore drag on past the rational point to quit (Mitchell, 1991). One is reminded here of Dr. Prentice, a character in Joe Orton's play *What the Butler Saw*. His attempts to cover up an adulterous affair put him in such absurd positions that the damage done was greater than that which would have arisen from exposure. Yet when his partner in adultery suggests that they ought to tell the truth to save themselves more trouble, his response is to exclaim that 'that's a thoroughly defeatist attitude'.

An example of entrapment occurred in Northern Ireland after the signing of the Anglo-Irish agreement in 1985. The agreement was disliked by Protestants because it gave the Irish government a consultative role in the running of Northern Ireland, and the Unionist parties responded with slogans such as 'Ulster says No'. 'No surrender' and 'Not an inch'. Very quickly the leaders of these parties found themselves trapped in a negative position of refusing to talk about the political future of Northern Ireland until the Agreement was abolished. This did not happen, and it took over five years of political paralysis before serious talks could get off the ground again as the Unionist politicians eased their way back from their initial negative response. This bears out Deutsch's claim (1991, p. 43) that 'parties to a conflict also frequently get committed to perpetuating the conflict by the investments they have made in conducting the conflict', and that such entrapment can lead to issue rigidity, cognitive rigidity and the premature closure of viable options.

A particularly powerful form of entrapment is the 'sacrifice trap', a term devised by Boulding, who has pointed out how 'sacrifice creates value' (quoted in Stedman, 1991, p. 19). For it is very difficult to admit that lives have been lost in vain. Indeed, the continuation of a violent conflict may be justified, not according to the initial reasons for the conflict that resulted in the loss of life, but in terms of the loss of life itself. The workings of the sacrifice trap can be seen in the Catholic community in Northern Ireland, where republicans committed to a united Ireland are brought up in a long historical tradition of martyrdom and sacrifice, which is itself linked to the more general Christian ideal of self-sacrifice, redemption and resurrection. This is very evident in the writings of one of the key republican heroes, Padraig Pearse, who was one of the leaders of the 1916 uprising against British rule (Falconer, 1990, p. 275; Kearney, 1985, p. 67; Kee, 1976, p. 272; Moran, 1991). On the eve of his execution he wrote a poem identifying his own death with the sacrifice of Christ and so made a significant contribution to the Irish republican tradition of martyrdom. The rebellion he led took place at Easter, the time of sacrifice and resurrection. As a result, in the words of Connor Cruise O'Brien, a 'festival of Resurrection becomes an insurrection'. But it was the heavy-handed British reaction to this insurrection that turned this small revolutionary group into martyrs and gave an enormous boost to militant nationalism in Ireland (Lyons, 1979, p. 100).

This tradition of martyrdom resurfaced during the hunger strikes of the early 1980s, when Republican prisoners in Northern Ireland starved themselves to death. According to Kearney, Irish republicanism has always operated in terms of two discourses. The secular, but slightly superficial discourse of class struggle and political action; and a deeper discourse deeply entrenched in the 'Gaelic, Catholic Nationalist' tradition. Kearney (1985, p. 68) goes on to claim that the electoral success of Sinn Fein after the hunger strikes was 'less because they represented a quasi-Marxist guerrilla movement of liberation than because they articulated a tribal voice of martyrdom'. But for whatever reason, in the heightened emotional atmosphere created by the hunger strikes, the militantly republican Sinn Fein could obtain 43 per cent of the Catholic vote in Northern Ireland in the 1983 British general election.

We should not forget that the Unionists in Northern Ireland have their own examples of the sacrifice an martyrdom which continue to resonate to the present day. The best known of them also arises from events in 1916, but instead of looking to the streets of Dublin, Unionists remember the thousands of Protestants who were killed or wounded at the battle of the Somme defending the British state.

Economic underdevelopment

Azar (1990) has placed a lot of emphasis on the way that protracted social conflict institutionalizes underdevelopment through the destruction of infrastructures and the diversion of wealth to excessive security expenditure. As he puts it, 'a vicious cycle of under-development and conflict deprives not only the victimized communities, but also the dominant groups, of the economic resources for satisfying their needs' (Azar, 1990, p. 16). One only needs to remember how Beirut, the financial capital of the Middle East, was almost turned into a wasteland by ethnic conflict and external invasion. In Northern Ireland an additional problem has been the movement of the brightest minds out of the province to reside elsewhere in the United Kingdom causing a massive haemorrhage of talent. One study at the height of the 'Troubles' found that 40 per cent of the province's brightest young people left to attend universities in Great Britain, and 63 per cent of these never returned to live in Northern Ireland. For those who remain the employment situation can be grim. In parts of Belfast male unemployment is as high as 85 per cent and there is very little inward investment to create new jobs. This might not be directly translated into violent behaviour, but it surely engenders certain negative attitudes. Whyte (1990, p. 53) , for example, has argued that if Northern Ireland was wealthier 'one might expect prosperity to alleviate community tensions'.

In the former Yugoslavia the various conflicts have destroyed the tourism, severely damaged the transport system and adversely affected foreign trade. According to Ramet (1992, p. 268), who used Yugoslavian Ministry of Information figures, GNP in Yugoslavia was cut by 20 per cent between 1990 and 1991 and industrial production was expected to fall by 50 per cent. Many skilled and talented people have also fled to less troubled regions. It is estimated, for example, that a quarter of the 5,000 scientists in Serbia have moved to other states since the introduction of the international embargo (*Guardian* 13 July, 1993).

Detailed analyses of the economic effects of violent conflict are difficult to carry out and are usually controversial. But one interesting study of the impact of ethnic conflict on the Sri Lankan economy between 1983 and 1988 makes rather depressing reading. Richardson and Samarasinghe (1991) have estimated that inter-ethnic conflict between Sinhalese and Tamils and the intra-ethnic conflict on the Sinhalese side between the government and the radical JVP over the handling of the Tamil issue has cost the country $US 4.2 billion. They make a useful distinction in their analysis between primary, secondary and tertiary costs. The primary costs were directly and unambiguously attributed to violent conflict', and included the destruction of property (69,400 houses and 8,000 businesses were destroyed in this period) and the need to care for victims. Secondary costs were spread over a period well beyond the time span of the conflict, were relatively more indirect and included factors other than the violent conflict. Such costs include the diversion of resources into non-productive areas to boost the military on each side, capital flight, the closure of universities, loss of tourist revenue, and the emigration of skilled manpower. Tertiary costs reveal themselves in the medium to long term and are related to the impact of the conflict on productivity and planning.[3]

Fatalism and powerlessness

Living through violent and protracted intercommunal conflict can lead to immobilism and negativism; a belief that little can be done to change the situation because constructive action is so difficult. Giddens (1990) has referred to this sort of adaptation as 'pragmatic acceptance', where the emphasis is on survival and the pursuit of temporary gains, since there is not much hope of long term improvement. He claims that this attitude implies a numbness that could reflect deep underlying anxieties (1990, p. 135). In Northern Ireland this sort of attitude is sometimes labelled alienation, which has been defined as

> dissatisfaction with government and leaders; a sense of remoteness from power; powerlessness to bring about change; a breakdown of social values; and a sense that policies and rules are meaningless or incomprehensible (Hamilton et al. 1990, p. 78).

Der Derian (1987, p. 13-14) makes use of the Oxford English Dictionary's definition of alienation: 'to convert into an alien or stranger...to turn away in feelings or affection to make adverse or hostile, or unwelcome'.[4] Alienation, hopelessness, resentment and powerlessness may have a profound impact on communities in conflict especially when it is combined with economic underdevelopment. When communities feel that state agencies are unresponsive, hostile or discriminatory there will be a temptation to turn to other groups. These include paramilitary organizations or messianic movements.

One interesting line of thinking about alienation concentrates on the development of a sense of victimization. Montville (1990) for example, draws on the work of Jeanne Knutson and attempts to relate the inclination to engage in terrorist acts in ethnic conflict with a victimizing 'conversion experience' that acts as a catalyst for violent behaviour. Victimhood produces an exaggerated sense of vulnerability and is caused by three factors (Montville, 1990, p. 169). A personal experience of physical or psychological violence against the victim or someone close to the victim. A feeling that this violence is unjustifiable by almost any standard. And the association of the violence with a continuous threat posed by the adversary group. The result, in Knutson's words, is a victim who 'grieves over the past and fears the future' (Montville, 1990, p. 170).

There are many accounts of the awfulness of large scale violence and the psychological and material consequences to individuals and societies that this results in.[5] One study of the Protestant Shankill area of Belfast found that 80 per cent of young people feel depressed (Opsahl Commission, 1993, p. 44). But perhaps one should not always exaggerate the psychological distress that living in violent conflict is assumed to bring. Cairns and Wilson (1991) have shown how people in such situations devise coping mechanisms that can limit psychological distress. One such mechanism which can limit the impact of stressors is denial. But whatever the mechanisms used they seem to work. Cairns (1987, p. 70) claims that although some children in Northern Ireland have suffered serious psychological damage and many others have suffered for short periods of time 'contrary to expectations...the vast majority of children in Northern Ireland have not become psychological casualties of the troubles'. Yet one cannot help wondering what is happening to the 62,000 children under the age of 14 who are living in Sarajevo. What seeds of aggression, resentment and hatred are being sown there? How will the trauma they have experienced express itself in the years to come?

Conclusions: Implications for Conflict Resolution Work

To conclude we will examine the implications of the previous analysis for conflict resolution. We have shown in this chapter how violent ethnic conflict can trigger or reinforce certain destructive processes such as militarization, residential segregation, heightened ethnocentrism, psychological distancing, entrapment, economic underdevelopment and alienation. We have also shown how these processes tend to privilege certain groups (specialists in violence), ideas (distrust, pessimism, separation) and images (stereotyping, demonization etc.). These engender ways of thinking and acting which tend to drive the communities in conflict into their own cultural cocoons as the processes associated with violent conflict harden and strengthen negative practices and beliefs which already exist in multi-ethnic states.[6]

This hardened shell around the communities, built out of fear, suspicion, hatred, intolerance and misunderstanding is a powerful barrier to peace work. It also impoverishes the lives of people who live within these cocoons, since it can be seen as a form of self-imprisonment and exile. In Canada, for example, reference has been made to the dangers of the 'two solitudes'. A wall, Gunter Grass once stated, is the enemy of all cultures, and Karl Popper (1992, pp. 122-4) has written about the enlightening effect of culture clash, claiming that societies such as Periclean Athens and Vienna from Haydn to Bruckner owed much to intercultural between east and west. On the other hand, cultural separation tends to reinforce what Kuper has called uncompromising dualism and a corresponding simplification of issues.

Encouraging people to break out of these cocoons is thus an important aspect of peace work, and has been recognised as such by several commentators on the Northern Ireland problem. Fitzduff (1991), for example, has talked about the need to move from 'monism' to 'pluralism'; from tribal simplicities based on intolerance, simplistic analysis, ethnocentrism and a zero-sum mentality to an acceptance of complexity, uncertainty, tolerance, respect and win-win thinking. Whilst Hayes (1991) has called for the creation in Northern Ireland of an 'open, self-critical society which can cope with cultural diversity'. Such contemporary statements were mirrored by the historian Herbert Butterfield (1951), who once wrote that when we are deeply engaged in conflict we are under an obligation 'not to be too blindly secure, too wilfully confident, in the contemporary ways of formulating that conflict'. Less self-righteousness, he claimed, would allow us to face the world more squarely and to move away from an 'heroic' narrative based on clear ideas of right and wrong to an account which could reveal the 'terrible predicaments' that underlie great conflicts.

Before we move on, however, two qualifications have to be made.

The first is that although, it seems to this author, all of these destructive processes operate with varying degrees of intensity in most, if not all ethnic conflicts, in any specific ethnic conflict there will be considerable variations in violence in time and space. We are not claiming that such processes operate evenly in either the temporal or spatial dimensions. As Whyte (1990, p. 111) has noted in his study of Northern Ireland

> On issue after issue in preceding chapters we have found great local differences...These make the community divide much more complex than one might imagine from drawing on region-wide generalizations. The sharpness of the divide varies from one place to another. The mix of religious, economic, political, and psychological factors which underpins it varies from one place to another.

In his study of Israeli society Shamir (1991, p. 1020) has also noted these variations and has attempted to explain differences in levels of tolerance in terms of variations in the threat environment, perception, personality characteristics, and the socialization process.

The second qualification is that alongside these destructive processes there will also operate, in Darby's phrase, controls on conflict, that can contain the negative effects of violence (Darby, 1986). There are a number of ways that such conflicts can be held in check. A power equilibrium may deter violence because of a fear of effective retaliation. Effective state security policies may make it difficult to engage in violence, or the presence of an outside peace-keeping force may help to prevent unintended escalations of violence. The middle ground may remain quite strong and cross-cutting cleavages or common interests may restrict the move towards the extremes. An interesting phenomenon is that even in situations of bitter ethnic conflict bonds with the other side are rarely broken completely. For example, Bell (1990) has found that working class Protestant youths who are defiantly anti-Catholic quite frequently went out with Catholic girls from nearby estates. In Cyprus, to this day, the Republic of Cyprus continues to provide electricity to the self-proclaimed Turkish Republic of Northern Cyprus despite having imposed an economic embargo on this part of the island. In return the Turkish Cypriots supply the Greek Cypriots with water. Sometimes, despite bitter violence, the parties will even retain an overarching loyalty to the state, which may also be a factor in limiting violence. This seems to have been the case in Lebanon (Azar, 1990). A final control on violence is that people living in the middle of a violent conflict will eventually come to suffer from war-weariness and may desire a return to palmier days and a normal life. Kant is well known for the observation in his *Idea for a Universal*

he English translation of the name of the pro-IRA party, Sinn Fein, is 'ourselves
lone'.

ewarding participant observation studies of Northern Ireland include Belfrage
1988), Burton (1978), and Conroy (1988). One of the best books on Sri Lanka
English has been written by the American journalist McGowan (1992) and in the
ase of Cyprus excellent studies have been produced by the anthropologist, Peter
oizos (1975, 1981, 1989). See also Drakulic (1993) for an excellent illustration
f how the pressures of war (in this case in the former Yugoslavia) change people.

History with a Cosmopolitan Purpose (in Reiss, 1991) that there is
nothing like exposure to violence to stimulate a longing for peace.

We can now turn to the implications for conflict resolution work of
the existence of these destructive processes. Firstly, the view from
inside the cocoon is very different from the view from outside. Thus
there is a wide gap in interpretations of conflicts between those who
have lived through the destructive processes we have examined and
those who come to such conflicts from the outside and who are
untainted by the bitter experiences that the parties to the conflict have
experienced. This can be an advantage to the extent that an outsider can
have a fresh, less distorted view of what is happening. But it must not
lead to an underestimation of the experiences of the victims and
participants, that will exert a powerful hold on their attitudes to peace
builders, mediators and peace-keepers. The victims of violent conflict
have to come to terms with their sense of loss, victimhood and grief;
their fears, insecurities and suspicions; their bitterness and desire for
revenge; their humiliation and vulnerability; their anger and a whole
host of other emotions. The usual response of the outsider is to attack
the people who hold these attitudes and to think of them as uneducated
bigots or backward 'primitives' engaged in 'tribal warfare'. Support
for 'extremist' parties is attributed to an 'illiterate electorate' or to
intimidation. But this is to profoundly misunderstand the nature of the
problem, and ignores Lippmann's observation that the 'attempts of
theorists to explain man's successes as rational acts and his failures as
lapses of reason have always ended in a dismal and misty unreality'
(Lippmann, 1962, p. 164). From the insider's perspective the
emphasis on abstract reason often appears the truly irrational approach
to the conflict.

Apter (1990, p. 152) has pointed out in one study of ethnic conflict
that 'if one begins with explanations of causes that are entirely
rationalistic and logical, the social as well as the conceptual
consequences will require going beyond a rationalistic model to a more
interpretive one, or what might be called a phenomenology of violence'.
Loughlin (*Irish News*, 15 Feb. 1991) has condemned the attitudes of
some 'moderate, middle-class reconcilers' in Northern Ireland because
of their 'inability to grasp the profound despair and the material, social
and psychological alienation which drives parts of the working-classes
to take up arms'. Clearly what is needed here is a more
'anthropological' approach to our understanding of violent ethnic
conflict. Indeed, many of the most illuminating of the studies of ethnic
conflicts have come from people who have engaged in participant
observation work at the grass roots level.[7]

This call for greater understanding of the attitudes and perceptions
is not to excuse murder, human rights abuses, ethnic cleansing and other

excesses carried out during violent intercommunal conflict. Furthermore, one only has to read eye-witness accounts of intercommunal atrocities to realize the terrifyingly savage emotions they can release. Nor should the need for greater anthropological understanding tempt us down the road of what Gellner (1992), in a strong attack on relativism, has called postmodernist hermeneutic egalitarianism. For, as he points out, the fact of cultural difference should not be confused with the idea of cognitive relativism, which he vigorously condemns. Cognitive relativism is not a solution to social problems but is a problem itself. There are, indeed, more or less accurate pictures of social reality. The need for *verstehen* is not the same as the endorsement of all cocoons. Thus the perspective of the outsider is useful in that he or she can identify distortions, stereotypes, misunderstandings and other factors that might be standing in the way of a peaceful resolution of intercommunal conflict. But third parties are likely to be less effective when they bring with them a ready made 'rational' solution to violent conflict that lacks a resonance in the minds of the parties to the conflict itself.

The second implication for conflict resolution work is that the most common responses to ethnic conflict by outside third parties wishing to intervene constructively do not address the impact of these destructive processes directly. Peace-making, the attempt to mediate in ethnic conflict to bring about a political solution, focuses on political elites and the perceived incompatible interests which divide the communities. It tends to ignore grass-roots action. Peace-keeping, which involves a military intervention to separate the groups who want to fight, can actually reinforce the physical and psychological divisions. So what is needed is a greater emphasis on peace-building, which has been defined as the strategy most appropriate for responding to these destructive processes (Ryan 1991).

However, it is important to resist the temptation to argue that peace-building on its own will result in a move from unpeaceful to peaceful societies. Even if all of the destructive processes identified here are brought under control or are reversed, the perceived incompatibility of interests which probably caused the violent conflict in the first place may remain. These perceived incompatible goals have to be addressed directly through negotiation, usually with the assistance of outside mediators or facilitators. As the Irish journalist Eamonn McCann once remarked, the parties in Ireland have had no problem communicating. The real problem is that they disagree fundamentally about whatever they talk about.

Finally, we should always remember that ethnic conflict is dynamic. It is not the inevitable clash of cultural monoliths who are implacably hostile to one another. Identities are not fixed in stone. Divisions will

exist within ethnic groups. People do weary of v conflict energy might find institutions and organizat have an input into violent situations. Individuals ar transformed and conflict formations are capable of b by peace-building work. If multi-ethnic states can be negative sense by the outbreak of serious viole destructive processes, could not the management a violent behaviour open doors for positive conflict tra it may be that it is not the ethnic difference but t direct and structural)that is the key variable in situat intercommunal conflict. So rather than condemn behaviour of those caught up in violent situations we s learn more about the processes that cause such behavic be a necessary pre-requisite for successful peace-build of the tension between the insider's and outsider's p end this chapter with a quote from an article by Z (*Balkan War Report*, No. 15 1992, p. 16).

There is much less Sarajevo, and more grief a than one month ago. Everything has been rec survival cramp...Sarajevo trusts no-one anymo learning through its wounds and through the lies the world outside. In some strange way it feels, its stomach, all the good things which were inte but never arrived. Maybe there's no other wa life. Those on the outside will understand less like here on the inside.

Notes

1. The quotation that forms the title of the chapter is from a Se poem about Northern Ireland, 'Whatever You Say, Say Nothii in the analysis of the ethnic conflict in Lebanon by Fisk (199
2. In the Yugoslavian case Ramet (1992a, p. 22) notes a stud which found that the ethnic groups there had a strong proclivit stereotyping.
3. Of course there are some who also benefit from violent ethni lead to an increase in funds for certain areas such as the secur system etc. The presence of UN peace-keeping forces h economy of Lebanon and Cyprus. In Cyprus, for example, t became known as the 'permanent tourists of Cyprus' (Markid
4. One recalls the comment by the distinguished Irish historia xiv), that the Irish 'contrary to popular impression, have li -what they have is a sense of grievance, which they choose to history.
5. See, for example, International Alert (1991).

6.

7.

4 Peace-keeping and peace-making

Albert Einstein said that the 'formulation of a problem is often more essential than its solution, which may be merely a matter of mathematics or experimental skill. To raise new questions, new possibilities, to regard old questions from a new angle, requires creative imagination.' Learning to handle the many protracted conflicts of our world requires new and creative ways of defining such problems. (Jay Rothman, 1992, p. 189)

Introduction

The previous chapter was concerned with the dynamics of violent ethnic conflict, and it identified destructive processes that can create a momentum that may become self-sustaining. There is nothing new in this observation. In a famous passage Clausewitz argued that the intrinsic nature of war was total, for

> The overthrow of the enemy is the natural end of the act of war; and that if we keep within the strictly philosophical limit of the idea, there can be no other in reality...it must follow, that there can be no suspension of the military act, and peace cannot take place   until   one or other of the parties   concerned   is

overthrown (Clausewitz, 1968, pp. 367-8).

This would seem to rule out the idea of ever resolving or managing conflict, short of outside victory for one side or another. In practice, however, Clausewitz realised that this 'Platonic ideal' (Howard, 1986, p. 4) is never found because certain frictions inhibit the logical development of total war. Therefore, the natural tendency of war to escalate is often checked. In real wars, as opposed to philosophical war, aims remain limited, warriors remain under the control of political leaders and people are weighed down by 'preponderousness', laziness and boredom - all of which 'devitalise' war (Rapaport, 1968, p. 293).

Also, as Darby (1986) has demonstrated, people caught up in a violent ethnic conflict do not, necessarily, career blindly towards total destruction. They are often very adept at managing their own conflicts so as to make life bearable even in the midst of violence. The existence of these controls on conflict, which involve avoidance, selective contact and functional integration (business and professional contact), means that conflict is often cyclical rather than cumulative (Darby, 1986, p. 27). One of the most interesting insights of Darby's work is that ordinary people are often better at working out mechanisms to control their conflicts than their leaders. For various reasons, then, a stage may be reached even in the most bitter conflicts where an opportunity for constructive action presents itself.

In this and the next chapter we shall first set out a framework of conflict resolution that can then be used as a yardstick to assess such interventions in ethnic conflicts. To do this it is necessary to explore the main features of ethnic conflict that have to be addressed and the strategies employed to deal with them. Too often conflict resolution is used as a cover-all term that fails to identify the different processes of conflict resolution. We will avoid this pitfall by adopting the work of two specialists in peace and conflict research, both of whom identify a tripartite system when thinking about the resolution of conflict.

The first specialist is Galtung (1976; 1985), who argues that conflict resolution involves three distinct, but interrelated strategies. These he has called peace-keeping, peace-building and peace-making. Harbottle (1979a and 1979b), has also adopted this system of classification, and in the course of examining each within the narrower context of UN activity suggests some definitions. Peace-keeping is the strategy that aims to 'halt and reduce the manifest violence of the conflict through the intervention of military forces in an interpository role'. Peace-building, a term Harbottle replaces with peace-servicing, is defined as the 'practical implementation of peaceful social change through socio-economic reconstruction and development'. A weakness in this definition is that no mention is made of strategies to change attitudes as apart of the peace-building process, even though this can be at least as important as material change. The importance of attitudes has been pointed out by Allport, who claims that they 'determine for each individual what he will see and hear, what he will think and what he will do (Hewstone, 1986, p. 58). To borrow a phrase from William James, they "engender meaning upon the world"; they draw lines about, and segregate, an otherwise chaotic environment; they are our methods for finding our way about in an ambiguous universe.'

Peace-making is a political and diplomatic activity 'directed at reconciling political and strategical attitudes through mediation, negotiation, arbitration or conciliation'. There is also a weakness of definition here, for it seems to confine peace-making to traditional methods of dispute settlement and ignores much interesting work on conflict resolution in the field of alternative dispute resolution. We shall examine this later in the chapter.

To this trio of peace strategies introduced by Galtung can be added another tripartite system suggested by Mitchell (1981a). He sets out the various aspects of conflict that need to be addressed in order to reduce or eliminate violent conflict. These are the perception of an underlying incompatibility of interest among the parties to the conflict; the negative and destructive attitudes that develop during the conflict; and the violent behaviour which both feed the negative attitudes and also feeds off them. By combining these typologies we can arrive at a general framework for the resolution of violent ethnic conflict (Table 4:1). This framework is, of course, over-simplified, but it is hoped that it can be shown to have both a heuristic and analytical value. The exploration of this framework will be the focus of this and the following chapter.

Peace-keeping and the reduction of violent behaviour

As Harbottle has already indicated, peace-keeping is an activity which involves the interposition of military and/or police forces between armed groups either to stop violence or to prevent it. The groups to be kept apart could be state agents, paramilitaries, militia, guerrilla groups or even mobs. What they will share is a desire to use violence against the other side as a way of conducting their conflict. The attitude of such groups is often more belligerent than than that of the general public, and they are often more committed to a military solution. The public will tend to be less committed to such a course of action, and will tend to share or reject such values as the general inter-communal situation and the activities of the warriors changes.

Most peace-keeping most of the time is the responsibility of the governments of sovereign states. However, there are certain types of internal conflicts where the very legitimacy of the state is being questioned (e.g. by movements calling for ethnic secession), and where the state agents will be seen more as a part of the conflict than part of the solution. Sometimes heavy-handed tactics by the military and the

Table 4:1. A Framework for Conflict Resolution

Problem	Strategy	Target Group
Violent behaviour	peace-keeping (military activity)	Armed groups ('warriors')
Perceived incompatibility of interests	peace-making	Decision-makers ('leaders')
Negative attitudes and socio-economic structures	peace-building	Ordinary people ('followers')

police will reinforce this perception of illegitimacy. Often, they will be working under special legislation that has declared martial law or a state of emergency. Between 1985-89, for example, states of emergency or martial law were declared by a number of states experiencing ethnic conflict, including Fiji, Bangladesh, Turkey, Pakistan, Sudan, Sri Lanka and Zimbabwe (UN Doc. E/CN.4/Sub. 2/1987/19, July 1987). Such legislation may well be regarded by certain ethnic groups as instruments of continuing oppression and so will do nothing to help reduce the conflict. Certainly the use of such measures may sometimes be seen as a move by the state away from dialogue with other groups in favour of policies of control. Hannum (1990, p. 169) shows how the implementation of certain provisions of the Indian National Security Act in the Punjab bred resentment by Sikhs and McGowan (1993, p. 178-9) points to the negative impact on the Tamils of the Sri Lankan 1979

Prevention of Terrorism Act. In Northern Ireland unease has been expressed by human rights groups about the special legislation introduced to combat terrorism, in particular the Prevention of Terrorism Act (which was the model for the Sri Lankan Act of the same name) and the Northern Ireland (Emergency Provisions) Act.

It cannot be denied that in certain ethnic conflicts the state and its agencies are not honest brokers, but are rather used as the instrument of a dominant group against other cultures. Galtung (1981), has pointed out how, in many situations, the state is not a neutral arbitrator of conflicting interests (a third party), but is a part of the conflict (a second party). Similarly, Horowitz (1985, p. 443), has noted that the use of military force may help control ethnic rioting, but if the army favours one group over another, its intervention may exacerbate the violence. One only has to think of the activities of the security forces in responding to ethnic unrest in certain states to see how this type of partial intervention develops. Amnesty International, for example, has condemned both Sri Lanka (1984) and Turkey (1989) for the way they have treated members of ethnic minorities (Tamils and Kurds respectively).

In situations where the state is proving to be an ineffective peace-keeper, governments might turn to international peace-keeping forces to bring about a de-escalation in violence. A definition of this type of peace-keeping force has been attempted by the International Peace Academy. It states that international peace-keeping involves

> the prevention, containment, moderation and termination of hostilities between or within states, through the medium of a peaceful third party intervention organised and directed internationally, using multi-national force of soldiers, police and civilians to restore and maintain peace (Child, 1980).

In fact, peace-keeping need not involve multi-national forces, though this would be the most common form of intervention. In recent years, we have seen peace-keeping forces organised by the UN (UNIFIL in Lebanon, UNFICYP in Cyprus, UNPROFOR in the former Yugoslavia), by regional organisations (Arab League in Lebanon, OAU in Chad), and by a grouping of states (MNF in Beirut and the MFO in Sinai). But we have also seen a unilateral peace-keeping initiative by India in Sri Lanka. All peace-keeping requires its participants to act as constabulary rather than as military forces (Segal and Gravino, 1985). That is, they are deployed to create and preserve the peace, not fight and win a war. They are, as a consequence, lightly armed and should use force only in self-defence. However, it may be that the growing interest in humanitarian intervention and peace enforcement will result in a more forceful role for UN peace-keepers, though opinions are divided about whether this would be a welcome development.

When ethnic groups are engaged in a violent conflict, peace-keeping is often the most urgent and necessary of all peace-strategies for it is the only one which deals directly with the warriors on all sides who are engaged in mutual destruction. Until this violent behaviour is stopped, or at least managed, it is unlikely that any attempts to resolve competing interests, to change negative attitudes, or to alter socio-economic conditions will be successful. Stopping the conflict usually involves separating the parties by constructing physical barriers such as the Green Line in Cyprus.[1]

Peace-keeping on its own cannot reverse destructive processes, but it can, by reducing violence, hold them in check and so provide a breathing space or cooling off period which might be used for constructive ends. This is not the place to go into the relative successes of various peace-keeping initiatives. This will be attempted in chapter six. The main point to be made here is that such initiatives can, at best, deal only with the symptoms of the conflict. This point has been made by Urquhart (1988), who has compared peace-keeping to nursing care. He writes

> Peace-keeping is a sort of daily nursing care. It's like the staff in a hospital engaged in getting the patient's temperature down and keeping him reasonably healthy. And when you get to a certain point, a great surgeon may be able to to arrive and deal with the problem. Maybe there isn't a great surgeon, maybe the case is not operable, in which case the aim must be to keep the patient reasonably comfortable. One's got to be realistic about the difficulty of settling the basic disputes which give rise to peace-keeping (Urquhart, 1988, p. 13).

So if peace-keeping is analogous to nursing care, the role of the surgeon is played by peace-makers, who have to devise new political and constitutional arrangements to end conflicts of interest. There is no automatic link between peace-keeping and peace-making. Indeed, successful peace-keeping is often not matched by progress in other areas (e.g. Cyprus). Peace-keeping is a palliative and not a cure. This depends on effective mediation.

Peace-making and the resolution of conflicting interests

Peace-making is concerned with the search for a negotiated resolution of the perceived conflicts of interests between the parties. Those interested in the general area of mediation should consult some of the excellent studies that exist (e.g. Bercovitch and Rubin, 1991; Mitchell, 1981; Mitchell and Webb, 1988; Woodhouse, 1991; Zartman, 1989). Assuming that the parties do not want to yield or withdraw, there are three main ways in which they can try to deal with conflicts of interests. The first method is to try and impose a solution either through violence or through power. These two strategies are not the same, since the more power one has the less direct violence one has to use, but they share a common approach, which is the attempt to impose one's own will on the other parties. There are several problems with this method, quite apart from the moral one that unilateral impositions are unjust It does not, for example, deal with the perceived incompatibility of interest which underlies the conflict. As this is left unresolved, the conflict will simply be suppressed and will probably reemerge at a future date. For this reason, although the exercise of power to impose ones own will may be effective in the short run, in the long term it will often undermine the legitimacy of the dominant group and force the underdogs to resort to violence. The continuing suppression of grievances will also often be bloody and violate widely accepted standards of behaviour. In addition, as we have already seen in the previous chapter, violence fuels several destructive processes which deepen conflicts and escalate them to levels where the politicians lose control of events. Finally the use of violence and power can be costly in terms of lives, resources and international sympathy.

The second way of trying to resolve ethnic conflicts is through the law. However, in deeply-rooted ethnic conflicts this is not a viable option. For it is the very legitimacy of the state which is usually being questioned, and in such circumstances turning to the law of that state to resolve an ethnic conflict will not be a popular option with the dissatisfied group, especially if the instruments of legal enforcement are deemed to be biased. Furthermore, recent experience has shown that the constitutional framework in certain multi-ethnic states, which was meant to resolve ethnic conflicts, can simply become another battle-ground for such conflicts. One only has to think of the battles that took place in Cyprus in the early years of the new Republic over the 1960 Constitution. This lead President Makarios to propose thirteen amendments to it, which led directly to the outbreak in 1963 of a long intercommunal conflict. The National Pact in the Lebanon, long hailed as a remarkably successful example of constitutional engineering, broke down, partly because of demands that it be reformed to reflect new population ratios. Even where a legal approach is applicable there might still be problems associated with it. It is costly, it takes control of the conflict out of the hands of the parties, it is inflexible, and it can leave all parties feeling dissatisfied.

The various problems with the use of violence/power and the inappropriateness of the recourse to law has led many to regard negotiation as the best method of ethnic conflict resolution. When negotiation involves the use of a third party or parties it becomes mediation. Mediators can play a number of important roles. They can ensure accurate communication, they can help keep the negotiations going they can construct the correct environment for negotiations by setting agendas and suggesting processes, they can explore options and offer alternatives, and they can help with the problem of disengagement from the talks and with reentry.

Mediation can be sub-divided into two broad categories. The first is traditional mediation, on which there is a large body of literature (e.g. Lall, 1985; Merrills, 1984; Northedge and Donelan, 1971; Touval and Zartman, 1985). Criticisms of these conventional approaches to conflict resolution has led to the growth of another approach, usually referred to as alternative dispute resolution (ADR) or track two diplomacy.[2] There is now also a growing body of literature about the various approaches that come under the ADR heading. Unlike the literature on traditional methods, which tends to concentrate on inter-state conflicts, much of the writings about ADR directly address the issues of ethnic conflict resolution (Burton, 1979; Azar and Burton, 1986; Mitchell, 1981a and 1981b; Mitchell and Webb, 1988). This reflects one of the differences between the two approaches. Traditional dispute settlement tends to work within frameworks of institutional legitimacy and established procedures. So Burton (1990, p. 27) has noted that

> Traditional means of settling disputes and conflicts follow from a framework that attaches importance to the preservation of institutions, to the socialization of the individual into certain behaviours, to the role of power in relationships, and to the application of elite norms.

One of the best examples of this is the attempt by UN Secretary General Waldheim to resolve the Cyprus problem. Shortly before standing down as Secretary-General, and following long years of deadlock in the intercommunal talks, the Secretary-General tabled a document which became known as the Waldheim initiative, though initiative is perhaps too generous an adjective to use in this case. The document submitted by Waldheim set out the points of agreement which already existed between the two sides. However, where no such agreement existed Waldheim suggested 'points of equidistance' which, as the name suggests, took what the UN negotiators thought was the middle ground between the negotiating positions. Not surprisingly, both communities rejected this plan. Or consider Lord Owen's comment during his mediation attempt in the former Yugoslavia. He argued that 'the task of the mediator is to define the positions of the warring parties and to try to bring them together' (*Guardian*, 12 August 1993). This is a typical example of traditional diplomacy. Such unimaginative responses to conflict situations has led even supporters of the UN to call for a reevaluation of mediation techniques. Lord Caradon, for example, has stated that

> Merely to bring both sides together even under the chairmanship of the UN Secretary-General cannot in itself provide an agreed solution...there must be a new method, some new initiative, if deadlock by inaction, disaster by drift, is to be avoided (Brademas Lecture, 1980, unpublished).

Alternative approaches are freer to step outside such restraints. Therefore ADR is able to engage with all relevant parties groups and some within the field put much emphasis on the importance of 'identity groups', even when these are deemed to be illegitimate by existing power structures. Van der Merwe (1989, p. 96) has noted how private individuals have more freedom to disregard protocol in order to 'suggest unconventional remedies or procedures, to widen or restrict agenda or change the order of items, to propose partial solutions or package deals, to press the case for constructive initiatives or magnanimous gestures'. For example, where governments are reluctant to talk directly to opposition groups, then private persons might fill the 'mediation gap'. This has certainly been the case with Britain and the IRA, Israel and the PLO and South Africa and the ANC. Other examples include private mediation between the Nigerian government and the Biafrans (Curle, 1990, p. 40-45) and the World Council of Churches role between the Moslem Sudanese government and southern Christian and anamist separatist groups (Assefa, 1987; Mitchell, 1989). The Carter Centre has used eminent persons as informal mediators in the Ethiopian-Eritrean, Liberian and Sudanese conflicts.[3]

It is also a lot easier for ADR to take place in private, away from the international spotlight. This, many observers believe, increases the chances of progress. Lijphart (1977, p. 155), for example, quotes an observation by Gordon Means about the ethnic situation in Malaysia. He stated that 'significant communal compromise was more likely to emerge from semi-secret and "off-the-record" negotiations conducted by communal leaders'.

Jandt (1985, p. 187), claims that

> Any fool can say, 'Take it or leave it.' And you don't have to be much smarter to say, 'Let's split the difference.' What separates the professional negotiator from the amateur - or from the

non-negotiator - is the professionals ability to find *creative solutions* that helps *all parties* obtain their interests (emphasis in original).

ADR has attempted to provide ideas and techniques to enable the parties can obtain such outcomes, what are sometimes referred to as win/win solutions. Two writers deserve particular mention for their work in this area. The first is Roger Fisher, who works with the Harvard Negotiations Project, and who, with William Ury, has written one of the most influential works on conflict resolution called *Getting to Yes* (Fisher and Ury, 1987). This work begins with the claim that negotiation is the best way to deal with differences. Yet it is an activity which is frequently done so badly that a 'wise outcome, efficiently and amicably reached' is a rare event. The book goes on to provide a guide for negotiators to allow such outcomes to be reached more frequently. They call their approach principled negotiation, and it has four basic features. The focus of the negotiations should be on the interests of the parties, not their current positions. The people should be separated from the problem, so that negotiations do not become a battle of egos. The participants should think about a variety of options before they start negotiating. And finally, agreements should be based on objective criteria or a fair standard acceptable to all.

One of the most important figures in the field of ADR and ethnic conflict resolution is John Burton, who since the 1960s has been involved in action research through academic interventions in actual conflict situations. As a result he has developed both a theory and a technique of conflict resolution. The theory, based on basic human needs, was developed in reaction to power politics ideas. It became closely associated with an approach in the international relations discipline known as the world society perspective, which directly challenged realist thinking. So, according to Banks (1984, p. 20)

> Their objective was to discover, in the literature of social science, ideas which would enable the international relations discipline, for the first time, to view conflict much as the physician regards pain. In medicine, to suppress pain with sedatives and painkillers is not enough; the main therapeutic effort must be directed at the underlying disorder. So, in the world society, the forcible conflict-suppressing devices so long employed - power balancing, peacekeeping, hostile intervention - would need to be replaced with other procedures which would not only control conflict symptoms, but also develop the capacity of the world society to become a self-regulating system capable of avoiding destructive conflict.

110

Human needs theory claims to meet this requirement and proposes that there are certain basic and universal human needs and that the denial of these needs is the major cause of protracted social conflicts. Although states may be able to repress and coerce groups in situations where their member's needs are being denied, at the end of the day the power of these needs will break through control mechanisms to produce overt violent conflict. Nothing can compensate individuals for the denial of their basic needs. Therefore,

> The state and sovereignty, legal authority, legitimate monopoly of force, are not useful tools of analysis. The nation and small group, legitimisation, values attached to relationships are tools more relevant to problem-solving within and between groups (Burton, 1982, p. 132).

The analysis of social life from a basic human needs perspective is not new. It can be found in the work of Fromm (e.g. 1974) and Maslow (1968). It is an important part of Lippmann's (1962) belief in a 'humanly centred politics', and more recently appears in Fukuyama (1992), who believes that one of the driving forces of political behaviour is the need for *thymos* (recognition). This is a theme developed by Charles Taylor (1992) in a recent study of the 'politics of recognition'. But it was Burton who was the first to apply these ideas to conflict resolution. He uses a list of human needs drawn up by Sites: consistency in response, stimulation, security, response, distributive justice, rationality, meaning, a sense of control, and he regards these needs as the basic starting point of behavioural analysis (Burton, 1979, ch. 3). They are, he believes, the navigation points of conflict theory.

Although Burton believes the human needs are universal, take priority over social norms, and cannot be permanently suppressed or traded away, their introduction into conflict theory does not make conflicts more intractable. For the whole point of this approach, the fact that makes it so attractive for conflict resolvers, is that human needs do not exists in a zero-sum relationship. They are not a scarce resource. Recognising your right to identity, for example, does not take away from my right to identity the way that your desire for sovereignty over my territory threatens my sovereignty. So it has been argued that

> Unlike material goods and interests, non-material human needs are not necessarily in short supply. Satisfaction of security and recognition one party to a relationship experiences, the more others are likely to experience. (Burton, 1990, p. 242)

Therefore, we should accept that

> conflict at all levels may not be over scarce resources, such as
> territory, but over social goods that are not in short supply...it is
> this paradigm shift that is the explanation of the win-win concept
> inherent in conflict problem-solving (Burton, 1984, p.140).

Of course, the human needs approach to conflict resolution has attracted criticisms. One attack on the theory disputes Burton's claim that human needs are universal. This, it has been argued, undervalues cultural differences that have to be addressed in attempting constructive third party involvement in conflict (see, e.g. Avruch, Black and Scimecca, 1991). Mack (1991, p. 95) claims that an important weakness in Burton's writings is that although he states that human needs can form the basis of a generic theory of conflict resolution there is, in fact, very little evidence presented to support the assertion that needs are biologically rather than socially determined. Mack also believes that Burton cannot explain why some conflicts remain stable over extended periods when there is systematic denial of basic human needs.

Other criticisms of need theory concentrate on questions such as the extent to which needs have to fulfilled to ensure peace and on whether there is a hierarchy of needs, with some having priority over others. Finally, Burton also presents little evidence to support the claim that most protracted ethnic conflicts arise out of need denial rather than ideological commitment or a lust for power or resources. Is it really true, in other words, that need is more important than creed or greed?

Burton is, perhaps, too much of an enlightenment rationalist when describing human nature. There is nowhere in his theory an acceptance that people can be driven by darker gods such as the desire for power and domination. All of Burton's needs are 'reasonable' ones, none of them take into account the existence of a sub-conscious mind. For this reason a response to a Nietzsche or a Freud is needed in his work before it can be accepted uncritically. Burton's image of individuals pursuing their basic needs and responding positively to open communication and analysis seems to rely on children of light rather than children of darkness. But how can such a view work with people committed to the post-enlightenment, anti-cosmopolitan, exclusivist passions inspired by nationalism?

The practical method of conflict resolution pioneered by Burton is the problem solving workshop (PSW), an approach that is subjected to a comprehensive analysis in Mitchell (1981b). Burton, himself, has developed fifty-six rules for the organizing and running of such exercises (Burton, 1987). The aim of the workshops is to promote 'facilitated conflict resolution' which assists the parties to a conflict to be 'analytical about their relationships' and enables the facilitators to draw on their understanding of social dynamics to point out the 'consequences of behaviours and decisions' (Burton, 1990, p. 169). As Oppenheim (1984, p. 124) points out, the problem-solving approach is novel to most participants 'in that it gets away from legalistic, territorial, logical, historical and military issues and focuses, instead, on the deeper level of human needs, fears and insecurities, hostile images, misperceptions and misunderstandings'. Mitchell (in Woodhouse, 1991, p. 48) shows how the workshop approach is supportive, analytical, non-directive, non-condemnatory, and self-determinate - the actors themselves must decide on the solutions. Attendance at such workshops also involves relatively low entry and exit costs for the parties.

Burton's ideas have inspired a number of academics to develop the theory and practice of academic interventions in violent conflicts. Kelman, for example, has used the PSW in the Jewish-Palestinian conflict (e.g. Kelman,1985; Kelman and Cohen, 1976). He argues that such academic, unofficial interventions should not propose solutions to complex problems but should help solutions emerge out of facilitated interaction. Academics can help this along through their choice of participants, the way they construct the setting and atmosphere, and the quality and nature of their interventions in discussions. For the joint analysis which these workshops promote can correct the participants systematic underestimation of the possibility of change, can provide them with a 'binocular orientation' so that each party can view the situation from the other's perspective, and can encourage the participants to question their 'conflict norms'. Kelman (1990, p. 152) argues that there have been several positive outcomes from the workshops he has been involved with: participants learn that they have something to talk about with the other side; they gain insights into the perspective of the other parties; they develop greater awareness of how the other parties may have changed and how they can promote such change through their own actions; and they become more aware of the significance of gestures and symbolic acts.

Azar (1990), from a base at the University of Maryland also organised several workshop exercises around the Lebanese and Sri Lankan conflicts. He claimed that the workshops allowed the participants to discover common needs and values, to establish informal networks, and to widen their agendas. He found that the parties who attended were sometimes able to depart from prepared positions and embark on self-discovery.

Before we end this section it is important to mention several recent trends in ethnic conflict resolution thinking. Firstly, there is the question about the timing of interventions. This has been examined by

Zartman, who has played a pivotal role with his idea of the hurting stalemate. He is mainly concerned with how outside states can use leverage to promote conflict resolution, and it is his belief that such constructive involvement may only be possible when certain prerequisites are in place: when the moment is ripe. Zartman (1989, p. 273) writes

> Conceptually, the moment stands out, but in reality it is buried in the rubble of events. Even when clearly defined, it may be recognised only after it has passed....Like any metaphor, the idea of the ripe moment should not be taken too literally. Moments, when ripe, do not fall into one's hands; they have to be taken with skill. Furthermore, in an imperfect world, moments are rarely totally ripe, or, no matter how ripe they are, there are usually counter indications and communications problems that can make them most unready for treatment if mishandled....Thus, for the conciliating power, it is a question not only of correctly identifying the right times to move but also of moving the times with skill.

Ripeness seems to exist where there is a mutually hurting stalemate; where unilateral solutions are blocked and a continuation of the violence will damage both sides; and where there exists a moment that calls for a decision to escalate or deescalate.

One implication of Zartman's work is a scepticism towards the idea of constructive involvement before violence breaks out. For the experience of violence is an important factor in establishing the hurting stalemate, which in turn makes the parties willing to consider third party intervention. From this perspective there is not much hope of preventive diplomacy. Curle (1990) has also examined, from a different perspective, the idea of 'unmediable violence'.

Zartman's idea of 'ripeness' has been tested and refined by Stedman (1991) in an excellent analysis of the negotiations that ended white minority rule in Rhodesia/Zimbabwe. He is convinced that the concept of ripeness should be a cornerstone of mediation theory, but he wishes to build on Zartman's ideas by exploring the intra-party debates about the acceptance of mediation and the way that the idea of ripeness can emerge from internal changes within the parties to the conflict.

Other recent works on conflict resolution have also concentrated on issues of timing. This line of thinking already existed in the work of supporters of PSW approach who, unlike Burton, did not see it as a substitute for conventional diplomacy. Kelman (1990), for example, has talked about such workshops as being part of the pre-negotiation process, where they can complement negotiations rather than substituting for them, and he accepts that binding agreements can only be achieved through official negotiations. This should be compared with Burton's linking of the needs approach to a paradigm shift in conflict resolution theory. Azar (1990, p. 26) supports Kelman, and has claimed that the workshop approach 'does not substitute for the ultimate need for formal diplomacy'. But it might 'prepare the ground for productive official negotiations'. This immediately raises the problem about how to decide which strategy is the most appropriate at what particular point in a conflict.

This is a question taken up by Fisher, who has developed a 'contingency model' of conflict resolution. He is generally supportive of the workshop approach, but points out that 'few outcomes have been successfully transferred to the wider relationship and conflict between the parties' (Fisher, 1989, p. 446). Therefore more research is needed into workshop practice before the full potential of the technique can be assessed. He appears to believe that their main value lies in the attitude change that can be induced. The workshop/facilitation approach should, however, be seen as a strategy within a range of possibilities, and the contingency model approach attempts to explore the sequencing and coordination of complementary interventions, matching each strategy to the appropriate point in the dynamics of the conflict. For 'conflict is a dynamic process of structural and social-psychological elements...in which the primacy of any element's influence varies throughout the course of any single conflict and over different conflicts' (Keashly and Fisher, 1990, p. 426). One way this moves us away from Burton's rejection of power politics is the possibility that at some stages of a conflict the use of leverage rather than analysis may be the most appropriate strategy. Indeed, Zartman (1989, ch. 16) has claimed that mediators tend to be more effective if they possess credible sanctions. He has even stated that the most important feature of effective mediation is leverage, which is the ability to produce a broadly acceptable outcome (Zartman, 1986, p. 27).[4]

This is not to suggest that one can impose a solution on the parties against their will, rather it is to propose that some arm twisting or some bribery might sometimes aid the resolution process. For example it seems that the imposition of sanctions against the government of South Africa did play a role in ending apartheid. Stedman (1991) has shown how leverage exerted on Mugabe by front-line African states contributed to the 1979 Lancaster House Agreement that ended the civil war in Zimbabwe. Who could object to the military interventions against Saddam Hussein in order to stop him attacking the Kurds in his country? Was the Syrian imposed peace in Lebanon, resulting in the 1989 Taif agreement, a good or a bad thing? Presently, there is a debate about whether military air strikes in Bosnia and Hercegovina would aid or hinder the search for a negotiated settlement. Would it deter or encourage further Serbian aggression? There can be no easy answers to such questions, but one should not dismiss the constructive aspects of power and leverage in the way that Burton has done.

Rupesinghe (1992) has proposed his own contingency model to guide third party involvement in ethnic conflict. He sees conflicts passing through distinct phases and proposes appropriate approaches for each phase of the conflict process. The stages and the strategies are as follows: conflict formation (early warning and conflict prevention); conflict escalation (crisis intervention); conflict endurance (empowerment and mediation); conflict improvement (negotiation and problem solving); conflict transformation (new institutions and projects). Rothman (1992) has also developed a sequential approach to intervention strategies based on his own experiences in organizing workshops around the Jewish-Palestinian problem. Effective conflict resolution work, he believes, has to move the parties from an adversarial to an integrative approach through the introduction of a reflexive stage that can promote reinterpretations of attitudes and reassessments of expectations.

Another recent development in thinking about ethnic conflict resolution is a growing emphasis on the prevention (or what Burton has called the prevention) of conflict rather than the resolution of conflict. This emphasizes constructive third party intervention in conflict when the violence is latent rather than manifest and there is now a rapidly expanding bibliography on early warning as academics and non-governmental organizations try to devise ways of identifying potential targets for preventative action (see, for example, Rupesinghe and Kuroda, 1992). The interest in early warning has also led to a growing collaboration between academics and intergovernmental (especially UNHCR) and non-governmental organizations (such as International Alert) in the establishment of data banks that measure indices of conflict such as human rights violations, refugee flows etc. Other aspects of conflict prevention include the limitation of arms flows into conflict regions and the training of local groups in peaceful conflict resolution strategies.

A final development worthy of note is a growing literature on the idea of conflict transformation. We shall examine this in the next chapter, so here we can restrict our comments to the identification of a growing awareness of the importance of transformation in the mediation literature. Vayrynen (1991, p. 4), for example, has argued that 'many intractable conflicts of interest or values may find their solutions only through the process of transformation' and goes on to explore different types of transformation: of actors, issues, rules, or structures. One problem with the transformation approach, however, is the lack of clarity about what is meant by transformation. Some of the literature uses the term in such a way that it appears to mean nothing more than change. But the idea that change is an important part of conflict resolution hardly adds anything new to our understanding of conflict. Kriesberg, Northrup and Thorson (1989) have also edited an interesting collection of papers on the theme of transforming intractable conflicts. As we shall see, the emphasis in the literature of transformation tends to be on grass roots action and the building of peace from the bottom up rather than the top down (Rupesinghe, forthcoming; Calliess and Merkel, 1993).

The need for a comprehensive peace strategy

So far we have examined two of the three main peace strategies. Before discussing peace-building it is necessary to explore some of the inter-relationships between them all. The argument to be made is that all three strategies are essential for effective ethnic conflict resolution, and it will be presented by examining what is likely to happen if each of them is neglected by any peace initiative.

(a) Ineffective peace-keeping

To begin, we can suggest what the consequences will be if peace-making and peace-building initiatives are attempted without successful peace-keeping. We have seen that peace-keeping tries to restrain the armed groups on all sides and this helps to hold in check the destructive processes associated with violent interaction. If this is not part of a conflict resolution strategy these processes will continue and will probably overwhelm peace-building and peace-making initiatives. Furthermore, in the absence of successful peace-keeping any group wishing to sabotage a peace initiative will find it easier to provoke armed clashes with the other side, since there will not be an impartial buffer between the sides which can act as a restraining influence. The absence of a suitable control mechanism may enable even a small group of people committed to violence to wreak enormous havoc, whereas the presence of an impartial third force can be an important factor for stability. Peace-keeping forces can also help the peace-making and peace-building process by providing inter-communal gatherings with secure meeting places and safe escorts to and from negotiations. This has happened many times in Cyprus, for example, where the Ledra Palace Hotel, located in the UN zone in Nicosia, has been used for intercommunal meetings.

There has been a tendency in some of the conflict resolution literature to dismiss peace-keeping as conflict management rather than conflict resolution, a device that may reduce the violence in the short term but something that will do nothing to address the real causes of violence. Such a view would see conflict management in general and peace-keeping in particular, as an attempt to contain violence rather than ending it. It has been referred to, rather dismissively, as a 'band aid' approach. However, instead of regarding the conflict management and conflict resolution approaches as being alternatives it may be more fruitful to see them as complementary (Ryan, 1990b). What is needed is not a narrow definition of conflict resolution which excluded management approaches, but a broadening of this perspective so that it can accommodate peace-keeping strategies. So Azar (1990, p. 127) has stated that 'conflict management may be regarded as a necessary preliminary step in the process of conflict resolution' and Heradsteveit (1974, p. 84-5) has argued that

A strict distinction is often made between what is called conflict management and conflict resolution....But at the same time it is clear that once there is obtained conflict management there is also obtained some elements of conflict resolution. And it is difficult to imagine a process towards conflict resolution that does not at some stage start with management of conflict.

Of course, insensitive and heavy peace-keeping tactics may escalate the violence and reduce the chances of successful conflict resolution, but this is not inevitable. In fact, good and effective peace-keeping may make a significant contribution to the overall resolution of an ethnic conflict.

(b) Ineffective peace-building

If peace-making and peace-building is attempted without proper peace-building the ordinary people will be left out of the peace process, and this can harm attempts at conflict resolution if decision-makers lose the support of their communities because they appear to be too ready to talk peace. This gives rise to what conflict theorists have termed the re-entry problem, which arises when new insights are created in the minds of a small group through negotiation, but then have to be passed on to the population as a whole. If leaders exceed the limits of tolerance of their followers they will be accused of having 'gone soft', and new hard line leaders may emerge to challenge for power. Intra-communal conflict will then be added to the intercommunal conflict, and attention will be diverted away from dialogue with other ethnic groups in order to concentrate on the struggles for leadership within the group.

Three examples of what happens when leaders move too quickly for their followers can be offered. The first example occurred in Sri Lanka, when on 26 July, 1957 the Sinhalese Prime Minister signed an agreement with the Tamil community (de Silva, 1986). This Bandaranaike-Chelvanayakan Pact proposed that Tamil would become an official language in Tamil areas; that regional councils would be created; and that limits would be placed on Sinhalese migration into Tamil areas to allow the Tamils to retain a majority in these areas. However a violent backlash by the Sinhalese community forced Bandaranaike to abandon the Pact shortly after signing it, and he was assassinated in 1959. Interestingly, a similar initiative in the late 1960s was also brought down by popular protest. This followed a deal between the ruling UNP (Sinhalese) party and its Tamil coalition partners by which power would be devolved to the regions and Tamil could become an official language in the North and East of the island. Popular Sinhalese protest led to the breakdown of the coalition in 1969 and the UNP lost the next general election, held in 1970, by an overwhelming majority.

The second dramatic example of supporters forcing their leaders to abandon a peace process occurred in Northern Ireland in 1974 when the Ulster Workers' Council forced Protestant leaders and the British government to abandon an initiative to share power with the Catholic minority (Fisk, 1975; Rees, 1985, ch. 3). In March 1972 the British government abandoned the regional Northern Ireland Parliament at Stormont and initiated a system of direct rule from Westminster through a Secretary of State for Northern Ireland. He was not elected by the people of Northern Ireland and it was hoped that this effective disenfranchisement of the Northern Ireland people would be a temporary measure. As part of the gradual transfer of power back to the people of Northern Ireland an attempt was made to establish a new Assembly, elected on a system of proportional representation (which is not used elsewhere in the UK) to guarantee the Catholics a reasonable number of seats. After ten years there was to be a plebiscite on the future of the province, and in the interim period a more active involvement by the Republic of Ireland in the affairs of Northern Ireland was envisaged through the creation of a Council of Ireland. Certain of these provisions were deemed to be unacceptable by many on the Protestant side, and through a policy of industrial action and intimidation they were able to destroy the initiative during the summer of 1974, even though some Protestant leaders were prepared to give it a chance to work.

Another example of a backlash to concessions to one ethnic group by the leaders of another has occurred in Bulgaria at the start of 1990. Although not the result of an agreement between elites in the manner of the Bandaranaike-Chelvanayakan Pact, apparently unilateral initiatives by the newly 'liberalised' Bulgarian government to ease the plight of the country's ethnic Turks caused mass demonstrations by nationalists demanding 'Bulgaria for Bulgarians'. Opponents of reform established Committees for the Defence of the National Interest throughout the country and did force the government to water down some of the proposed concessions (Poulton, 1991, p. 164-5).

The above examples should warn us, therefore, that ordinary people cannot be taken for granted and left out of the conflict resolution process. Yet there is a tendency in the literature to ignore this dimension, and in much of the literature, including that of Burton and Fisher, there seems to be an unwritten assumption that negotiations between decision makers take place in a social vacuum. This is particularly ironic in the case of Burton, who, as we have seen, emphasises the importance of an individual basic human needs approach. Yet his approach concentrates almost entirely on elite interaction and peace-making. It is as though the broader social context within which this elite interaction takes place does not exist. Yet, as Sherif (1967, p. 136), has noted

> Being an integral part of the group, the leader himself is not immune to the corrective sanctions applied to any member who steps out of the acceptable bounds of outlook and the developing trends in his group...In some matters he has more leeway than members with less power, but it is precisely in the most crucial issues that he must be exemplary of the group's values and stay within their narrow bounds.

It is therefore necessary, if progress is to be made in peace-making, that the attitudes and values of ordinary people be addressed by anyone interested in conflict resolution.

(c) Ineffective peace-making

Peace-keeping and peace-building without peace-making is not likely to be an effective conflict resolution strategy because the perceived conflicts of interest which are the cause of the conflicts will remain unresolved. If this is the case, any cessation of violence is likely to be short lived. Frank McKinney Hubbard once stated that no-one ever forgets where they bury the hatchet, and the festering of unresolved conflicts of interest will mean that they are eventually dug up again. So improvements that are the result of good peace-keeping and good peace-building will remain shaky and are too easily reversed if a final political resolution is absent. This was the experience of Cyprus between 1968 and 1974.

Here, effective peace-keeping and a very limited amount of peace-building has resulted in several years of relative peace and security for Greek and Turkish Cypriots. However, there was no resolution of the question of the status of the two communities within a general constitutional settlement. Therefore suspicions remained, and open warfare returned in 1974 following the coup against Makarios sponsored by Greece and the Turkish invasion which led to the de facto partition of the island. Zartman (1989, p. 279) has warned us that 'management is not enough and the idea that managed conflicts can be forgotten even though the basic conflict is not touched is a dangerous illusion'.

For it is generally accepted that third party peace-keeping can only be effective if a desire to avoid violence exists among all the important parties to the conflict. Indeed, one of the rules of UN peace-keeping as developed by Hammarskjold in the 1950s, is that it relies on the consent of the host state to operate at all (Mackinlay, 1989; James, 1984). So clearly, if the leaders of a state are opposed to negotiations and a peace process and prefer to pursue a policy of repression or armed confrontation with an ethnic group within its borders, then effective international peace-keeping will not be possible. A minority ethnic group will not have the same sort of *de jure* veto power, but if it is opposed to a peace-keeping operation it can seriously undermine its effectiveness, as has happened to the UN force in Lebanon. Therefore, if no commitment to peace-making exists among key decision makers, and if they prefer to conduct their conflict through the use of power and/or violence, then the prior consent necessary will be lacking, as will the commitment of the parties to avoiding violence. This is not to suggest that an agreement not to fight is the same as an agreement to resolve the conflict, but there has to be an awareness that negotiations are preferable to fighting. As Zartman has noted (1985, p. 25)

> A peacekeeping force can perform only minimal law-and-order functions and can do so only when the parties are agreed not to challenge or to circumvent it in that role. It is unlikely that the members of a peacekeeping force will feel their interests affected enough to take the heavy casualties required to impose a solution or to contain a conflict if the parties have the will and the means to pursue it.

In fact, the failure of peace-making would tend to condemn peace-keeping operations to passivity in the face of violent conflict, as in Rwanda; to perpetual conflict management, as seems to be the case in Cyprus; or it will force peace-keepers to become more deeply embroiled in the actual fighting, as was the case with the Indian Peace

Keeping Force in Sri Lanka. UNPROFOR in the former Yugoslavia is already facing these unattractive options.[5] All of these situations will test the will of contributing states. In Cyprus the lack of effective peace-making has led several governments to withdraw their contingents from the peace-keeping force. Here some of the contributing states were eventually unwilling to continue supporting the long established policy of automatic renewal of UNFICYP's mandate by the Security Council. So, as the UN Secretary-General noted in his annual report for 1990

> Formerly, peace-keeping was understood to mean essentially to control or contain conflicts while peace-making was meant to resolve them. A deeper and more active involvement of the United Nations has over time, however, increasingly shown that peace-making itself determines, as it should, the size, scope and duration of peace-keeping as conventionally understood and that it is often by the fusion of the two in an integrated undertaking that peace can generally be brought to troubled areas. (De Cuellar, 1990, p. 5)

There are some who seem to believe that deeply rooted, violent ethnic conflict can be resolved by methods which bypass the need for political settlements. McAllister and Rose (1982), for example, have examined proposals for resolving the Northern Ireland conflict that emphasise social change not political agreements. Such proposals fit into one of four categories: secularisation, greater material prosperity, modernisation and generational change. McAllister and Rose are critical of all such theories, however, and argue that political conflicts can be resolved by political agreements. They write

> The conflict in Northern Ireland is a political conflict. Facing up to the violent constitutional conflict about how Northern Ireland should be governed is the same as being faced with a Gordian knot. Such a knot cannot be undone by the erosion of time. It can only be cut by actions directed at its core (McAllister and Rose, 1982, p. 21).

Kelman (1990, p. 202-3), in support of such a view, has written that 'overcoming the psychological barriers does not in itself resolve the conflict. A settlement must ultimately take place at the political level through political and diplomatic processes'. This is similar to an argument made by the historian Herbert Butterfield (1951, p. 26), who once argued that after many of the incidental features of a particular case are peeled away 'we shall find at the heart of everything a kernel of difficulty which is essentially a problem of diplomacy as such'. O'Connell (1988, p. 157) agrees, and argues that it is 'unlikely that approaches can be made to resolving or reducing conflict without facing up to conflicts of interest'. These writers are quite right to claim that peace-building cannot resolve political conflict, but we should also note that the model of conflict resolution we are examining does not claim that this will be the case. What is of interest here is the extent to which peace-building can contribute to conflict resolution in general.

Lack of effective peace-making will undermine not just peace-keeping work. It can also frustrate peace-building. For if elites are not prepared to negotiate about the problems they have with other parties they may be suspicious of attempts to forge contacts between ordinary people. As a result, elites might block contacts, or take action against those who press ahead with intercommunal meetings. Supporters of peace-building often claim that the empowerment of people is one of their main aims. Yet there are many elites who would find this idea rather worrying. Furthermore, elites may be able to take counteraction to stop such initiatives. In extreme cases this might even involve the murder of opponents of hard line policies. The Jayawardenes (1984), for example, have shown how Tamil separatist leaders have supported the murder of moderates such as the mayor of Jaffna, Alfred Duraiappa, who was killed in July 1975. In South Africa, Inkatha and ANC community leaders who were able to conclude local peace agreements have been murdered by the 'third force' which is opposed to the moves to a unitary, democratic South Africa. This secret organization appears to have received support from high ranking members of the South African security forces.

In some states, legal restrictions were introduced by governments to restrict intercommunal contact. In Israel a law was introduced which made it illegal to have contacts with members of the PLO. Those who broke the law could be imprisoned for three years, irrespective of the motives behind the contact. In South Africa the Prohibition of Political Interference Act (1968) made it a crime to engage in 'mixed' politics and banned inter-racial political parties or inter-racial political cooperation (Kuper, 1977, p. 213).

Governments can restrict contact by withholding travel permits to prevent inter-communal meetings held abroad. In 1986 the Cyprus government stopped one of its football teams from travelling to Turkey to play a match against a Turkish team it had been drawn against. This led the Turkish government spokesman to comment that a leadership that was not prepared to play football with Turks could not sincerely be entertaining a federal solution to the Cyprus problem that would respect Turkish Cypriot fears and wishes. However, the Turkish Cypriots are not blameless in this area either. In October 1989 it was reported in the

Greek Cypriot press that Denktash, President of the unrecognised (except by Turkey) Turkish Republic of Northern Cyprus, had stopped Turkish Cypriot women attending a joint meeting with Greek Cypriot women at the UN controlled Ledra Palace Hotel in Nicosia (*Cyprus Bulletin*, 8 November 1989, p. 3). In 1991 the Turkish Cypriot Movement for an Independent Cyprus attempted to take the Denktash regime to the European Court of Human Rights because it was prohibited from travelling to the Greek Cypriot part of the island. This failed, ironically, because the Greek Cypriot controlled government of the Republic of Cyprus had not recognised the right of individual petitions to the Court.

In July 1987, 58 white South Africans travelled to Dakar, Senegal, to meet with representatives of the African National Congress (ANC), one of dozens of meetings held in the 1980s with white South Africans. The leader of the white delegation, Dr. Frederik van Zyl Slabbert, described the meeting as a 'peace-seeking operation' (*Guardian*, 1 August 1987). However the meeting was condemned by the South African government in what one British newspaper called a 'propaganda broadside' because it gave credibility to the ANC, which Pretoria regards as a terrorist organisation (*Guardian*, 27 July, 1987). Extreme nationalist groups such as the Afrikaner Resistance Movement threatened to take revenge against those whites who had travelled to Dakar. Nor could South African journalists who attended the meeting give full accounts of it in their own press because of government imposed press restrictions. Nevertheless, contacts continued. In June, 1989, for example, ANC lawyers met with South African Supreme Court Justices in Oxfordshire, at a conference on the law in South Africa funded by the Ford Foundation (*Guardian*, 24 June, 1989).

One month before the meeting in Dakar a group of left wing Israelis met with a PLO delegation in Budapest. During their stay in the Hungarian capital they issued a statement calling on the government of Israel to recognise the PLO as the legitimate representatives of the Palestinian people and to grant them the right of self-determination. However, the meeting violated an Israeli law of 1986 banning contacts with the PLO because it was a 'hostile' organisation, and so when the leader of the Israeli delegation, Charlie Biton, returned to Israel he was handed a police summons. In October 1989 the Israeli peace activist, Abie Nathan became the first individual to be imprisoned under the 1986 law, for meeting with PLO leader Yassir Arafat. The Israeli government has shown similar negative attitudes towards Israeli citizens (Jews and Arabs), who have attended conferences organised by the UN Committee on the Exercise of the Inalienable Right of the Palestinian People to Self-Determination. Indeed, it has also penalised members of its own government for contacts with the PLO. A recent example of this is the furore caused at the end of 1989 when it was revealed that the Israeli science minister, Ezer Weizman, had had secret meetings with the PLO in an attempt to establish a dialogue between the two parties. Prime Minister Shamir threatened to sack him, but after opposition to this move from his Labour coalition members, it was agreed that Weizman would be demoted from the 'inner cabinet'.

Curle (1990, p. 143), argues that the Community Relations Commission, established by the British government in Northern Ireland, was closed down in 1974 because it was working so well that the government felt that it was losing control of the situation. He also claims that the government was happier dealing with clearly defined and separate Protestant and Catholic areas. This interpretation is supported by Frazer and Fitzduff (1991, pp. 8-9), who write that 'the possible radical nature of a successful community development programme, independent of government control, was thought by many in the Commission to be inevitably threatening to ministry and politicians alike'. Part of the reason for closing the CRC down, therefore, was to silence grass-roots criticism of its work (Weiner, 1974).

Serious difficulties, then, can arise when peace-building is attempted without support from the leaders of the various communities. The hope is always that peace-building will promote 'peace from below' and push the political leaders to negotiate a resolution of violent conflict. Such demonstrations of the desire for peace may be especially necessary in the light of research by Pruitt (1981, p. 44), who claims that

> In the absence of indications to the contrary, representatives tend to view their constituents as desiring a tough, non- conciliatory approach to bargaining of the kind that is produced by a win/lose orientation. Therefore, the more motivated they are to please their constituents, the less conciliatory they will be in their dealings with the other party.

Demonstrations that ordinary people favour negotiation, not confrontation, may therefore modify elite attitudes, but this need not always be the case. For, as Mills (1960, p.86), has warned us

> Better understanding between peoples does not necessarily result in, much less determine, changes in the policies of their respective elites. To believe that it does is to assume that the policies of all governments are a simple mirror of the opinions of national populations.

Furthermore, elites can resist pressure for peace from below by promoting intransigence from above. As we have seen, people who meet with the other side can be penalised, restrictions can be imposed on intercommunal contacts, the control of the media or of education can be used to influence attitudes. There tends to be too much easy optimism in the literature on peace-building that contacts at the grass roots level will inevitably spill over on to the level of elite interaction. In fact there is nothing automatic about this process, and much more work needs to be done on how peace-building feeds into the peace-making process. Peace-building is sometimes called track-two diplomacy, though diplomacy is a word that would tend to confuse the aims of peace-building with peace-making, or track-one diplomacy. The hope is that track-two diplomacy will spill-over onto track-one, but there is a real danger in many instances that the tracks will not converge at all and will continue into the distance unconnected. Peace-building emphasises the need to overcome the blindness and hatred of ordinary people, but it often overlooks the folly and stubbornness of their leaders.

Conclusions

This chapter and the next chapter is concerned with the different strategies and processes involved in ethnic conflict resolution. It is argued that there are three main strategies, peace-keeping, peace-building and peace-making; and all three are needed if efforts to resolve ethnic conflict are to be fruitful. Failures in any peace initiative are probably due to inappropriate strategies in one or more of these areas. The final point to be made is that all three strategies often need external involvement to be successful.

We have already seen how the legitimacy of peace-keeping work by the agents of the state is often questioned by ethnic groups during deeply rooted conflict. This will probably be because these agents are deemed to be biased or the representatives of an illegitimate entity. In some cases this has led some states to turn to an outside agency to provide a peace-keeping force. This could be another state (India in Sri Lanka), a group of states (MNF in Beirut), or an international organisation (UN in Cyprus, OAU in Chad). We will evaluate the history of such initiatives in chapter five.

External involvement in peace-building initiatives is often required because projects aimed at improving socio-economic conditions are expensive and local resources may not be adequate to meet the necessary expense. Or local resources may be adequate, but will not be made available to those engaging in peace-building. Alternatively, local sources of funding will be too compromised to be acceptable to one or more of the parties. In all of these cases outside funding will be vital.

This has been recognised in recent discussions about how to consolidate the peace process in Israel, South Africa and Northern Ireland. In all of these cases progress towards a negotiated settlement has led to promises of economic assistance aimed at placing peace on a firmer foundtation.

In the final area, peace-making, external involvement is often needed because the parties to the conflict become locked in to a violent confrontation and are unable to carry out important tasks necessary for conflict resolution. These tasks have been identified by many conflict theorists. Wall (1981), in examining the literature on conflict mediation uncovered approximately 100 techniques which could be employed by a mediator. Kriesberg (1982), lists the most important of these tasks. They are: providing a neutral setting; providing accurate information; reducing interpersonal barriers; improving procedures; inventing options; adding resources; and building up support for an agreement. Moore (1986, p. 182), also provides a list of important functions. For him they are: opening channels of communication; legitimising; process facilitation; training; expending resources; exploring problems; being an agent of reality; playing the role of scapegoat; and being a leader. Such outside involvement could involve exercising leverage on recalcitrant groups. Economic sanctions, for example, helped to move the whites in South Africa towards a negotiated settlement with the ANC. Similarly, strong US pressure on Israel, which included threats to withold loan guarantees, forced the Likud led coalition into talks with Palestinians in Madrid and Washington in 1991. But outsiders can also provide assistance that is not related to power. The involvement of Norway in the Israeli-Palestinian peace process points out how a private, neutral venue can also be a significant aspect of peace-making because it creates a space for quiet track-two diplomacy.

Part three of this book will analyse actual international initiatives, with special emphasis on the work of the UN. We shall see how close international practice is to our ideal framework. In chapter six we analyse the role of the UN as peace-keeper, peace-builder and peace-maker. Then, finally, in chapter seven we shall explore the dimension of ethnic conflict prevention, which we have not addressed here, but which deserves some attention. Under this strategy we place particular emphasis on the idea that an international regime for minority protection could be created as a way of preventing violent ethnic conflict. However, before we do this it is important to say more about peace-building.

Notes

1. The term green line derives from the action of the commander of the British peace-keeping force in Cyprus just after the outbreak of intercommunal violence in December 1963. He drew a line on a map of Nicosia with a green pencil to indicate where the the barricades should be constructed between the Greek and Turkish communities.
2. The term track two diplomacy was devised by J. Montville (1987).
3. More information on the work of the Carter Centre and the International Negotiations Network can be found in Carter Centre (1993).
4. My thanks to Mark Hoffman for stimulating an interest in these issues. See his 'Regional conflicts, third party mediation and conflict resolution in the post-cold war international system' (unpublished).
5. These cases are discussed in chapter six.

5 Peace-building and conflict transformation

And if an atmosphere of fear does not encourage accurate thinking, then they must first of all come to terms with fear (Albert Camus, *Neither Victims nor Executioners*).

Introduction

Peace-building is the strategy which most directly tries to reverse those destructive processes that accompany violence which we have already examined in chapter three. This involves a shift of focus away from the warriors, with whom peace-keepers are mainly concerned, to the attitudes and socio-economic circumstances of ordinary people. Therefore it tends to concentrate on the context of the conflict rather than on the issues which divide the parties. All peace-building strategies involve greater inter-party contact. So whereas peace-keeping is about building barriers between the warriors, peace-building tries to build bridges between the ordinary people; and whereas peace-making is concerned with elites, peace-building directs it attention at grass-roots work. It wants to transform conflicts from the bottom-up.

Peace-building is also the most under-researched aspect of conflict resolution, though there is now a growing recognition of its importance, partly prompted by recent demonstrations of 'people power' in Eastern

Europe. Also of interest here is South Africa's move towards a democratic and pluralist society, and especially the National Peace Accord of September 1991. This established the National Peace Council (with its regional and local Peace Committees) and the Goldstone Commission of Inquiry for the Prevention of Public Violence and Intimidation which can investigate cases of violence and intimidation and can advise the President of South Africa on matters that are within its remit.

As we noted in the previous chapter, there is now a growing interest in conflict transformation in the literature on conflict resolution. Curle (1990) has identified three 'tools for transformation': peace-making, development (defined as purposeful growth and change) and education. Boulding (1990, p. xxii) has pointed out the need for 'learning sites' to ensure contact between different groups. Garcia (e.g. Garcia and Hernandez, 1989) has done pioneering work on grass-roots peace-building in the Philippines in areas such as the creation of peace zones, the promotion of cultural pluralism, the establishment of codes of conduct for all armed groups and the involvement of all people in conflict resolution work. Walker (1988) has examined the way that critical social movements can challenge our inherited notions of authority, legitimacy and power and suggests areas where they can concentrate their analysis: economic development, gender, environment, militarization, human rights and culture. Groom (1986, p. 133) has argued that in attempting conflict resolution 'it is more fruitful to start with behaviour, building local ties of a practical nature, not with great issues of constitutional principle'. Esman (1989, p. 63) believes it is important to address the 'atmospherics' that surround violent intercommunal conflict. So perhaps Alger (1991, p. 245) is correct to claim that there has been a broadening of the definition of peace in recent years which reveals that it is impossible to 'attain a strong and lasting peace without widespread knowledge, participation and support from the people of the world'.

Practitioners are also realising the importance of the peace-building approach. The Anglo-Irish agreement of November 1985, for example, makes explicit reference to economic and social development in the three paragraphs of Article 10. This commits the British and Irish governments to cooperate to promote development in areas worst hit by political instability; allows the Intergovernmental Conference, which was established by the Agreement, to be the framework for some cross-border cooperation in economic, social and cultural matters; and looks at the need for machinery for cross-border cooperation if there is devolution of power to local politicians.

A 1987 report on Cyprus by the UN Secretary-General noted that

A major cause of the present difficulties is, of course, the deepening distrust between the two sides and the lack of contact, at all levels, between the two communities. Continuation of this trend will further undermine the prospects for a negotiated settlement. *A climate must be created in which effective negotiations can take place.* (UN Doc. S/18880, 29 May 1987. Emphasis added)

In the case of Cyprus this has resulted in a greater emphasis on confidence building measures (especially the resettlement of Varosha and the reopening of Nicosia International Airport) in recent intercommunal mediation efforts by the UN. A recent study of intercommunal relations in Canada since the failure of the Meech Lake Accord notes that recent events have demonstrated that 'an accommodation among political elites, often made behind closed doors, no longer satisfied interest groups and individual citizens who felt empowered by a written charter of rights and freedoms' (Simpson, 1990-91, p. 73).

The contact hypothesis

The most simplistic approach to peace-building is the contact hypothesis, defined as 'the widely held belief that interaction between individuals belonging to different groups will reduce ethnic prejudice and inter-group tension'. This contact could come about through trade, through business or trade union interaction, through meetings of professional bodies (doctors, teachers, journalists etc.), or through sport (what might be called the de Coubertin dream). Individual schemes run from the mundane to the eccentric. The general argument that just inter-group contact will force people to revise negative and hostile attitudes to each other is, however, unconvincing. Such an idea can be criticised for a number of reasons, and they have been set out persuasively by Hewstone and Brown (1986).

Firstly, there is much research to suggest that contact between individuals belonging to different, hostile groups will only improve attitudes if certain conditions are met, and in their absence it is unlikely that conflict will be reduced, and it may even increase. For it is the quality of the contact, rather than the quantity of interaction, which is the crucial variable. Five conditions seem to be especially important. The contact should be between persons of equal status. The social climate should favour such interaction (clearly a problem during violent ethnic conflict). The contact should be intimate, not casual. It should also be pleasant and rewarding. Finally, there should be important common goals.

The second problem with the contact hypothesis which Hewstone and Brown identify is the questionable assumptions upon which it is based. Three of these receive particular attention. The first is the idea that the inter-ethnic conflict is merely a mistake due to misperceptions, misunderstandings and ignorance. This might be partially true, but the conflict might also arise out of a real, rather than perceived, clash of interests. The second assumption of the hypothesis concerns the direction of causality. Is it, as the hypothesis claims, that unfavourable attitudes are the cause of the conflict, or is the conflict the cause of the unfavourable attitudes? Hewstone and Brown suggest that there is no clear evidence available to resolve this question and so it is safer to assume a mutual causality. This weakens the contact hypothesis by making the negative attitudes a dependent as well as an independent variable.

The third dubious assumption is the idea that inter-*personal* contact can resolve inter-*group* conflict. The problem with such an approach is that ethnic conflict is as much about social identity as it is about personal identity. The conflict is not just between me and you but is also between us and them. The distinction has been put as follows

> Both interpersonal and intergroup behaviour are the actions of individuals, but in one case they are the actions of individuals qua individuals, while in the other they are the actions of individuals qua group members. (Hewstone and Brown, 1986, p. 14)

Condor and Brown (1988, p. 19) claim that 'intergroup conflict is, by definition, a collective phenomenon, and requires a suitable collective "model of man". The psychological factors associated with intergroup hostility are best sought in *collective* social cognition and motivation' (emphasis in original). In protracted and violent ethnic conflict, with all the pressures that exist to conform to group norms, it may be that identification in terms of us/them is more powerful than identification in terms of me/you. Foster and Finchilescu (1986, p. 119), put it this way

> In a deeply divided social structure, riven by a long history of conflict and power imbalance, social identity penetrates the personal sphere to such an extent that interpersonal contact per se, even under the most favourable conditions, is not likely to alter substantially established social relations.

Such arguments are also borne out by the findings of Murphy in a UNESCO study of the early 1950s (Sherif, 1969, p. 13-14). He found that in the Indian sub-continent being a good Hindu or Moslem implied believing all the nasty qualities that one group attributed to the other. Hewstone and Brown (1986) conclude, therefore, that inter-personal relations may be the effect of more general changes in inter-group relations, but are unlikely to be the cause of such changes.

The third problem with the contact hypothesis is closely linked to the previous point. It is known as the re-entry problem. It is concerned with what happens to individuals, who as a result of inter-personal contacts with members of other groups, change their own negative attitudes to them. How will they be treated when they return to their own communities and to the pressures to conform to negative images of the other side? If they do conform and allow these group pressures to overpower their personal experiences then the contact will have no practical value. If, on the other hand, they refuse to conform they will be treated with suspicion and could be eliminated or marginalised. Supporters of the contact hypothesis have so far not addressed this reentry problem in an adequate way.

It can be argued, then, that the idea that contact between ordinary people from warring communities will result in changed attitudes is simplistic and flawed. It assumes too readily that contact always broadens the mind. However, it has been pointed out that it might have the opposite effect. Stroebe et al. (1988, p. 171) for example, in a study of student exchange programmes, challenge the idea that getting to know people in another country will produce a more favourable attitude. They cite studies that show how attitudes to a host state can deteriorate during an extended period of contact. Lijphart (1977, pp. 88-9) is also suspicious of inter-ethnic contact, and in defending a plea for clear boundaries between ethnic groups claims that 'close contacts are as likely to lead to strain and hostility'.

If, for example, a distinct cultural group feels that its identity is being threatened by contact with other cultures, increased exposure to these cultures may make things worse. Lawler (1976, p. 786-7), recounts an interesting case of contact escalating conflict. In the Aboisso region of the Ivory Coast there existed a Sanwi secessionist movement. In an attempt to reduce this ethnic conflict the government decided to increase contact between the capital and the Sanwi region by building a bridge to ease communications. However, as Lawler points out, since the Sanwi already thought that there was too much contact with outsiders, the building of the bridge was 'probably counter-productive'. So it seems that bridge building is not always the best way to build bridges.

Amir, Ben-Ari and Bizman (1986) have tested the contact hypothesis in Palestine. The three investigators carried out an attitude test on 279 Palestinian students in a West Bank vocational training centre and another 83 applicants registered at West bank employment offices. This test was then repeated nine months later. Of the 210 who responded to the request for a second interview 82 had worked in Israel. However, this experience had not changed their attitudes to Israelis. However, in another survey undertaken by the authors, this time into the attitudes of 254 men and 48 women, all Palestinians who had worked for at least a year in Israel, a softening of attitudes towards Israelis was noticed, if the Palestinians had worked in a job with perceived high status.

Here one should also note the point made by Schiff and Ya'ari (1990, p. 84) about Palestinian workers in Israel who travel from the West Bank and Gaza. They state

> Every night tens of thousands of laborers who had left their homes before dawn to eke out a living in Israel returned with an ever greater burden of repressed anger against the country that mocked their right to equality and ravaged their dignity. They were discriminated against in wages, barred from joining Israeli unions, and forbidden to form workers' committees of their own, while huge sums of money were deducted from their pay for benefits (such as social security and pensions) they would never receive.

There are clearly, therefore, serious problems with the simplistic approach embraced by the contact hypothesis. However, rather than reject the idea that contact can result in a change of attitudes, it seems a more fruitful approach to argue that something needs to be added to the contact to make it more effective as a way of reducing stereotypes, avoiding scapegoating and reversing dehumanisation. For as Ben-Ari and Amir (1988, p. 153) note, contact 'should be regarded as a necessary but not sufficient condition for producing a positive change in ethnic attitudes and relations'. The question, then, is what is the extra dimension that needs to be added? The main suggestions seem to be the following.

Contact plus forgiveness

This is a strategy adopted by those who belong to religious peace traditions. What they all emphasise is the need for reconciliation, and they obtain their inspiration for this view from the great religious texts, and the teachings of modern peace activists such as Gandhi and Martin Luther King Jr. It was an idea supported by Tolstoy, and it has also influenced the Quaker approach to conflict resolution (Mendle, 1974), which Wink has stated believes that 'faith in God means believing that *anyone* can be transformed, regardless of the past (Van Der Merwe, 1989, p. 93). Reconciliation is also an important theme in the work of the Jewish writer Martin Buber (1992) and his idea of the I-Thou relationship. All approaches appeal to the human duty to obey a higher, divine law.

Gallagher and Worrall (1982, p. 3) regard reconciliation as more than just pragmatic accommodation because it is 'the attainment of a higher synthesis made possible by common acceptance of a destiny transcending the sectional interests that have led to conflict'. The main features of the reconciliation approach seem to be: the experience of common suffering as a basis for common understanding and redemption; adherence to the idea of a common humanity; the willingness to take responsibility for the wrongs committed against the other side; and the religious imperative to act with kindness, love and forgiveness towards your enemy (Falconer, 1988; Toth, 1988).

King (C. S. King, 1983, p. 27), for example, talked about the need for forgiveness, not as an occasional act but as a permanent attitude. He also taught that

> He who is devoid of the power to forgive is devoid of the power to love. There is some good in the worst of us and some evil in the best of us. When we discover this we are less prone to hate our enemies.

The civil rights leader also stated that we 'must somehow believe that unearned suffering is redemptive' (King, 1983, p. 67). This is a theme developed by Robert Kennedy. On the night of the assassination of Martin Luther King, and two weeks before his own assassination at the hands of a Palestinian, he quoted his favourite poet, Aeschylus, a group of blacks on a street corner in an Indianapolis ghetto: 'in our sleep, pain which cannot forgive falls drop by drop upon the heart until, in our despair, against our will, comes wisdom through the awful grace of God' (Schlesinger Jr., 1978, p. 875).

Gandhi organised his nonviolent campaigns around the concepts of *satyagraha* (the power of truth) and *ahimsa* (the obligation not to harm others). Parekh (1988), has pointed out that one of his important contributions to Indian moral thinking was the way he transformed the concept of *ahimsa* from its original meaning of a passive acceptance into a positive and active political idea.

Examples of the reconciliation approach in action can also be found at various religious communities around the world. These include Corrymeela in Northern Ireland, Agape in Italy, Taize in France, Neve Shalom in Israel, and Koinonia (from the Greek word for communion) in South Africa. Corrymeela was founded in 1965 and offers facilities for inter-communal dialogue. It also runs meetings on such topics as the two cultures, violence, and mixed marriages. In addition it helps twin segregated schools. To be a member of Corrymeela it is necessary to be committed to the community's Christian beliefs.[1] Koinonia describes itself as a 'ministry for reconciliation and preparation for a new South Africa'. It began work in 1982, largely due to the influence of Dr Nico Smith after he resigned as a minister from the Dutch Reformed Church. It now has groups functioning in many towns and cities, where it promotes inter-racial contacts in small groups. The usual format for such meetings is that four couples (two white and two black) share meals with each in turn acting as host. Each of these groups then divide into two and invite new couples to join in. Inter-racial camps, picnics and houses are also being planned. Reconciliation conferences are organised and outreach groups have been established. Neve Shalom/Wahat al-Salam (Oasis for peace) was founded in 1971 by the Jesuit Father Bruno. It is an 'experiment in co-existence' where Jewish and Palestinians farmers can live together. A school for peace is also organised, and over 10,000 Jewish and Palestinian children have made use of its facilities. It also helps with teacher training and every spring sponsors a fair dedicated to mutual understanding (Rothman, 1992, p. 27).

An important criticism of the reconciliation idea is that it explains protracted violent conflict in terms of cultural rather than structural factors. This is a point made by Ruane and Todd (1991), who have examined explanations of the conflict in Northern Ireland and have argued that there are those who see the cause as cultural (mis-understanding, prejudice etc.) and those who blame structural factors (exploitation, oppression etc.). They are drawn more towards the structural explanation and write that

> For many writers the roots of the Northern Ireland conflict lie in the anachronistic ideas and ideals, mistaken perceptions or exaggerated fears of the people of Northern Ireland. We have argued that this idealist position mistakes the cultural expressions and manifestations of the conflict for its deep causes. It subjectivises the conflict and supposes that a change of ideas and perceptions will resolve it. It ignores its structural basis. Even descriptively, the cultural approach is mistaken (Ruane and Todd, 1990, p. 39).

Because of the lack of interest in structural factors, the reconciliation approach to ethnic conflict also tends to emphasise individual change as the best way forward. Yet, as Cairns (1987, p. 160) argues, 'the conflict in Northern Ireland is almost certainly an intergroup phenomenon related to the importance of social identity in Northern Irish society. This in turn suggests that if reconciliation is to be achieved then contact should take place at an intergroup level and not simply at an interpersonal level'. A similar point is made by Hofman (1988, p. 90), who recounts what happened at a series of meetings for Jewish and Arab children at a community centre in Haifa:

> For the first few meetings everyone is all smiles. Then, almost inevitably, someone raises a political issue, and, as if a switch had been thrown, all revert to ingroup justification and outgroup condemnation. Jewish and Arab persons begin to perform as group members.

It cannot be denied that reconciliation groups have a great impact on certain individuals; but one is left wondering if this approach, with its emphasis on otherworldly obligation, is pragmatic enough to become a successful large scale solution to the problems of violent ethnic conflict. The experience in Northern Ireland, where there are scores of such groups working at the grass roots level, seems to suggest it does not. For they seem to have had only a negligible effect on the intercommunal problems there. So perhaps Darby (1986, p. 172), is correct to suggest that common interest has been a more important catalyst for contact than religious faith, and 'in districts which had experienced sectarian violence, the argument that people should get together because they were hostile towards each other was not persuasive'.

Contact plus the pursuit of superordinate goals

Following Darby's suggestion that common interest, rather than reconciliation, is a more appropriate device to promote inter-ethnic contact we can examine the work of the Sherifs, who developed the idea of superordinate goals. The term was invented by them in the course of a series of experiments, conducted in the 1950s, on children aged eleven and twelve who were attending summer schools in the US (Sherif 1967 and 1969). The experimenters were testing an hypothesis that for intergroup contact to be effective as a mechanism for reducing conflict a 'motive base' was required. This they termed a superordinate goal, defined as an urgent goal that could only be achieved by cooperation between the conflicting groups. Thus a superordinate goal is not the same as a common goal, which could be achieved through unilateral action.

In their experiments a group of boys was randomly divided into two groups, and conflicts between these groups were then encouraged. As inter-group hostility increased so did intra-group solidarity, and interaction between the groups was characterised by name calling and negative ratings of the other group. Simply bringing the groups into contact did not reduce the conflict. In fact such contacts just provided the opportunity for the groups to attack each other. The mutual hostility was only overcome by getting the groups to engage in cooperative acts for common ends which they could not obtain on their own. Only this pursuit of superordinate goals would overcome stereotyping and reduce hostility. This led Muzafer Sherif (1969, p. 74), to conclude that

> Social contact...may only serve as occasions for intensifying conflict. Favourable information about a disliked group may be ignored or reinterpreted to fit stereotyped notions about the group....What our experiments have shown is that that the possibilities for achieving harmony are greatly enhanced when groups are brought together to work toward common ends....In short, hostility gives way when groups pull together to achieve overriding goals which are real and compelling to all concerned.

Can this insight into group dynamics be applied to protracted and violent ethnic conflict? It is certainly advisable to avoid over-optimism. For the differences that separate ethnic communities are clearly deeper and more fundamental than differences created by artificially dividing up schoolchildren in an American summer camp. However, those who think that introducing superordinate goals into conflict situations will help ease ethnic antagonism often draw inspiration from the European Community, and the functionalist perspective developed by writers such as Mitrany (1975), and activists such as Monnet (1978). Both argue that the creation of supranational bodies that have the responsibility for fulfilling key economic and social needs will gradually bring about a transfer of loyalty from the narrow cultural group to the supranational bodies. Eventually particularist antagonisms will be dissolved as the participants become caught up in a web of mutual dependence and political differences will then become less important. Monnet believed that

> Human nature does not change, but when nations and men accept the same rules and the same institutions to make sure they are applied, their behaviour towards each other changes. This is the process of civilisation itself (Sampson, 1968, p. 8).

Both the reconciliation and functionalist approaches attempt to transcend national egotism, but they do so in different ways. Whereas reconciliation appeals to a pre-existing moral community, functionalism tries to create an interdependent community to meet welfare needs. Reconcilers emphasise the replacement of self-interest with an ethic of brotherly (and sisterly) love. Functionalists use self-interest as the basic motivator of change. Issues of common concern seem to offer real opportunities for peace-building and can emerge across a wide range of subjects, including: the environment; housing; policing; the rights, treatment and exchange of prisoners; status of women; and the provision of public services. As Pruitt and Rubin (1986, p. 136-7) point out

> Having and working on superordinate goals enhances bonds with the other party in a number of ways. One is by the principle of psychological balance-my enemy's enemy is my friend...Another is by reducing the salience of group boundaries; people who are working toward common goals are in some sense members of the same group and hence are not so likely to be antagonistic toward one another...A third is by a reinforcement mechanism; as we work together, each of us rewards the other and produces a sense of gratitude and warmth in the other. Pursuing superordinate goals also means that Party sees itself as working on behalf of Other, a view that is likely to foster positive attitudes.

However, the European experience has shown that the creation of supranational bodies such as the European Coal and Steel Community and the European Economic Community do not automatically lead to an abandonment of narrowly defined identities (e.g. de Gaulle's withdrawal from the Community for six months or the recent popular backlash against the Maastricht Agreement). Interdependence may not necessarily result in an equal sharing of costs and benefits, and this can be the cause of conflict. Also, physical interdependence need not lead on to a feeling of psychological interdependence, which is necessary if a new supranational community is to be created. The entry of Ireland and the UK into the European Community in 1973 did nothing to solve the problem of violence in Northern Ireland. In fact a leading theorist of integration has warned us that 'the world has got more violent as interdependence has increased' (Haas, 1987a, p. 116). One should also bear in mind that the status of Brussels, the 'capital city' of the European Union has been the subject of bitter disputes between the French and Dutch speaking peoples of Belgium,a country that is now rigidly divided monolingual areas. In fact the disintegration of the unified Belgian state has coincided with European economic integration. What better example can one find of the conflicting and contradictory responses to such integration?

The European Community is an example of the pursuit of superordinate goals at the macro-level. There have also been numerous projects at the micro-level. The Sarvodaya Society in Sri Lanka has created multi-ethnic teams of volunteers to dig wells and reconstruct houses (Thomas, 1985, p. 81). In Cyprus in the early 1970s the Cyprus Resettlement Project, made up of volunteers from the American Friends Service Committee and the Shanti Sena (the Indian peace brigade inspired by Gandhi), developed a project in collaboration with the International Peace Academy to rebuild villages destroyed by intercommunal warfare so as to allow refugees to return to their homes. It was hoped that work camps involving Greek and Turkish Cypriot young people could be created to do the actual construction work, but, sadly, this phase of the project was meant to start in July 1974, and had to be abandoned following the overthrow of President Makarios by the Athens Junta and the subsequent Turkish invasion (Hare, 1985). In the Middle East the need to jointly manage water resources may yet prove to be a factor encouraging Jewish-Palestinian cooperation.

Examples of micro-level superordinate projects can also be found in Northern Ireland. In the town of Dungannon a mid-Ulster Basketball Club was established in an attempt to bring together schoolchildren, unemployed teenagers and parents from both communities. Basketball is a sport with no sectarian connotations and so is ideally suited to this type of work. Impartiality was further maintained through the use of an American as the club's coach. Another imaginative project was the establishment of a city farm on the Springmartin Road, along the infamous 'peace' line that divides the Protestant and Catholic housing estates of West Belfast. This brings children from both communities together to care for the animals on the farm. In the words of the manager of the farm, Jack Hewitt, 'everyone in Northern Ireland...claims they're working for peace...but the best thing to do is not work for peace, the best thing to do is to work for something else - to improve the environment, to improve education, to improve housing' (*Guardian*, 10 August, 1985).

To end this discussion of superordinate goals and interdependence we can turn to G.K. Chesterton's (undated, p. 244) relationship with a typewriter. Arguing that only friendliness produces friendship he wrote

> I resent the suggestion that a machine can make me bad. But I resent quite equally the suggestion that a machine can make me good. It might be the unfortunate fact that a coolness had arisen between myself and Mr. Fitzarlington Blenkinsop, inhabiting the suburban villa next to mine...but if somebody told me that a new kind of lawn-mower had just been invented, of so cunning a

structure that I should be forced to become a bosom friend of Mr. Blenkinsop whether I liked it or not, I should be very much annoyed. I should be moved to say that if that was the only way of cutting my grass, I would not cut my grass but continue to cut my neighbour....Reasonably spirited human beings will not be ordered about by bicycles and sewing machines; and a sane man will not be made good, let alone bad, by the things he has himself made. I have occasionally dictated to a typewriter, but I will not be dictated to by a typewriter .

Contact plus economic development

Perhaps the most significant of all superordinate goals is economic development. A region experiencing protracted ethnic conflict will also often suffer from economic underdevelopment. New capital will tend to avoid dangerous areas, which threaten company lives and property. Existing capital will tend to leave and not be replaced. The best minds will often seek their fortune elsewhere. Therefore, it seems reasonable to link the peace process with economic development (Azar, 1990), though even if it is true that violent ethnic conflict causes underdevelopment, it does not follow that economic development will cause a reduction in ethnic violence. Economic development may depend on the effective management or resolution of the conflict, and in this case it is development that is the dependent variable. Indeed, there are several reasons for doubting such an argument, which smacks of what Gellner has termed 'cornucopianism', which is rather crude materialistic argument about stability in contemporary society that is too much concerned with economic indicators.

Firstly, there seems to be no satisfactory evidence that economic development will alter deeply held cultural orientations or political beliefs, at least in the short run. Industrialization need not lead to convergence (Stone, 1985, p. 84f). In arguing that it does we would be close to adopting the now largely discredited modernisation theory approach so prevalent in the 1960s. Connor (1972), has pointed out that one of the weaknesses of this theory is that it overstated the power of economic development to change identity and underestimated the attachment to ethnic identity, whatever the economic situation. In addition, recent studies have tended to stress that modernisation is a cause of nationalism, not a cure for it (Gellner, 1983; Hechter, 1975; Schou, 1989).

Secondly, McAllister and Rose (1982), have shown that the period leading up to the outbreak of intercommunal violence in Northern Ireland was a period of rising living standards. Indeed the Prime

Minister of the time, O'Neill, argued that 'if you give Roman Catholics a good job and a good house, they will live like Protestants' (McAllister and Rose, 1982, p. 12). In fact this didn't happen because violent conflicts can break out when development begins and expectations rise rather than when an area or a group remains underdeveloped. An upsurge of black action against segregation in the deep south of the US, for example, developed in the 1950s in part precisely because of this revolution of rising expectations following the post war economic boom. Similarly, in Canada the modernization of Quebec since the 1960s has not reduced ethnic tensions between English and French speakers. It seems to have hastened the province's move towards separatism.

Thirdly, during the process of economic development it may be that conflicts will arise over the distribution of the wealth being created. As a UN report has pointed out

> Conflicts are likely to intensify when there is unequal development and some ethnic groups or minorities lag behind others in the overall national development....Ideally, developmental processes should remove or reduce economic and social obstacles to cooperation and mutual respect among all groups in national society; if development processes are misdirected, they may unfortunately have the opposite effect. (UN Doc. E/CN.4/Sub.2/1990/46 par. 35)

Fourthly, it is important not to confuse economic development with economic justice. The two do not necessarily go together. The former is about shares, the latter about rights (Glazer, 1983, ch.2). More wealth, if it is distributed in an unequal way, may just deepen the ethnic divisions. It may also be the case that a prosperous economy may exist in a situation of political oppression and the denial of basic rights. Greenburg (Giliomee and Gagiano, 1990, p. 2) attacks the 'growth hypothesis' by pointing out how division and discrimination can remain despite development. In such circumstances prosperity will not be able to buy peace. Consider, for example, the point made by a Palestinian in Minns (1990, p. 140)

> Today we have comforts we did not have in the past. We have electricity in our homes, running water and machines. Even now we can rent a tractor for twenty shekels an hour for farming. But what's the use of all this when life is so bitter under the Israelis? If we trespass on Jewish land, we are fined or imprisoned, but they can trespass on mine, ruin my crops, and steal my land. They are free to do what they like, while I'm robbed of my rights and

livelihood.

Economic development is often an example of what Sherif termed a common goal, not a superordinate goal. That is it is a goal which may be achieved by one or other ethnic groups on their own. This will be especially true where the ethnic groups are geographically separated and the violent conflict can be contained in just one region of the country. Cyprus, for example, experienced considerable economic growth in the years between 1964 and 1974, but this was not shared with the Turkish Cypriots who had withdrawn into their own enclaves. Of course in especially violent ethnic conflict (Lebanon), or where the conflict cannot be isolated in one part of the territory (Northern Ireland), or where considerable resources have to be diverted to institutions responsible for law and order or the continuation of the struggle, it may be possible to argue that resolving violent ethnic conflicts does become a superordinate goal rather than a common goal, and unilateral actions by one group will not be able to bring about the desired wealth creation.

Fifthly, we should remember Rose's observation (Whyte, 1990, p. 192) that some conflicts are so intractable precisely because material factors, which are negotiable, are not as important as values such as identity, culture and security, which are non-negotiable. Finally, there is very little evidence to support the peace through development idea. Esman, for example, claims that the causal link between economic growth and the mitigation of conflict has never been demonstrated. He believes that a full investigation into this link will reveal that 'macroeconomic performance has only marginal effects on ethnic conflict - quite insufficient to confirm the crude expectation that growth, however vigorous and sustained, has beneficial consequences for inter-ethnic relations' (Esman, 1990, p. 489). All in all, therefore, the claim that development brings peace is not entirely convincing. It tends to overstate the political and social benefits of rising prosperity without noting the dangers of rising expectations, dislocation, fear and anxiety, and unequal distribution.

Nevertheless, Azar is surely right to argue that what he calls balanced and redistributive development strategies should complement, and cannot be a substitute for, political dialogue. Here Stavenhagen's idea of ethnodevelopment is of particular interest. With this concept he is suggesting that greater sensitivity to cultural differences is needed in the design and implementation of development programmes. Ethnodevelopment means 'finding in the group's own culture the resources and creative force necessary to confront the challenges of the modern, changing world' (Stavenhagen, 1990, p. 90). Ethno-development would involve 'redefining the nature of nation-building and enriching the complex multicultural fabric of many modern states'

(Stavenhagen, 1990, p. 148). Cole (1990) has pointed to the increasing concern about the relationship between culture and development and has called on UNESCO to play a role in cultural forecasting so as to allow the articulation of alternative development scenarios. Azar has also placed great emphasis on 'development diplomacy' and the links between structural inequalities and protracted social conflicts. In particular, he wants more attention given to the fulfilment of local needs and to local participation. So although we should be aware that the peace through development approach is flawed, we should not reject outright the thought that economic development which can help the need fulfilment of all groups and which involves the participation of all cultures is of value in conflict resolution initiatives.

An interesting test case for the influence of development diplomacy on ethnic conflict is about to take place in the Occupied Territories of Gaza and parts of the West Bank. The international community has recognised, in the light of the 1993 accord between the PLO and Israel, that economic development of these areas should make an important contribution to a lasting peace between Jews and Palestinians. The World Bank has estimated that the Occupied Territories will need $2.5 billion over the next five years for projects such as roads, sewage and other infrastructure (*Guardian*, 1 October 1993). Forty seven international donors pledged $2 billion for this work at a meeting in October 1993. Other tests of the link between peace and development can be found in Russia and South Africa, both of whom have made demands for western financial help to maintain stable societies. Northern Ireland has also obtained significant international funding for projects related to peace work.[2]

Malaysia is an interesting case when assessing the link between development and peace. Up until 1969 it experienced large annual growth rates of about six per cent per annum, but this benefited the urban-based Chinese and other non-Malay communities more than the 'native' Malays, who make up about 47 per cent of the population. Following riots in 1969, a symptom of growing ethnic tension, the governing Alliance Party introduced a New Economic Policy(NEP), which attempted to distribute the benefits of growth more widely. This involved setting job quotas to encourage the recruitment of more Malay workers at all levels of industry and finance. As a result of the NEP income imbalances did decline and more Malays were employed in non-agricultural work. Perhaps as a result of these policies direct ethnic violence has not been common in Malaysia, but tensions are evident, and they indicate the problems that could arise in implementing development strategies.

There seems little doubt that the policies adopted by the government over the past 20 years has caused resentment in the Chinese and Indian communities, who feel that positive discrimination in favour of Malays has involved negative discrimination against them. Secondly, it has been argued that the emphasis placed on inter-ethnic balancing has distracted attention from intra-ethnic inequalities, and all the NEP had done is enabled the creation of a new Malay upper class without improving by much the lot of the ordinary Malay. It seems that the gap between the rich and poor Malays is widening, not decreasing (Ali, 1991). Many of these poorer Malays are now arguing that the NEP has not worked and that even more positive discrimination in their favour is needed. This is, inevitably, increasing fears in non-Malay communities. A final problem is that the move towards state-enforced economic redistribution was accompanied by a drift away from consociational politics. Even if the government was able to retain cross-community support at the elite level, the quality of democracy in the country has suffered. Indeed, one commentator has described the Malaysian system as 'coercive consociationalism'. (Mauzy, 1993).

Contact plus confidence building

In violent ethnic conflicts the parties usually develop a distrust of one another, and this distrust can then inhibit the search for a peaceful solution. Some writers, therefore, stress the importance of re-establishing trust between the parties an an important prerequisite of constructive intercommunal dialogue. However, although there has been a lot of interest in confidence building in inter-state relations, and especially superpower relations (Berg and Rotfeld, 1986; Byers, Larrabe and Lynch, 1987; Harbottle, 1986) there has been very little written on confidence building in ethnic conflict.

One area to which attention could be fruitfully directed is the strategy of Gradual Reduction in Tension (GRIT), developed by Osgood (1985; 1986; Mitchell, 1986). This aims to reduce tension levels and build up trust between adversaries by suggesting a series of steps which might help promote negotiation. The key features of GRIT are as follows. One side unilaterally makes an unambiguous concession to the other side which is, ideally, open to full verification. This action is accompanied by a clear signal that a reciprocal action is expected. If the other side responds positively, and also makes a concession, the process is continued through a series of unilateral initiatives. If no reciprocal action is forthcoming no-one really loses since the initial concession will be chosen so that it does not affect the security and safety of the community making it. Osgood suggests that unilateral initiatives by one side only should even be continued over a period regardless of the unresponsiveness of the other side in an effort to change aggressive interpretations into conciliatory responses. Pruitt and Rubin (1986, p. 39) argue that such action can build confidence especially when the helpful behaviour is seen to be voluntary and involves some costs for the gesturing party.

Confidence building can also be eased by the presence of an impartial third party who can verify cease-fires and agreements not to engage in military build-ups in sensitive areas. The parties may even be willing to surrender control of such areas to such a third party as part of a disengagement process. In Cyprus in 1989 the UN force (UNFICYP) was able to implement de-confrontation measures along the Green Line in Nicosia where Greek and Turkish armed forces are only yards apart. After much patient negotiating the UN was able to get the parties to pull their troops back to a safer distance.

Souter (1989), has recently examined other ways that confidence building measures can be introduced into the ethnic conflict in Cyprus. He argues, correctly in this author's view, that there are a series of initiatives which could improve intercommunal trust and which are not related to the basic security needs of each side. Measures Souter proposes include the ending of the Greek Cypriot economic blockade against the Turkish Cypriot controlled area of the island and an acceptance by the Turkish side that Greek Cypriots be allowed to resettle the new town of Varosha, which is presently deserted.

In Northern Ireland confidence building initiatives could include reforms in the administration of justice, sensitivity in the way sectarian parades are conducted, and the abandonment of the territorial claim over Northern Ireland that is written into the Irish constitution. The building up of cooperation at the local council level is another promising avenue to explore. Several of these councils in Northern Ireland have been able to develop schemes that allow the sharing of power between the Catholic SDLP and the main Unionist party the Ulster Unionists.

However, there is bound to be some resistance to confidence building attempts. Hewstone (1988) claims that the psychological tendency for 'hypothesis confirmation' means that contradictory information will be reinterpreted to confirm either negative or positive interpretation of the actions of others. So positive and well meaning confidence building initiatives could be interpreted as an attempt to lull one's own side into a false sense of security. Or the gesturing group might be accused of trying to foster divisions within the target group. In chapter three we also noted how Hewstone (1988) shows that a positive act committed by an enemy group may be interpreted in terms of situational (or external) attributes rather than in terms of a disposition (or internal) to act positively. In other words the enemy is acting in a positive way because the group is forced by circumstances beyond their control to act well not because they have good intentions.

Contact plus education for mutual understanding

Here the emphasis is on the attitudes of children and young adults, and the hope is that peace can be obtained through generational change. This involves a view of education which is broader than the emphasis on the transmission of knowledge. For education for mutual understanding (or multi-cultural education) also involves the nurturing of certain values such as tolerance and respect and the emphasis is on education *for* as well as education *about* something (UN Doc. E/CN.4/Sub.2/40 Rev.1). Parekh (1986), has set out in more detail the goals of education for mutual understanding. They are: the cultivation of basic human capacities such as critical reflection, imagination and reason; the fostering of intellectual and moral qualities such as openness, love of truth, objectivity and scepticism; and the familiarisation of students with the great intellectual, moral, religious and literary achievements of the human spirit in general and not just their own cultures. This latter goal involves exposing the students to the language, history, religion and culture of other societies.

Formal education is the way that national culture and historical enmities are transmitted (see, e.g. Rogers, 1990). Said (1993, p. 37). notes how 'every scheme of education known to me...purifies the national culture in the process of indoctrinating the young'. Nevertheless, even though education is used to launder the past (Said, 1993, p. 39), examples of practical initiatives to improve inter-communal relations through education do exist. Cases worthy of study include the recent emphasis given to education for mutual understanding (EMU) in Northern Ireland and the role of the Van Leer Jerusalem Institute. There has been growing support in Northern Ireland, where there is a segregated education system, for the ideals of EMU. Indeed, the Northern Ireland Council for Educational Development (1988, p. 8) has called for a fourth 'R' to be placed on the school curriculum-relationships, and argues that 'there is a considerable body of empirical evidence in Northern Ireland to support the view that education has an important role to play in the promotion of community relations'. EMU could be especially important in encouraging children to: learn to respect and value themselves and others; know about and value their own and other cultural traditions; learn the importance of resolving differences by peaceful and creative means (p. 9). Also of note in Northern Ireland is the development of integrated schools open to all children irrespective of their religious beliefs. There are still only a handful of these schools, but Whyte (1990, pp 210-11) claims that some psychological studies have revealed that they do have a beneficial effect on the intercommunal attitudes of children who attend them (see also Dunn, 1993, p. 72).

In Israel, the Van Leer Institute has established a programme in civic education on Arab-Israeli relations for secondary school children and also conducts joint courses for Arab and Jewish teachers. Whilst in Cyprus the recently created University of Cyprus, which is in the Greek Cypriot part of the island, is to have the first Turkish Studies Department in the Hellenic world. But to date the University has not been able to attract Turkish or Turkish Cypriot students.

The area of education for mutual understanding is an important and fascinating topic, and the brief treatment given to it here, which concentrates on general rather than specific issues, cannot do it full justice. It cannot be denied that the whole process of child raising has a crucial impact on attitudes and beliefs in later life. It is also obvious that if the hostile attitudes and negative perceptions of one generation are not passed on to the next, the younger generation might be able to deal with inter-ethnic problems in a more constructive atmosphere. However, formal schooling is just one part of child raising and just one way in which values are transmitted across generations. There is no agreement on the relative influence of schooling on attitudes, but it could plausibly be argued that in a deeply divided society, education will reflect these divisions more than they can heal them. Furthermore, hopes that educational reform can stop the transmission of deeply held in-group attitudes will probably be dashed if supportive changes do not happen elsewhere in society. Education for mutual understanding might be a necessary step towards attitude change, but it is not a sufficient cause of such changes. A child exposed to more positive images of an 'enemy' culture might reassess the negative images held by his or her own group, but this is unlikely if other in-group institutions (the churches, the media, the family) continue to reinforce prejudices.

This assumption has been tested by Campbell (Jones, 1972, p. 104), who conducted tests into the effects of integrated schooling on inter-group attitudes of US children. In fact, he could uncover no clear evidence that desegregated schooling resulted in improvements in negative attitudes. Rather he found that such attitudes would increase or decrease depending on the attitudes of the child's friends and parents. Parekh (1986), makes a similar point when he points out the need to address ways in which the social context can frustrate the aims of multi-cultural education and explore why the rhetoric of such education is often so different from the practice.

Some writers have argued that the psychological foundations of the enemy concept are laid long before formal schooling begins. Volkan (1989) has claimed that it is at the age of thirty six months that a cohesive sense of the self emerges, along with the need to externalize certain unintegrated images. This need, filtered through certain 'cultural amplifiers' (like food, clothes, symbols) leads to an early linkage of 'good' with the ingroup and 'bad' with other ethnic groups.

This is not to argue that educational projects cannot have an impact. However, it is likely that gains will be small unless such initiatives are part of broader changes in society. Rhode (1980), reports on a UNESCO sponsored programme in Kawasaki, Japan which attempted to change Japanese attitudes towards its Korean minority. This involved teaching Japanese students Korean culture, history and geography, and a letter exchange programme with Koreans was started. As a result, the number of Japanese children who said they could be friends with Korean children increased from 20 per cent to 70 per cent, and those who said that Koreans were dirty and could not be accepted fell from 60 per cent to ten per cent. It must, however, be pointed out that this project involved communities that were not at war with one another.

Prejudice reduction

It is not only children who need to reassess their attitudes and beliefs. Prejudice reduction for adults, which may result in 'disarmament of the mind', has always been recognised as an important part of peace-building. Allport (1954, ch. 30) has set out several ways that prejudice can be reduced, whilst also noting that it can be so deeply embedded in an individual's personality that it is not easily removed. For him, the main strategies are formal education methods; contact and acquaintance programmes (e.g. neighbourhood festivals, community conferences etc.) group retraining methods; positive action by the mass media; exhortation by community leaders such as churchmen and politicians; and individual therapy. In Northern Ireland there are many examples of organizations involved in prejudice reduction and mutual understanding work, and in an attempt to boost their role the government created a Community Relations Council in 1990 to 'foster a shared respect and mutual understanding of...[its]... social, cultural and religious diversity' (Arthur, 1990, p. 417).

There are formidable difficulties to be faced, however, in attempting to reduce prejudice. We have already mentioned the problem of the reinterpretation of information to confirm a negative assessment of the other side when we examined confidence building. As well as this Volkan (1990) has pointed out how we become emotionally attached to an enemy image, the need for which can arise out of our own need to project our own negative features on to others. Such images are therefore difficult to renounce, and the existence of psychological barriers to prejudice reduction is a reminder that grass-roots peace-building is not without its difficulties. A whole host of problems can be encountered. Deutsch has examined some of these as a problem of defensiveness (1964, p. 157-8), which, he claims arises out of fears about losing status, vested interests in the status quo, and a lack of confidence

Exploring cultures

Cultural differences are often presumed to be at the heart of ethnic conflict. In many situations, especially in the case of ethnies struggling for recognition and self-determination, intellectuals and artists play a vital role in constructing a romantic 'national identity' that can be exclusivist (Smith, 1991, ch. 4). Nevertheless, the exploration of culture may be an interesting way of transcending difference. In Northern Ireland, for example, a company of world famous playwrights, poets and actors have established the Field Day project, which is attempting to reappraise the cultural and political traditions in Ireland through the deconstruction of inherited myths. As Bell (1991, p. 85) puts it, 'Field Day's genius has been to engage with the political via a theatrical and literary practice. This politico-cultural project, despite its apparent utopianism, indeed perhaps because of it, has considerable appeal, particularly in the North where alienation from politics is prevalent among both communities'. Ireland is divided into four ancient provinces. The goal of Field Day is to create a 'fifth province' of the imagination, free of sectarianism and stereotyping, where there can emerge an understanding that Ireland as a whole shares a single cultural tradition enriched by all groups on the island. One of its themes is the need to replace the romantic, Celtic approach to Irish culture, as typified by Yeats, with the pluralistic, demythologizing approach found in the work of Joyce and Beckett. Yeats was searching for the essence of Irishness, whereas Joyce, in particular, used his genius to explore the multiple aspects of Irish society. The most important of Field Day's projects to date has been the publication of an anthology of Irish literature from AD 550 that aims to show that the intermingling of the different traditions in Ireland has produced a unique literature. There is a constructive and a destructive aspect to this enterprise. The constructive aspect is that it hopes to make all Irish people both aware and proud of this literature. The destructive intention is to induce a questioning of what Deane (1992, p. 27) has called the 'lethal premise, that there is a stable identity called Irishness'.

A slightly different justification for an artistic/literary approach to conflict transformation can be found in the work of the American pragmatist philosopher, Richard Rorty. In a recent stimulating study he has pointed out the importance of literature in building up a sense of solidarity by helping us to be less cruel. Great authors like Orwell and Nabokov, he suggests, inspire us not by the 'truth' of their writings but by the images they present (Rorty, 1989). Similar claims have been advanced by Lippmann (1962, p. 86-7), who has written that 'art enlarges experience by admitting us to the inner life of others...literature in particular elaborates our insight into human life, and therefore, enables us to center our institutions more truly'.

Conclusions

All of the peace-building strategies discussed above are not mutually exclusive. Indeed it has already been hinted that they can be mutually supporting. Economic development, the build up of mutual trust, the existence of superordinate goals, education for mutual understanding and reconciliation and forgiveness can be powerful weapons in the armoury of any peace-builder, particularly if the various strategies can be combined. Here it may be possible to borrow a term from Alger (1984). He has called for the creation of a 'learning community', whereby attempts to change attitudes involve a collaborative effort by many groups, including schools and universities, adult education institutions, trade unions, churches and various non-governmental groups. This networking of possible bridge building groups will then allow for the assault on negative attitudes to be made on a broad front. To use Galtung's terminology, this broad front approach would improve the chances of symbiosis (the creation of interdependence), would broaden the scope of interdependence (through a multitude of spheres and widening agendas) and might create a superstructure for planning, problem articulation and resolution (Galtung, 1981).

Peace-building initiatives are often tentative, precarious and easily reversed. As yet we are not in a position to offer any conclusive conclusion about their value in conflict resolution work, but there is at least a plausible argument that peace-building can make an important contribution, even if the gains from peace-building tend to be small and undramatic. For grass roots peace-building will not have immediate dramatic effects on conflict situations. It works to a different time frame and agenda. If it is effective it may lead to the establishment of new networks and new institutions. According to Walker (1988), critical social movements, in particular, can explore new political spaces, extend horizons and establish connections. They may develop a new language of dialogue to replace the language of conflict and sectarianism. In so doing it may help 'deconstruct' and reconceptualize the inherited history of myth and symbol that fuels confrontation and which channels the mind into a rigid interpretation of intercommunal relationships. It can empower ordinary people and release constructive energy, and this might stimulate creative thinking. Therefore we might agree with Allport that

> Since the problem (of prejudice) is many sided there can be no sovereign formula. The wisest thing to do is to attack on all fronts simultaneously. If no one single attack has large effect, yet many small attacks from many directions can have large cumulative results (Allport, 1954, p. 507).

This idea of a plurality of small moves forward rather than one break-though is an attractive one, not least because it recognises that peace is more than successful mediation. It also involves justice, the empowerment of ordinary people, demilitarization, education, the revitalization of democracy, and respect for diversity. Initiatives to achieve these goals may result in increased conflict, which is not necessarily a bad thing. As people make increased demands on the political system, it may be an effective way of contributing to the resolution of bitter, violent, destructive and seemingly intractable intercommunal conflict. We do not just have to see the need for conflict transformation, we also need to recognise that conflict is also a means of transformation.

Notes

1. For more on Corrymeela see McCreary (1974). A comprehensive survey of reconciliation projects in Ireland can be found in Ellis (1986). This begins with a quote from Matthew, 'Blessed are the peacemakers'. Another survey of reconciliation work is Lampen (1987). He makes two important comments on such activities. Progress in easily reversed and it fails to take hold in working class areas. The idea of redemption through suffering is also a theme developed by playwrights. See, for example, *Pentecost,* by the Northern Ireland writer Stuart Parker.
2. In the case of Northern Ireland the International Fund for Ireland has provided money for cross-border economic projects such as ACUMEN and MENTOR and the European Union has provided money through its INTERREG programme, which aims to accelerate the integration of 'internal border areas' (Ryan, 1993).

Part III
The United Nations and Ethnic Conflict

6 The United Nations and ethnic conflict resolution

> People from the United Nations form a club unto themselves.
> Many of them are pretentious: they look on everything and
> everyone from a global perspective, which means, simply, that
> they look down. They repeat the word 'global' in every sentence,
> which makes it difficult to settle everyday problems with them
> (Ryszard Kapuscinski, 1987, p. 73).

Introduction

To some it may appear a strange or unproductive course of action to
attempt to link together the United Nations and ethnic conflict. For the
UN, despite its name, is an organization of states, not of nations, and is
concerned primarily with relations between these sovereign entities.
Furthermore, as many states feel threatened by ethnic sentiments held
by groups of their population, they have a vested interest in keeping
ethnic issues of the UN agenda. Pierre van den Burghe, for example,
has claimed that

> The UN is first and foremost an organization of states, not of
> nations, and since most states are, in fact threatened by the claims
> of nations, it is little wonder that the UN is pro-state and

anti-nation (quoted in Kuper, 1981, p. 161).

This is an argument echoed by Shiels (1984, p. 10), who claims that 'ethnic separatist movements are not likely to be aided by the United Nations or regional groups, which tend to have pro nation-state biases'.

In addition, since most, but by no means all, ethnic conflicts are fought out within the borders of a single sovereign state they can be characterised as being within the domestic jurisdiction of the state concerned, which effectively inhibits UN involvement under Article 2 (7) of the Charter, which states that

> Nothing contained in the present Charter shall authorize the United Nations to intervene in matters which are essentially within the domestic jurisdiction of any State or shall require the Members to submit such matters to settlement under the present Charter.

The only qualification to this clause is that the principle of non-intervention 'shall not prejudice the application of enforcement measures under Chapter VII'. Intervention by the UN is therefore permissible if the Security Council deems there to be a threat to international peace and security, however there has been a traditional reluctance to invoke this justification for intervention in ethnic conflict. So during the Biafran conflict the then UN Secretary-General decided

> It was... impossible for me to act during one of the most tragic events of the decade of my tenure: the civil war in Nigeria in 1967... There was never any doubt in my mind that the conflict was strictly an internal matter and, therefore, outside the jurisdiction of the United Nations. (U Thant, 1977, p. 53)

Indeed one could provide a long list of serious ethnic conflicts from which the UN has been excluded. For example, despite the limited humanitarian role played by the UN during the Bangladeshi war of secession in 1971 (Ramcharan, 1983, ch.4), its involvement has been described as 'limited and ineffective' (Buckheit, 1978, p. 209). When intercommunal riots broke out in Northern Ireland in 1969, the Irish Premier Jack Lynch called publicly for UN troops to be sent to the city of Derry, but privately he must have known that the UK government could have prevented such a move by its use of a veto on the Security Council or by invoking Article 2(7) of the Charter.

Nevertheless it has not been possible either to keep the ethnic issue off the UN agenda entirely, or to keep the UN out of all ethnic conflicts. There are several reasons to explain this overlapping interest. The first of these is that as long as the UN remains true in even a minor way to the ideals enshrined in Article 1 of its Charter it will have to, on occasions, respond to ethnic violence. Article 1 states that two of the purposes of the UN are to maintain international peace and security and to promote and encourage respect for human rights and fundamental freedoms for all. The recent past has clearly shown that ethnic violence can become a threat to international peace and security and will often involve widespread infringements of human rights. Article 1 also includes a reference to the principle of the self-determination of peoples. This was not intended to be an open invitation to all groups who considered themselves a distinct people to break from existing sovereign entities. Far from it. Nevertheless it is a principle enshrined in rather ambiguous language in the Charter, and it can be argued that this has important implications for ethnic conflict. Finally, states themselves, when they have not been able to resolve their own internal problems and cannot keep the peace without outside assistance, have turned on several occasions to the UN to request this organization's involvement. This will usually happen when, as in the case of Cyprus and Lebanon, there is a danger of intervention by another state or states.

There are good reasons for believing that the UN might be able to play a more constructive third party role than the government of the multi-ethnic state itself or other states. For we have already argued that the government of the state experiencing ethnic conflict frequently becomes a party to that conflict, or at the very least is unable to devise policies to reduce ethnic violence, and that external involvement by other states often escalates conflict through biased affective or self-interested interventions. In the face of these problems associated with other types of official third party involvement, some have looked to the UN as the best conflict resolving/managing institution. This is mainly because the UN, as the supposed guardian of international peace and security has no particular stake in an outcome apart from a satisfactory reduction in violence. It is therefore less likely than states to exploit ethnic conflict for its own ends, since it does not have a 'national interest' of its own to protect and promote. This is a point made hesitatingly by Beitz (1979, p. 85), who argues that the problem of partiality in intervention may be resolved by 'intervention under the auspices of an international organization (like the UN) which might not (I do not say will not) be subject to the partiality that characterises the decisions of particular governments'.

In this chapter we will explore the extent to which the UN can involve itself constructively in protracted and violent ethnic conflict. There are several ways the UN has attempted this. Miller (1967) has identified these involvements in 'local disorder' under the headings of mediation, peace-keeping, observer missions and resolutions. Schachter

(1974) has offered a more detailed and comprehensive list that is comprised of: public debate and the expression of international concern; quiet diplomacy, good offices and conciliation; inquiry and reporting; assistance to ascertain the will of the people; observation and surveillance; peace-keeping and policing; economic assistance and technical cooperation; determination of the government entitled to representation at the UN; sanctions and enforcement measures; and the elaboration of norms and criteria of conduct. For the purposes of this study, however, we shall examine UN activity under our three headings of peace-keeping, peace-making and peace-building.

The UN, despite the restraints on its activities already mentioned, has been involved in all these types of action with varying degrees of enthusiasm and commitment. The hope here is that an analysis of the UN record will provide a realistic basis upon which to judge the worth of the international organization in this area. We can then avoid either the temptation to embrace the UN too enthusiastically, or reject it too quickly. The organization is neither a panacea nor a nonentity. Its record is mixed, as the following examination will reveal.

Peace-keeping and the United Nations

The most visible and dramatic form of UN involvement in ethnic conflict is the installation of peace-keeping forces between the warring sides in certain multi-ethnic states. At present there are three such operations underway. The United Nations Force in Cyprus (UNFICYP), which was established in 1964 by Security Council Resolution 186; the United Nations Interim Force in Lebanon (UNIFIL), which has been in this troubled country since its establishment by Security Council Resolution 425 in March 1978; and the United Nations Protection Force in Yugoslavia (UNPROFOR) which is now operating in different ways in Croatia, Bosnia and Hercegovina and Macedonia. We can also examine the recent experiences of the UN observer mission in Angola (UNAVEM). There is one other instance when the UN established a peace-keeping force in a state experiencing ethnic conflict. This is the force that was stationed in the Belgian Congo (ONUC) between 1960 and 1964, when there was a secessionist attempt by the province of Katanga. There are, in addition, small observer missions in Kashmir (UNMOGIP) and Georgia (UNOMIG). The former, which has been in operation along the India-Pakistan border since 1948 has never involved more than 70 observers (see Alam, 1982; James 1990, pp. 158-163), and could play no significant role in the fighting that erupted between the two states in 1965 and 1971, when the cease fire broke down. There were to be 88 military observers in Georgia to monitor a July 1993 cease-fire agreement between the Republic of Georgia and the leaders of the secession movement in Abkhazia. However, because of the break-down of this agreement the deployment of the observers was suspended and very few were actually in place at the end of 1993.

The main aim of peace-keeping forces is clear enough. It is essentially to reduce the violence by positioning military units between the warring factions. In addition to this the specific mandate of each force may call on it to perform additional tasks. Here, however, we are concerned with the primary role of reducing violence through military interposition. Peace-keeping is, therefore, a military activity, but unlike the actions of the army in, for example, Ulster, UN forces do not try to enforce a particular solution. Rather they try to keep the sides apart without prejudging a final political solution. So Rikhye (1983, p. 6) has argued that enforcement plays no part in UN peace-keeping and that the fundamental principles of such operations are 'objectivity and nonalignment with the parties to the dispute, ideally to the extent of total impartiality from the controversial issues at stake'. The problem with non-UN international peace-keeping efforts is that this impartiality has usually been lost (OAU in Chad, MNF in Beirut, Indian Peace-Keeping Force in Sri Lanka).

Of course such impartiality is only possible if the parties to the conflict have already accepted that the maintenance of a cease fire and the separation of the warring groups is in their own interests. The UN would clearly lose its reputation for impartiality if one side accepted the enforcement of a cease fire, whilst the other side wanted to continue fighting. In such circumstances the UN presence would clearly be seen to be favouring the interests of the party that wanted to stop the fighting. This is why, as we noted in chapter four, a commitment to a non-violent solution is needed from leaders before there can be an effective UN peace-keeping operation. For, as James (1989b, p. 372) has pointed out, UN peace-keepers are in the business of 'providing assistance rather than banging heads'. He develops this point (1989c, p. 500) by arguing that the success of such operations 'are dependent on the will of the parties towards peace. If one or both of them are bent on war, the peacekeeping body will not offer a serious obstruction...What it does provide a barrier against, however, is an unwanted war'.

The impartiality of the UN, together with the fact that the blue berets are meant to fire only in self-defence; do not interfere in the internal affairs of the host state; and represent an organization with no particular national interest to pursue, helps to maintain the impartiality of the UN and preserves whatever moral force it can bring to bear. This is vital if a peace-keeping force is to avoid becoming part of the problem rather than part of the solution to the problem.

Although we will concentrate on the role of UN peace-keeping in separating the warring factions, this should not be taken to imply that peace-keeping forces do not do valuable work in other areas or that they do not need certain other skills. They can facilitate the withdrawal of the parties from direct confrontation (Skjelsbaek 1989). Peace-keepers often have to negotiate with local commanders of rival parties, and therefore, at the micro-level also act as peace-makers. As we shall see, they also participate in work that can be regarded as peace-building. However, these activities are secondary to their main role, for as Thakur (1988) reminds us, the main purpose of peace-keeping is to bring about and preserve a cessation of hostilities.

(a) The United Nations Force in Cyprus (UNFICYP)

In December 1963, a fragile intercommunal peace that had existed in Cyprus between the Greek Cypriot majority (80 per cent of the population) and the Turkish Cypriot minority (18 per cent of the population) broke down. During the preceding months the central government of the Republic was paralysed by a number of disagreements. In November 1963, in an attempt to overcome this paralysis, President Makarios proposed 13 changes to the constitution, which in its original form was very favourable to the Turkish Cypriots. The 'thirteen points' were regarded by many Turkish Cypriots as the first stage of a Greek Cypriot plan to bring about *enosis* (union with Greece), which the Turkish Cypriots were pledged to resist. So in this atmosphere of heightened inter-communal tension a clash between Greek Cypriot policemen and some Turkish Cypriots escalated into major violence and began a process that led to the Turkish invasion of 1974 and to the *de facto* partition of the island into Greek Cypriot and Turkish Cypriot areas.

When intercommunal fighting began at the end of 1963 the British took on the responsibility of peace-keeping, but were prepared to do this work only on a short term basis. With no end to the fighting in sight, the British and the Americans hoped that NATO could take over this role. However, this was unacceptable to Makarios, who had been one of the founder members of the Non-Aligned Movement, and so the problem was passed on to the UN Security Council, which established the United Nation Force in Cyprus (UNFICYP). At its strongest the force was composed of 6,500 troops from the UK, Canada, Sweden, Denmark, Finland, Austria, and Ireland. Between 1964 and 1974 the force did much good work in reducing intercommunal tensions and preventing an escalation of violence, though it was not able to do this on all occasions (see e.g. Efthymiadou, 1979; Harbottle, 1971; James, 1969; Kaloudis, 1982, Ryan, 1984, Stegenga, 1968). James (1990, p. 229) argues that during this period the force 'made a very significant contribution to the maintenance of peace', and Hart (1990,p. 120) claims that until 1974 it 'proved vital to the maintenance of general peace'.

UNFICYP was unable to take decisive action against either the Greek sponsored coup against Makarios in July 1974 or the Turkish invasion which resulted from this. This is not to suggest that the peace-keeping force changed into a war watching force, for it was able to do valuable work. It helped with the evacuation of foreign nationals and offered sanctuary to people fleeing the fighting It took over control of Nicosia airport and the Ledra Palace Hotel, which might have otherwise become the focus of bitter fighting. The force helped arrange local cease-fires and supervised the surrender of Turkish Cypriots to UK forces. Following the establishment of a general cease-fire it was able to patrol the short lived Security Zone created by the July 1974 Geneva Agreement. It assisted in the control of anti-American riots, delivered essential supplies to those in need, went to Turkish Cypriot or mixed villages to protect inhabitants and repaired water pipes and electricity and telephone lines. The exchange of prisoners was eased because of the UN presence. Perhaps the most unpleasant task was the investigation of alleged atrocities committed by both sides. These reports remain classified and were sent only to the governments concerned. As the situation stabilized it became clear that the role of the force had now changed from being a 'law and order' force, patrolling in areas of mixed population, into a 'buffer force'. For after the Turkish invasion the two communities in Cyprus were separated and day to day contact was made impossible. The role of UNFICYP since then has been to police the zone which divides the communities. This zone stretches from Kato Pyrgos on the west coast of the island right across to Dherinia on the east coast. It comprises three per cent of the territory of Cyprus, and varies in width from ten metres in parts of Nicosia to three kilometres.

Since the Turkish invasion of 1974, then, UNFICYP has controlled this buffer zone between the Greek and Turkish Cypriot positions. Here it has installed observation posts, which together with mobile patrols, try to spot quickly any breeches of the cease fire agreement. If this breech is a shooting, attempts are made to stop the incident escalating. If it involves the construction of new fortifications, or encroachment into the buffer zone, UNFICYP tries to persuade the guilty party to return to the status quo position, and is nearly always successful in doing so. In May 1992 UNFICYP was composed of 2,103 soldiers from seven states, together with a small 38 man civilian police contingent from Australia and Sweden (UN Doc. S/24050). These soldiers patrol the buffer zone, using 150 observation posts, 51 of which are permanently manned. UNFICYP also undertakes other tasks. It escorts farmers into the buffer zone to allow them to farm their land. The force performs a pastoral role, visiting the small number of Greek Cypriots resident in the North of the island (661 at the end of 1987), and a handful of Turkish Cypriots in the South. It provides an emergency medical service and a mine detection operation. It also facilitates meetings between professional bodies from both communities and negotiates the release of unfortunates that stray across into the territory of the other side.

An original, and successful feature of the UN operation in Cyprus was the creation of a civilian police unit, known as UNCIVPOL (Harbottle, 1971, p. 68). Initially this was composed of small contingents from Australia, Austria, Denmark, New Zealand and Sweden. Now this has been reduced to contingents from Australia and Sweden. Its main functions are to escort people on visits across the intercommunal divide and investigate complaints of criminal activity with an intercommunal content.

James (1989c) has argued that UNFICYP has contributed to crisis defusion, truce maintenance and the continuation of a 'calm stalemate'. It has, as we have seen, also carried out numerous humanitarian functions and has facilitated peace-building work. Although relatively quiet, intercommunal relations in Cyprus remain tense. There are numerous violations of the buffer zone by aircraft and of the maritime security zone by ships. Shots are still fired, either deliberately and accidentally, across the buffer zone. In recent years there have also been staged incursions into the buffer zone by Greek Cypriot groups seeking to draw international attention to the continuing partition of the island. These 'invasions' can become violent and have led to direct confrontations with Turkish soldiers and Turkish Cypriot police. For these reasons a UNFICYP review team decided in November 1990 that the status quo in Cyprus was not self-sustaining and that the number of troops could not be reduced without impairing the efficiency of the Force and its ability to implement its mandate. However, cuts in manpower have had to be made as certain governments have withdrawn their contingents, against the advice of the UN Secretary-General and the wishes of the Republic of Cyprus, for financial reasons and in reaction to the inability of the communities to reach a negotiated settlement. Sweden had already withdraw a contingent in January 1988. By the end of 1993 Canada and Denmark had removed their troops from the island and Britain had cut its contingent by 25 per cent. This has led to speculation that UNFICYP may be scaled down to become an observer mission. In the short term this has been avoided because of the arrival of an Argentinean contingent, which has helped to make up some of the losses in manpower that the force has incurred in recent years.

162

For nearly thirty years Lebanon seemed to many outside observers to be a first class example of a successful multi-ethnic state. It was more democratic than most of its neighbours and became the second most developed economy in the region after Israel. Because of the National Pact, a power sharing agreement that had been in operation since independence, the country had also avoided serious intercommunal violence between Christians and Moslems. In 1965 the Vatican declared it to be a pioneer country in the development of Islamic-Christian relations, and in 1974, in a speech at the UN Arafat stated that Lebanon could offer a model for Palestine. Yet in a relatively short period of time the country went from being one of the most successful examples of consociationalism to being the example which every multi-ethnic state would want to avoid.

There were several reasons for the breakup of the state (Cobban, 1985; Khalidi, 1979; Schou, 1989). The economic success of the Lebanon resulted in social changes that disrupted established ways of acting. Disagreements developed within the Lebanese oligarchy and between the oligarchs and their communities. Moslem politics became radicalized. The demographic profile changed so that the National Pact, which had been the cornerstone of inter-ethnic accommodation, became outdated. Then there were a series of external factors. The influx of Palestinians led to disagreements between Moslems and Christians about whether to support their struggle against Israel. The growth of pan-Arabism also led to increased polarisation. Interventions by Syria and Israel deepened the divisions. These tensions eventually resulted in a bloody civil war in 1975, which in turn led to a limited Israeli intervention (Operation Litani) into Lebanon in March 1978. In response to this invasion the Lebanese government turned to the UN, and in March 1978 Security Council Resolution 425 created the United Nations Interim Force in Lebanon (UNIFIL). In mid-1992 the force was composed of 5,807 troops from ten states, along with 65 members of the UN Truce Supervisory Organization (UNTSO) who are under the authority of the UNIFIL commander (UN Doc. S/24341).

UNIFIL operates under more difficult circumstances than UNFICYP. It was originally meant to be 4,000 strong, with contingents drawn from France, Nepal, Norway, Nigeria, Senegal, Iran, Sweden and Canada. The force was to confirm the withdrawal of Israeli forces, prevent a recurrence of the fighting, restore international peace and security, and assist the government of Lebanon in ensuring a return of its effective authority. It was deployed in the South of the country, in an area between the Litani river and the Israeli border, and even though the Secretary-General was able to use the Swedish and Canadian units that were then working for UNEF II in the Sinai and the Iranian detachment from UNDOF on the Golan Heights, there were still delays in establishing the force because of the difficulties in recruiting other contingents.

The situation in the Lebanon is much more fluid than in Cyprus, and the parties are often less willing to co-operate with the peace-keeping force. This is reflected in the fact that between 1978 and mid-1991 seventy UNIFIL personnel had been killed and 280 wounded in shooting incidents or by mines. (UN Doc. S/24341). UNIFIL troops have been harassed, even kidnapped, by various local militias and UN posts have been persistently attacked by the various factions. Indeed, nothing has happened in recent years to cause us to question the assessment of the UN in October 1985 that 'the conditions still do not exist in which UNIFIL can fully perform its functions or completely fulfil its mandate' (UN Doc. S/17557).

A major reason for this is that the government of Israel does not believe that UNIFIL can guarantee its security. As the Israeli representative at the UN Security Council put it in 1985, 'it is not able structurally to stop terrorism, because it can only serve as a buffer between two governments and because there is no sufficiently strong government on one side, it is structurally unable to fulfil the mandate' (UN Doc. S/PV 2623, p. 24). Therefore Israel has preferred to attempt to guarantee its security by armed raids into Lebanon and by supporting the forces of the Christian militias in South Lebanon which provides a buffer zone on Israel's borders. However, it must be pointed out that such actions only serve to increase the instability in Lebanon, and make it even more unlikely that a 'strong government on one side' will emerge. Interestingly, similar arguments about the ineffectiveness of UN peace-keeping operations have been presented by Turkish and Turkish Cypriot politicians and diplomats. In December 1982, for example, in defending the 1974 Turkish invasion of Cyprus, the Turkish representative Kirca told the Security Council that

> ...experience unfortunately teaches us that international forces have never been able to ensure the full security of populations, which is why, at the request of the Turkish Federated State of Cyprus, the Turkish armed forces will remain on the territory of that Federated State until the conclusion of the final agreement between all the parties concerned (UN Doc. S/PV 2405, p. 48).

Israeli lack of support for the UN can most clearly be demonstrated through two incidents. The first was the way that when they withdrew their forces from Lebanon after the first invasion of 1978, they handed thirty-five per cent of the area under their control not to the UN forces, but to the Christian militia of Major Haddad. His forces played a significant role in frustrating UNIFIL's attempts to fulfil its mandate. The second incident, of course, was the 1982 invasion, when the Israeli Defence Forces simply drove through UN positions. This did not come as a real surprise to the UN. Urquhart (1987, p. 342), recalls how in 1981 he had told the UNIFIL commander that if major hostilities broke out there should only be token UN resistance (protests, roadblocks etc.) and positions should be held as long as possible. But as Urquhart admits, this 'was largely cosmetic stuff and...the Israeli army would sweep through UNIFIL with little difficulty'. So even though UNIFIL's mandate called on it to confirm Israel's withdrawal from South Lebanon this has never been fully achieved. UNIFIL has not yet reached up to the Israeli border.

The lack of an effective government of Lebanon was another reason for the difficulties encountered by UNIFIL. Urquhart (1987, p. 291), has stated that meetings with the Lebanese government following the establishment of the force revealed its 'impotence and wretchedness' . For, 'there was no authority, no serviceable army, and an overwhelming desire to pass the buck' (p. 292). Therefore, self-evidently, UNIFIL was seriously handicapped in fulfilling the part of its mandate that required it to help reestablish the authority of the Lebanese government.

The force has had some success in controlling the movement of armed persons in the UN zone to prevent the recurrence of fighting and to ensure that its area of operation was not used for hostile activity of any kind. This is achieved through the use of observation posts and road blocks and these have resulted in the turning back of thousands of infiltration attempts. Like UNFICYP, UNIFIL also escorts farmers to allow the cultivation of land to take place, and provides mine clearing and emergency medical services. It has also helped negotiate the release of Lebanese abducted by the warring parties. In recognition of the importance of this role a humanitarian section has been established at UNIFIL headquarters and each contingent has been allocated a humanitarian assistance liaison officer.

The UN continues to believe that the force plays a 'significant role in controlling the level of violence in its area of operations and thus reducing the risk of a wider conflagration in the region' (UN Doc. S/20742, par. 34). Without UNIFIL, it could be argued, there would have been many more than the 144,240 official deaths caused by the Lebanese civil war. In a comprehensive analysis of the work of UNIFIL between 1978 and 1988 Skogmo (1988) states that there are three main arguments to support the case that the force should stay the course. The major one is the 'stability factor', and this is an argument that has been consistently made by the UN Secretariat. As Skogmo (1988, p. 260) notes, compared with the rest of Lebanon the UNIFIL area has been 'an area of relative peace and stability'. James (1990, 9. 347) agrees with this assessment and claims that 'Unifil does seem to have made a significant contribution towards reducing the number of arms, and has thus brought a reasonable measure of security to its exclusive area'. Even someone like Fisk (1990, p. 156), who is sceptical about the general work of UNIFIL, accepts that the force can 'up to a point' protect villagers in its area of operation.

The second argument in favour of UNIFIL's continuation is the need to preserve the option of maintaining a peace-keeping presence so that it can play a role in bolstering any future negotiated settlement. If the force was to withdraw it might not be easy to reassemble if it were needed to play such a role in the future. The third argument is that UNIFIL is upholding the prestige of the United Nations and respect for the Charter, and if the force were to withdraw because of difficult circumstances this would be to reward the most aggressive and uncooperative parties in this conflict. Until it is withdrawn the interim assessment of Urquhart in the introduction to the Skogmo (1988, p. viii) study is that it is an 'extraordinary tribute to the successive commanders and to the officers and men of UNIFIL...that after ten years the Force is still in place and is regarded as a valuable, indeed an essential, element of peace and stability in this extremely sensitive area, even by those who were once its main detractors'. Perhaps this is a major achievement for a poorly financed peace-keeping operation working under an impractical mandate, without the support of all of the key parties in a volatile and complex conflict.

(c) United Nations Angola Verification Mission (UNAVEM)

There has been a tendency, which was particularly strong during the Cold War, to see the civil violence in Angola in ideological terms. From this perspective, since 1975 the MPLA Marxist government was faced with a challenge from two anti-Marxist groups, UNITA and the FNLA. This interpretation is strengthened by the fact that the Cubans and the Soviet supported the MPLA and the CIA, South Africa and Zaire (along with China) were on the side of the opposition forces. However, as Mohanty (1992, p. 7) has pointed out 'many of the phenomena of African reality cannot be understood without taking the ethnic factor into account'. In particular this study of Angola argues that there is a very strong ethnic element to the Angolan civil war, and one of the main difficulties for the MPLA has been to moderate the attachment separate cultural identities with a 'civic loyalty'. Thus the MPLA drew much of its support from the Mbundu, the FNLA from the Bakonga and UNITA from the Ovimbunda. There is some justification, therefore, in including Angola in this study of ethnic conflict.

The end of the Cold War enabled the various interested parties in Angola and neighbouring Namibia to make a move towards negotiated settlements of these interrelated problems. As part of the overall settlement package UNAVEM 1 was deployed in Angola in January 1989 to monitor the withdrawal of Cuban troops at the request of the Angolan and Cuban governments. It was made up of 70 military observers and 22 international civilian staff (James, 1990, p. 255). In June 1991 the Secretary-General informed the Security Council that UNAVEM 1 had fulfilled its mandate. This added to a general optimism about the future of Angola that was based on an MPLA- UNITA peace agreement of May 1991, signed after fifteen years of civil war. This agreement envisaged UN monitoring of a cease fire, elections under international supervision and the integration of the two opposing armies into a single force, which was to occur before the elections.

UNAVEM 11 was established on 30 May, when Security Council resolution 696 provided it with a mandate to verify the cease-fire and police monitoring arrangements agreed by the parties. It was to be deployed at 46 locations where troops were to assemble and at other 'critical points'. Because of a lack of material support from UN member states UNAVEM 11 remained a small operation. (Fortna, 1993, p. 391). It contained 350 military observers from about two dozen states, 126 police observers from nine states, who were deployed in all 18 provinces, a military medical unit, 54 international civilian personnel and 41 locally recruited staff (Fortna, 1993, p. 395). Its main function was to monitor the groups who were made directly responsible for monitoring the cease-fire. especially the Joint Political-Military Commission composed of representatives from UNITA, the MPLA, and observers from Portugal, the US, and the Soviet Union. In March 1992 Security Council Resolution 747 extended the mandate of the mission to include election observation, and a small electoral division of 100 people was created within UNAVEM.

However, when elections were held in September and October 1992, accompanied by only minor violent clashes between MPLA and UNITA supporters, the defeated party of Jonas Savimbi refused to accept the results. UNITA, who obtained only 34.1 per cent of the vote compared to 53.7 per cent for the MPLA, withdrew its troops from the unified army and, at the end of October, restarted the civil war despite claims by international observers that the elections were, on the whole, free and fair. On the other hand, critics of the elections could point out that the UN did not control the election process and monitoring of the polling was not comprehensive as not enough resources or personnel had been sent to Angola, a huge country with 4.8 million voters. The speed with which UNITA forces were able to mobilize also revealed the extent of the non-compliance with the provisions of the Peace Accords that related to demobilization and weapons' storage. UNAVEM was unable to do much in the face of renewed fighting and another opportunity to end the sixteen-year civil war in Angola was lost. UNAVEM's mandate was extended for brief periods several times throughout 1992 and 1993 but its strength was reduced. By the end of 1993 it was made up of 50 military and 18 police observers as well as 11 military paramedics and 43 international civilian staff. It is deployed in five locations where it patrols areas, liaises with local authorities and renders support to the humanitarian assistance operation that is attempting to get aid to the millions of victims of the conflict. The Security Council has also indicated that it is ready to consider expanding the force if there is significant progress in the peace process.

(d) The United Nations Protection Force in the former Yugoslavia (UNPROFOR)

When the crisis that developed around the break-up of Yugoslavia first became an important issue for the interstate system at the start of the 1990s the first reaction of the United Nations was to consider this as a problem that the Europeans themselves should respond to. It was only after the repeated failures of the European Community to negotiate an end to the violence between Serbs and Croats in Croatia that the United Nations became involved as a significant actor. In December 1991 the UN Secretary-General dispatched a small military mission to the new state to assess the possibilities for a peace-keeping operation. Already, on 25 September 1991, the Security Council had called on states to implement a general and complete embargo on the delivery of weapons and military equipment to Yugoslavia.

Following a mediation initiative between October 1991 and January 1992 by the Secretary-General's Personal Envoy, Cyrus Vance, the parties in Croatia did agree a cease-fire and on 21 February 1992 Security Council Resolution 743 created the United Nations Protection Force for twelve months. The force was mandated to be deployed in Croatia, Bosnia and Hercegovina, Macedonia, Montenegro and Serbia. Slovenia was excluded from its mandate. This was the first use of a full-scale peace-keeping operation on continental Europe. However, it was initially deployed only in Croatia, where it was to police the United Nations Protected Areas (UNPAs). These are the Serbian areas of eastern Slavonia, western Slavonia and Krajina. Here the force was to ensure the demilitarization of the UNPAs and the protection of all persons residing in there. UNPROFOR also was to verify the withdrawal of the pro-Serbian Yugoslavian army (JNA) from Croatia.

It controls access to the UNPAs and monitors the local police there. Initially about 14,000 troops were deployed, but this number has been steadily increased. Six hundred civilian police have been authorised to monitor human rights abuses, identify people in need of humanitarian aid and carry out parallel investigations. Contributing states include France, the UK, Denmark, Egypt, Spain, Russia, Jordan, Poland, Nepal, Ukraine and Belgium.

The mandate of the force has since been expanded by the Security Council. Resolution 762 of June 1992 enables it to monitor the 'pink zones'; Serbian areas outside the UNPAs that were then controlled by the JNA. In August the same year Resolution 769 also passed on to UNPROFOR the task of controlling civilian entry into the UNPAs, and this involved performing immigration and customs duties at the international frontiers of the areas. Resolution 779 of October 1992 allowed UNPROFOR to monitor the demilitarization of the Prevlaka Peninsular near Dubrovnik and placed control of the Peruca Dam in UN hands.

With the harrowing scenes produced by media coverage of the civil war in Bosnia and Hercegovina the UN also came under pressure to extend deployment to this state, but a cease-fire agreement was more elusive in this conflict. As the parties seemed unwilling to stop the fighting it was not possible to deploy a peace-keeping operation similar to the one in Croatia, yet the continuing fighting added to the need for humanitarian operations. In April 1992 the Secretary-General sent 40 military observers to the Mostar region, but they had to be withdrawn for their own safety the following month. The same month the headquarters of UNPROFOR was moved from Sarajevo to Zagreb because of fears about their safety, leaving behind about 100 military personnel. Also in May Chapter VII of the Charter was invoked to impose sanctions on the rump state of Yugoslavia (Serbia and Montenegro) by resolution 757.

In June Security Council resolution 758 enlarged UNPROFOR's mandate to allow it to deploy observers to supervise the withdrawal of anti-aircraft weapons from Sarajevo and the concentration of heavy weapons at designated sites in the city. Eventually, on June 21, after a prolonged siege of the city by Serbian forces, resolution 761 again enlarged the mandate of UNPROFOR to include the securing of Sarajevo airport in order to ease the delivery of relief supplies to the victims of the violence. President Mitterrand of France had helped to speed the deployment of UN forces by a dramatic gesture on 28 June when he flew in to Sarajevo and ordered an emergency airlift of relief supplies from France to the city. The UN deployment was accomplished very speedily using Canadian troops based in Croatia. Resolution 776 of 14 September then extended UNPROFOR's role to include support

169

for the UNHCR in its delivery of humanitarian relief. In order to do this effectively the ability of the UN troops to open fire in self-defence was interpreted as meaning that they could use force to stop anyone trying to prevent the UN carrying out its mandate. In October resolution 781 banned all military flights (except those on humanitarian missions) in Bosnia and Hercegovina's airspace and instructed UNPROFOR to monitor compliance with the ban through the deployment of military observers at airfields in Bosnia and Hercegovina, Croatia, and the Federal Republic of Yugoslavia.

The UN's role in Bosnia and Hercegovina has been the subject of a great deal of criticism. There have been serious problems with the behaviour of certain contingents. It has not been able to ensure the flow of supplies through hostile areas to those who need it the most. The force has been associated with the European Union-UN mediation initiative which intends to carve up Bosnia and Hercegovina into three ethnic areas. The UN has also been criticised for its arms embargo, imposed on what was still a single Yugoslavian state in September 1991. This has effectively given the Serbs and Croats in Bosnia and Hercegovina a military advantage because they have access to weapons that are denied to the Moslems. There are some who would argue that the UN has therefore collaborated with a plan to disarm the Moslems in order to make it easier for the Serbs and Croats to partition the country (see Ali and Lifschultz, 1993). The hostility that is felt to the UN policy in Bosnia was all too visible on the faces of the demonstrators who turned out to jeer Secretary-General Boutros-Ghali on his brief visit to Sarajevo in January 1993. These people believed that the UN was doing nothing to stop the imposition of an unjust solution on their country.

In response to criticisms the UN has tried to play a stronger role. Sarajevo has been declared an international city under UN administration until there is a negotiated settlement. A 'safe area' was established in Sebrenica and its surroundings (Security Council Resolution 819, 16 April 1993) and this enabled UNPROFOR to successfully demilitarise the town. The following month resolution 824 made other towns 'safe areas' and in June resolution 836 used chapter seven of the Charter to authorise UNPROFOR to protect these areas and to respond with force to actions such as bombardments of 'safe areas', armed incursion or the deliberate obstruction of humanitarian convoys.

In November 1992 the President of Macedonia, with the support of Cyrus Vance and David Owen, requested the deployment of UN observers in his state. Macedonia had declared its independence in April 1992 but has contested borders with Serbia, Bulgaria, Albania and Greece, which has raised fears about territorial conflicts with its neighbours. A volatile situation in the region appeared to be worsening in November 1992 when there were clashes between ethnic Albanians in Macedonia (about 21 per cent of the total population) and police. The Secretary-General, in response to the request from the government of Macedonia, sent a group of military and civilian personnel to the area, and on the basis of their report recommended to the Security Council that UNPROFOR's mandate be expanded to include a conflict prevention role Macedonia. On 11 December 1992 Security Council resolution 795 authorised the dispatch of military, civilian and police personnel. At the end of 1992 Canadian troops were sent to Macedonia, in what is the first large scale deployment of UN peace-keepers in a conflict prevention role. By July 1993 there were about 1,000 UN soldiers engaged in this work, 700 from Scandinavia and 300 from the US (operation 'Able Sentry').

The overall record, in all the varied tasks UNPROFOR undertakes in the former Yugoslavia, has been a mixed one. Some aspects of its work seem to have contributed to the reduction of violence. For example, in Croatia it has overseen the withdrawal of the JNA from the country and its presence in the 'pink zones' may have helped reduce outbreaks of violence. However, other task have eluded the force. In the UNPAs local Serbian leaders have obstructed attempts to bring about demilitarization and human rights abuses continue. Croatian Serbs have also raided UN stockpiles of weapons. The forced expulsion of non-Serbs from these areas has also continued despite the UN presence, though in some cases the presence of UN troops has provided some protection for possible victims of this policy. UNPROFOR has not been able to establish border controls as envisaged in resolution 769, nor was it able to prevent renewed fighting between Croats and Serbs in January 1993. The final status of the UNPAs and the 'pink zones' is also undecided, and fighting may occur over whether they are part of Croatia or not. As UNPROFOR is treated with suspicion and distrust by both sides, new widespread fighting may place members of the force in extreme danger. Nevertheless, the Secretary-General believes that the withdrawal of the force would lead to widespread intercommunal violence and the Security Council continues to renew its mandate for set periods of time.

In Bosnia and Hercegovina UNPROFOR has been able to keep Sarajevo airport open and it has helped with the delivery of humanitarian relief, imperfect though this has been because of the attitudes of the warring factions. On several occasions relief operations have had to be suspended because of the threat posed to the lives of relief workers and UNPROFOR personnel have been fired at on a regular basis. There have been widespread violations of the no-fly ban and the record of the 'safe areas' policy has been a mixed one. Gross violations of human rights, especially through the implementation of 'ethnic cleansing', have continued and the laws of war have been consistently violated by actions such as indiscriminate bombardments and mass executions (Human Rights Watch, 1993, pp. 75-105). So although UNPROFOR has been given responsibility for humanitarian relief, it appears to be unable to stop the fighting that is causing the suffering. Several commentators have been understandably frustrated by this emphasis on dealing with symptoms rather than eliminating the causes of violence (see, for example, Fisk, 1992b).

UNPROFOR has been the largest and most controversial of UN peace-keeping missions. Its influence over events has been rather limited and, in the words of one commentator, 'the writ of the "international community" ran no further than 150 metres either side of the UN checkpoint' (Ignatieff, 1993, p. 2). Various disputes have arisen between the Secretary-General and member states on issues such as who controls troops from NATO states based in Bosnia and and who is to blame for the violence.[1] In July 1992 the Secretary-General bitterly criticised a Security Council decision that made UNPROFOR responsible for the control of heavy weapons in Bosnia and. Boutros-Ghali did not attend this meeting and afterwards made the claim that the British press were attacking him because he was a 'wog'. Divisions have also existed within the Security Council about the UN's role in the former Yugoslavia. The French have taken a very pro-Bosnian line, whilst the Russians have demonstrated unease about a strong anti-Serbian policy.

At the end of 1993 the force was composed of about 25,500 military personnel, 660 civilian police and 695 international civilian staff. 13,000 of these are deployed in Croatia, about 11,500 in Bosnia and Hercegovina and just over 1,000 in Macedonia. Despite these relative large numbers Human Rights Watch (1993, p. 85) argues that UN peace-keeping in both Croatia and Bosnia and Hercegovina have been marked by 'timidity, disorganization, unnecessary delay and political indecision'. Sanctions against Serbia have not been fully effective and it remains to be seen if the UN war crimes commission will be able to assist in the convictions of individuals responsible for breaches of international humanitarian law. Many commentators would like the UN to move to a peace enforcement role in Bosnia and Hercegovina, but others feel that this will compromise UNPROFOR's humanitarian efforts, which depend on a perception of neutrality. There is also no consensus on the Security Council in favour of a peace enforcement policy. Yet despite all the criticisms and controversies UNPROFOR remains the best last hope for the victims of the war. However, given all the problems associated with the force, one cannot assume that it will retain the support of troop contributing countries who are faced with escalating costs in resources and lives.

Several alternatives to a UN peace-keeping operation have been attempted. In recent years we have seen peace-keeping forces established by the Organization of African Unity in Chad (Kelley, 1986; Obaseki, 1983) and by the Arab League in Lebanon (Cobban, 1985; Haddad, 1985; Khalidi, 1979). A sub-regional organization, the Economic Community of West African States, has established a force that has been deployed in Liberia. There has been a Multi-National Force (MNF), also in Lebanon (Heiberg and Holst, 1986; Thakur 1987a and 1987b), and a unilateral initiative by India in Sri Lanka. (Tripathi 1987; 1988) Some commentators have also proposed that the Organization of American States should develop a peace-keeping capability (Childe, 1980). But so far this organization, which has traditionally emphasised non-intervention, has not responded favourably to an idea that they fear might become a fig leaf for US involvement in their internal affairs. We can now briefly examine the record of these alternatives to UN peace-keeping.

(a) The Organization of African Unity force in Chad

Chad is a landlocked state that is one of the poorest countries in the world. It obtained its independence from France in 1960. It is a culturally diverse state, with one of the main ethnic divisions, like other North African states, being between the Moslem and Arab north and the Christian and 'black' south, though within each region there are further ethnic differences. The country was ruled from independence by Tombalbaye, who created a one-party state in 1962 that benefited mainly the southern Saras. For a number of years before his assassination in 1975, Tombalbaye had to fight against the guerrilla forces of FROLINAT, an Arab group fighting against the Christian dominated government. This obtained Libyan backing. In order to shore up his power Tombalbaye had to invite in the French army.

The death of Tombalbaye led to several years of political instability which saw the Libyan seizure of a part of Chad known as the Aouzou strip, and a civil war in 1979 between the forces of President Habre (FAN) and the Chad army (ANT). This triggered widespread intercommunal violence and led to another French intervention, the deployment of a short lived Nigerian peace-keeping force and the establishment of a Government of National Unity (GUNT) in which Habre became Foreign Minister under his rival, President Goukouni Oueddei. However, there was only a short period of peace before a civil war broke out again in March 1980. At this time, through an Accord reached at Lagos, African governments committed themselves to establishing and funding a 'neutral OAU force in Chad', though the force was created outside of the formal OAU framework (Pelcovits, 1983). Its mandate was to supervise a cease fire, ensure freedom of movement, disarm the population and restore and maintain law and order. The force was to be composed of contingents from several African states, but eventually only that from the Congo turned up, and further action on such a force was delayed as a result of the renewed civil war. In this war the Libyans, who had previously offered aid to Habre, now supported Oueddei, and ensured his short term victory before withdrawing their forces in November 1981.

The Organization of African Unity (OAU) saw the Chad crisis as an opportunity to demonstrate its ability to find 'African solutions for African problems'. To this end they finally created an Inter-African Peace-keeping force in November 1981, following an agreement between the OAU and President Oueddei. This was meant to be composed of contingents of 2,000 troops from Nigeria and 600 troops each from Zaire, Senegal, Benin, Guinea and Togo. It was to be under the authority of the OAU Secretary-General and was to replace Libyan troops in Chad. Its mandate was to keep the peace in Chad, supervise elections at a date still to be agreed, and assist the integration of the Chadian army (Sesay, 1989b).

However the force was a 'total failure' (Sesay, 1989a, p. 2), did not live up to 'the ideal or to the interests' of the OAU (Zartman, 1986, p. 28) and was withdrawn 'in confusion' in 1982 (Zartman, p. 24). There were several reasons why the force was 'short lived and ineffectual' (Martin, 1990, p. 43). Firstly, the role of the French, who were worried by Libyan exploitation of the unrest in Chad, upset some states who had promised contingents. Indeed, in order to appease such worries the original signing of the OAU-Oueddei agreement in Paris had to be repeated in Nairobi later the same month. However, Togo and Guinea were never to send their promised contingents, in part because of the behind the scenes role of the French. As a result only 3,500 of the promised 5,000 troops were deployed.

A second reason for the failure of the force was that it was always badly financed. According to one estimate, it was to cost $150-300 million a year. Yet the total OAU budget had never been more than $30 million in any one year. The cost, which the OAU could not meet on its own, therefore fell on the contributing governments, who were not prepared to bear them for any length of time. The OAU did appeal to the UN Security Council for funding, but this was regarded as not permissible by the UN, since it was not an operation under its control. The Security Council did, however, set up a voluntary find which was to raise $35 million for the OAU force.

A third reason for the failure of the force was that it was deployed

174

without a cease-fire being agreed beforehand between the parties to the conflict. Indeed according to Sesay (1989b, p. 17), one of these parties had no intention of settling the conflict peacefully. A fourth reason for the failure was that members of the OAU, who one might have expected to support the peace-keeping operation, continued to support one or other of the parties. Sudan, for example, continued to provide arms and bases for the Habre forces.

All in all, then, the Inter-African Force lacked the resources, the prestige, the logistical capability and the experience of the UN (Sesay, 1989a; 1989b). Its dismal failure was a severe blow to the prestige of the OAU in the area of peace-keeping, and therefore reduces the chances that a similar force will be created in the near future. Even if the will existed at the OAU to create another force, and the funding was to be found for it, it has to be doubted whether the parties concerned would trust it to do its job properly. For President Oueddei, who had invited the Inter-African Force into Chad, was overthrown by Habre whilst the force was still operating in his country. After the force was withdrawn there was continuing Libyan and French (with US help) military involvement and the country was effectively partitioned between the Libyan dominated 'government ' in the north and the internationally recognised Habre regime in the south.

(b) The Arab League Peace-keeping force in Lebanon

In 1976 Syria intervened in the Lebanese Civil war that had been underway since the previous year. There were several motives for this intervention. They included a claim over Lebanese territory and a fear that the PLO would be victorious in their conflict with the Maronite Christians. President Assad may also have feared the spill-over of the conflict into Syria itself. The Syrian involvement seemed at first to benefit the Christians in Lebanon, and Damascus ensured that Elias Sarkis, a Christian banker, was installed as President of Lebanon.

In October 1976, in order to encourage a Syrian disengagement from the conflict, and, presumably, to enhance its status as a regional organization, the Arab League, first at a summit at Riyadh, and then at the Arab Heads of State meeting in Cairo, approved the creation of an 'Arab deterrent force' (ADF). The aim of the force was: to observe the cease fire between the various parties to the conflict; to promote internal security; and to implement the 1969 Cairo Agreement, part of which involved a commitment by the PLO not to carry arms in public or to interfere in Lebanese politics. It was made up of contingents from Saudi Arabia (2,200), Sudan (1,000), United Arab Emirates (1,000), South Yemen (700), and Libya (700). Egypt refused to contribute. But Syria was by far the largest contributor to the force, with a contingent that made up 25,000 of the 30,000 total. The force was meant to be under the personal command of the Lebanese President, though in practice the Syrian contingent took its commands from Baghdad. It was financed by a special fund open to all Arab League members. It operated under certain constraints worked out between the Syrian and Israeli governments with the help of US mediations - the so called 'red line agreement'. This included a Syrian acceptance that its forces would not interfere in Israeli operations against Palestinian guerrillas, that it would not attempt to close the port of Junieh, nor would it deploy troops south of Zahrani.

This was certainly not a peace-keeping force in the traditional UN sense, and a good argument could be made for not including it in this study of peace-keeping. For one of the parties to the Lebanese conflict was the main contributor and the Syrian contingent was prepared to use force not just in self-defence. Pogany (1987, p. 96) has therefore argued that the force was a peace-keeping force in the 'broad' rather than the 'narrow' sense. James (1990, p. 337) has doubted that the ADF can be regarded as a peace-keeping mission at all, given the Syrian geo-strategic aims in Lebanon and its aggressive attitude to certain Lebanese factions. These activities were complemented by the work of the Syrian secret police, the *mukhabarrat*, which engaged in covert operations against opponents of Syrian influence that probably included assassinations.

Although the mandate of the force did not expire until July 1982, by 1979 Syria was the only contributing state. In that year Sudan, Saudi Arabia and the United Arab Emirates all withdrew their contingents. The Libyan troops had already left in 1976 and the South Yemen contingent had been withdrawn in 1977. These contributing governments appeared to be convinced that the force was unable to fulfil its mandate and that there was no hope of a negotiated settlement (Pogany, 1987, p. 110). It should also be noted that the force was unable to deter two Israeli invasions of Lebanon. In fact it played a role in provoking them.

(c) The Multinational Force in Lebanon

Following the 1982 invasion of Lebanon by Israel an agreement was worked out whereby PLO fighters would be allowed to leave Beirut under the supervision of a Multinational Force (MNF), composed originally of contingents from the US, France and Italy. This evacuation began on 21 August 1982 and was completed by the 1 September. On 10 September the MNF left Beirut. That same week Presidential elections were held in Lebanon, which were won by Bashir Gemayel, the candidate favoured by Israel and the US. However, within days of his election victory Gemayel was assassinated, and was soon replaced in new elections by his brother Amin Gemayel.

Gemayel's Christian supporters were outraged by his murder, and with some collusion with the Israeli Defence Forces devised 'Operation Iron Mind' to take revenge by attacking the Palestinian refugee camps of Sabra and Shatila. The hundreds of deaths caused by this operation led to strong international condemnation of Israel and helped force Amin Gemayel to request the return of the MNF to Beirut. The three governments approached all agreed to this, with the US supplying 1,200, Italy 1,400 and France 1,500 troops. A small British contingent of 100 men was added at a later date.

The force was intended to operate in a conventional peace-keeping role (James, 1990, p. 356; Wiseman, 1983, p. 321). However, its presence was not welcomed by all groups. For the radical Islamic militias the American presence simply seemed to confirm their worst suspicions about US 'imperialism'. There were a series of ugly exchanges with local factions, but the most dramatic example of this opposition were the car bomb attacks by Islamic fundamentalists on the barracks of the American and French MNF contingents at 6.20 am on October 23 1983. This resulted in the deaths of 241 US marines and 58 French paratroopers. At the same time there were attacks on the US and French embassies in Kuwait. America retaliated, using the ships of the sixth fleet anchored off the Lebanese coast. This involved air attacks and the shelling of 'enemy' positions by the USS New Jersey. Such actions only increased Moslem opposition to the MNF presence, and towards the end of its life the force became more of a symbolic international commitment to the Gemayel government than an effective peace-keeping unit. In fact the US marines were withdrawn to ships anchored off the coast of Beirut. Here they lived in an atmosphere which Fisk (1990, p. 467), after attending a briefing on the *USS Independence*, described as a strange amalgam of 'political naivete, pseudo-scientific jargon and Christ-like goodwill'. When the US contingent was withdrawn by President Reagan in February 1984 the MNF collapsed, and Gemayel, denied active American support, was forced to turn even more to Syria to ensure his survival.

The differences between the UNIFIL and MNF operations in Lebanon have been analysed by Thakur (1987a and 1987b). He claims that the UN force has had some success, whereas the joint MNF operation was a failure. The reason for this, he suggests, is that UNIFIL based its operation on its authority, not its power; whereas the MNF relied on power, not authority. In fact the UN Secretary General rejected calls from the Lebanese government to act in a peace-enforcing manner (Skogmo, 1988, p. 85). As a result UNIFIL was regarded by the various Lebanese factions as a 'legitimate' presence that had the right to demand obedience, whereas the MNF, because of its coercive actions, was regarded as 'illegitimate' and became a besieged entity incapable of undertaking any positive action in Lebanon. Because of actions such as support for the Lebanese Army, the sharing of intelligence information with Israel and the bombardment of Druze villages by US naval forces the MNF, Thakur claims, lost even the passive acquiescence of large sections of the Lebanese population. Fisk (1990, p. 477) points out that by the spring of 1982 the MNF was 'supporting a Phalangist administration, openly acknowledging links with Israeli forces and, through the Americans, encouraging an unofficial peace treaty between Israel and Lebanon'.

It is hardly surprising, therefore, that the MNF suffered from its lack of perceived impartiality. Thakur writes that

> The decisions of the United Nations command authority because they are the outcome of an international political process of the assertion and reconciliation of national interests... States acting outside the UN framework...are suspected of espousing universalism to disguise special interests... The authority conferred by the claim to be acting in the interests of mankind can be legitimised only by the international community as a whole. The United Nations is so sanctified; the MNF was not... As Washington grew more firmly committed to the Gemayel government, so opposing factions identified the marines increasingly as part of the enemy forces. Once this happened, the presence of the marines was no longer impartial third party peacekeeping, but an obstacle to Lebanese reconciliation and peace. Such a transformation is inconceivable with UN forces. At worst they can become ineffectual peace-keepers, but never hurdles to peace. (Thakur, 1987b, p. 474)

He claims support for his conclusion from Brian Urquhart, and quotes the following passage written by the former Under Secretary-General approvingly. Urquhart states

> A peace-keeping force should never be expected to rely on force to achieve its ends. If it finds itself forced into such a position, it will already have lost its status as a peace-keeping operation and, in all probability, any reasonable hopes of remedying the situation as well. It will cease to be above the conflict and will have become part of it. (Thakur, 1987a, p. 175)

(d) The Indian Peace-keeping Force in Sri Lanka

Sri Lanka is an island state that has suffered various degrees of inter-communal conflict since its independence from Britain in 1948. The country can be divided into two large ethnic groups, the majority Sinhalese community which is Buddhist (74 per cent of the population), and the minority Hindu Tamil population (approximately 18.2 per cent), which is concentrated in the North and east of the island.[2] There are also two other ethnic groups: the Moslems and the Burghers. The Tamils had lived in their own state until Portuguese colonization, and even after that had a long history of separate administration. The Sinhalese had, however, traditionally regarded themselves as guardians of Buddhism and had perceived Tamils as barbarian invaders. The Tamil population can itself be subdivided into the native Tamils (12.6 per cent) and the plantation Tamils (5.6 per cent) who were brought from India during the colonial period to work in the plantations in the Central province, where the Sinhalese are the majority.

Reacting to the perceived 'Sinhala only' policy of the state; to claims of land colonization; and to perceived discrimination in areas of education, government employment and language policy, the Tamils officially proclaimed the establishment of the Liberation Tigers of Tamil Eelam in 1975. This was a militant group calling for an armed struggle to achieve an independent Tamil state. Support for a more militant approach was increased because of an economic downturn due to falling prices for tea and rubber, which led to increased Tamil unemployment (Arasaratnam, 1987). In the 1977 elections, for example, the separatist TULF party, founded in 1976, obtained 72 per cent of the vote in the Jaffna district, and won all 14 seats in the North (Kearney, 1985).

Relations between the Tamils and Sinhalese deteriorated significantly in the 1980s, especially after large scale violence against the Tamils in Colombo and surrounding areas in July 1983 (Hyndman, 1988). This was itself triggered by the murder of thirteen Sinhalese soldiers in a Tamil guerrilla ambush, which was caused, it was claimed, by the abduction and rape of three Tamil girls. As intercommunal violence deepened, so India was increasingly drawn into the problem in order to protect its own interests.

Firstly, it was concerned that the Sinhalese-Tamil conflict would spill over into its own state of Tamil Nadu, where there this a strong tradition of support for Sri Lankan Tamils because of ethnic ties. This was an issue which could be exploited by Tamil Nadu leaders in their own battles with the Indian government. There were even fears that disaffection in Tamil Nadu and other parts of India could ignite secessionist demands (Kodikara, 1987). Tamil secession in Sri Lanka could, therefore, encourage the break-up of India because of a demonstration effect and consequently the Sri Lankan conflict was both directly and indirectly linked to important ethnic issues in India. The Indian government felt that a reduction of the violence in Sri Lanka would also reduce opposition in Tamil Nadu to the policies of the central government and would help to limit the spread of secessionist feeling throughout India.

Second, continuing instability in Sri Lanka was a threat to Indian security, because it could lead to the direct involvement of unfriendly powers in a state close to the Indian mainland. This sensitivity was increased during the 1971 war between India and Pakistan, when the Sri Lankan government had allowed flights between East and West Pakistan to use the island; though the Sri Lankan P.M. Bandaranaike claimed that these flights were to transport evacuees, and were not engaged in military missions (Gupta, 1985). During the upsurge in violence in the 1980s Sri Lanka sought aid from Israel, South Africa and Pakistan, and there were rumours that it had asked for military assistance from the US. This had important implications, and in particular increased fears that the excellent harbour at Trincomalee could become a strategic base for the US, fears heightened by the visit of important US government officials to the island during this period, and rumours that the US was looking for an alternative to its naval base in the Philippines.

The importance of the fate of Trincomalee harbour for the Indians is underlined by a side letter, sent to P.M. Gandhi from the Sri Lankan President, to accompany the 1987 India-Sri Lankan Accord. It stated that Sri Lanka would not allow the port to be used in a way prejudicial to Indian interests. Instability in Sri Lanka also threatened the so called 'Indira Doctrine', never officially stated by the Indian government, but which has been described as follows: India has no intention of intervening in internal conflicts of a South Asian country, and it strongly opposes intervention by any other country in the internal affairs of any other. India will not tolerate external intervention in a conflict situation in any South Asian country if the intervention has any implicit or explicit anti-Indian implications. No South Asian government must therefore ask for external military assistance with an anti-Indian bias from any country (B.S. Gupta in Kodikara, 1987, p. 644-5).

The strain on Indian-Sri Lankan relations reached breaking point in 1987 when the government in Colombo, provoked by Tamil attacks in the capital which killed over one hundred people, launched 'Operation Liberation' and imposed an economic blockade on Tamil areas. When the Indian government, under strong domestic pressure, attempted to send relief supplies to the Tamils by sea they were turned back by the

Sri Lankan navy, so India sent the supplies by air instead. This resulted in strong protests by the Sri Lankan government to the UN.

It seems, however, that this confrontation did increase fears in both states about the way the conflict was escalating and so it helped to open the way for the Indian-Sri Lankan Accord of July 29 1987, which led to the dispatch of an Indian peace-keeping force to the Tamil areas of the island. India had been playing an active diplomatic role in the Sri Lankan conflict for a number of years. Activities included direct meetings between Sri Lankan President Jayawardene and Prime Minister Rajiv Gandhi; the use of the Indian foreign minister as a shuttle diplomat; and the arrangement of meetings between Tamil and Sinhalese leaders (see, for example, de Silva, 1991; Wilson, 1988). Now the July Accord led to a much greater Indian commitment to the peace process on the island.

In fact, the Accord itself did not mention the possibility of a peace-keeping force at all. Instead the document set out the measures by which it hoped peace and normalcy could be restored on the island. For example, the agreement acknowledged that Sri Lanka is a 'multi-ethnic and a multi-lingual plural society' (Article 1:1) and recognised that each ethnic group has a distinct cultural and linguistic identity which has to be carefully nurtured (1:2). Tamil was recognised as an official language (2:18). The two Tamil provinces would be joined to form a single administrative unit for an interim period, after which there would be a referendum in the eastern province to determine if its people wanted to retain this link or establish its own administration (2:2; 2:3). The state of emergency was to be lifted in these two provinces and all arms were to be surrendered to authorities designated by the Sri Lankan government (2:9). An annexure to the agreement stated that this hand over would take place in the presence of a senior representative of both the Sri Lankan Red Cross and the Indian Red Cross. Consequent to a cessation of hostilities and the surrender of arms the army and other security personnel would be confined to barracks (2:9). There would also be a general amnesty to political and other prisoners held under the Prevention of Terrorism Act and other emergency laws and special efforts would be made to bring them back into the mainstream of national life (2:11).

Although there is no mention of an Indian Peace-keeping force in the Accord the basis was provided for its introduction on to the island. Section 2:14, for example, states that 'the Government of India will underwrite and guarantee the resolutions, and co-operate in the implementation of these proposals'. And section 2:16 (c) states that 'in the event that the Government of Sri Lanka requests the Government of India to afford military assistance to implement these proposals the Government of India will co-operate by giving to the Government of

Sri Lanka such military assistance as and when requested'. Paragraph 6 of the annexure to the agreement goes on to state that 'the President of Sri Lanka and the prime Minister of India also agree that in terms of paragraph 2.15 and 2.16 (c) of the agreement, an Indian peace-keeping contingent may be invited by the President of Sri Lanka to guarantee and enforce the cessation of hostilities, if so required'.

Despite early optimism, the IPKF was not able to live up to expectations. There seem to be two main reasons for its failure. The first had to do with its relations with the Tamils, and in particular the group known as the Liberation Tigers of Tamil Eelam (LTTE). The LTTE leader, Prabhakaran, felt that India had presented him with a *fait accompli* , though Indian sources claim that he had consented to the Accord (Rupesinghe, 1989, p. 344). Whatever the truth is about this disagreement, in trying to implement its mandate the IPKF was forced into clashes with the LTTE, who, contrary to the India-Sri Lanka Accord, had not surrendered most of their weapons and continued to attack the Sinhalese population. As a result, the LTTE ambivalence about the Accord turned quickly into open hostility and in the face of LTTE attacks the IPKF often responded in a heavy-handed manner, indiscriminately strafing and shelling Tamil population centres and destroying crops (Shanmugaratnam, 1989). Inevitably many civilians were killed and many others became refugees. There were many accounts of deliberate human rights violations by the IPKF (see evidence by Martin Ennals to UN Sub-commission on the Prevention of Discrimination and the Protection of Minorities, UN Doc. E/CN.4/Sub. 2/1988/SR.14 par. 17). Causing such widespread misery in Tamil areas undermined the legitimacy of the force, which forced it to rely even more on military power. Indeed, its manpower was quickly increased from 6,000 to 50,000 troops and one estimate claims that, in the first year of its existence, the IPKF killed 2,000 civilians, damaged 50,000 buildings and created 200,000 refugees (*Guardian*, 29 July 1988).

The second reason for the failure of the force was the backlash it provoked against the Sri Lankan government by Sinhalese opposed to the introduction of Indian troops and to concessions to the Tamils. Many were so outraged by the Accord that they abandoned support for President Jayawardene and transferred their loyalties to the Janatha Viyaparaya Peramuna (JVP), a xenophobic body which organised extra-Parliamentary opposition in Sinhalese areas. This opposition included marches, strikes and violence against government officials and supporters. Fervent Sinhalese nationalists now redirected their hatred of Tamils and of India against their own government and this intra-Sinhalese violence degenerated into campaigns of terror and murder by both the government and the JVP (Campaign for Social Democracy, 1989).

Eventually the need to deal with this intra-Sinhalese violence became more important for the Sri Lankan government than allowing the IPKF to pacify the Tamils. JVP activities were destroying the economy of the island through intimidation, terror and protest. One thousand people were murdered, for example, in attacks in the run up to the parliamentary elections of February 1989 (McGowan, 1993, p. 371). Getting rid of the IPKF would help to undermine support for the JVP. Therefore on June 1 1989, President Premadasa, elected into office in December 1988 with just over 50 per cent of the vote, ordered the IPKF to leave by July 29, the second anniversary of the force's deployment. Premadasa, who as Prime Minister had opposed their deployment to begin with, did not consult with New Delhi before making the demand, which occurred in a speech he made to a public meeting. By then the IPKF had been discredited in the eyes of many Tamils and Sinhalese.

Gandhi, however, rejected this 'unilateral deadline', and was upset by the way it was presented to the Indian government. He was further annoyed when President Premadasa released private correspondence with Gandhi about the IPKF to the media. The Indian government was clearly in an awkward position. A continued IPKF involvement against the wishes of the Sri Lankan government could be interpreted as an act of armed intervention. On the other hand, there were many Tamils who had supported the IPKF and feared that its withdrawal would lead to reprisals against them by the LTTE. Indeed, there was a fear that a withdrawal of the IPKF would lead to an intra-Tamil civil war. Elections were also soon due in India, and Gandhi's reputation might have suffered had he been seen to be giving in to Premadasa's demand. Gandhi therefore rejected Premadasa's call until Tamil security could be secured and the withdrawal was linked to a plan to devolve power to the regions. The IPKF also began a new armed offensive against Tamil guerrillas in an attempt to build up the relative power of the pro-Indian EPRLF. This led more human rights abuses, including the massacre of 51 men, women and children by the IPKF at Valvedditturai in early August 1989.

At the end of July 1989 Premadasa sent a conciliatory letter to Gandhi and the Indian government ordered the token withdrawal of 600 troops. But this was interpreted as a climb down to India by Sinhalese nationalists, who appeared to step up their attacks on government supporters. This led to increased repression and reports of government opponents being murdered by death squads. At the Non Aligned Summit meeting in Belgrade in September 1989 India and Sri Lanka were able, finally, to agree on a timetable for the withdrawal of the IPKF. The force was eventually withdrawn at the end of March 1990. By then, in an ironic twist, the government of Premadasa and the

LTTE rebels were willing to talk to one another in order to speed up the ending of direct Indian military involvement on the island (Saravanamuttu, 1990). The fragile peace between the government and the Tamil guerrillas did not last long and inter-ethnic fighting resumed in June 1990.

(e) The Military Observer Group and the United Nations Observer Mission in Liberia

In 1847 Liberia became the first independent republic in Africa with a capital city, Monrovia, named after the US President James Monroe. It became an important source of US rubber and Firestone created the world's largest rubber plantation in the country. In 1980 the Afro-American elite, who had long dominated the country, were expelled from power when the government of William Tolbert was overthrown in a coup led by Samuel Doe. The Doe regime, which abandoned moves by Tolbert to improve relations with Libya, received large amounts of aid from the Reagan administration despite evidence of human rights abuse and corruption in the country (Chomsky, 1992, p. 240). O'Neill (1991) estimates that this aid amounted to $500 million between 1980 and 1985. This included the arming of Doe's troops, who were trained by the Israelis. In return Doe allowed the US government to make use of his country for their own geo-strategic purposes. It was the main centre for CIA intelligence operations in Africa and a satellite tracking station was located in the country. Robertsfield air base was designated for use by the US Rapid Deployment Force, and the Voice of America had an important transmitter there (Lawyers' Committee for Human Rights in Liberia, 1986).

Although elections were held in 1985, opponents of the government were intimidated and harassed and when it appeared that Doe's NDPL party was losing he imprisoned the leader of the would-be victorious party and ballot boxes disappeared and ballot papers were burnt (Lawyers' Committee for Human Rights in Liberia, 1986). The country was already 'fissured along ethnic lines' because of the Krahn domination of the government, even though they only made up four per cent of the population (Riley, 1993, p. 42). The frustration that the aborted election created prompted a coup attempt in November 1985, but this, in turn, resulted in reprisals by the Krahn against the Gio and Manos ethnic groups. The leader of the coup, Thomas Quiwonkpa, was castrated and dismembered and thousands of people were executed by the government. Yet Doe, who Reagan once mistakenly introduced as 'Chairman Moe', continued to obtain US support.

On Christmas Eve 1989 civil war erupted again when the Gio and Mano backed National Patriotic Front for Liberia (NPLF), led by

Charles Taylor, invaded the country from the Ivory Coast and eventually conquered most of Liberia outside of Monrovia. The NPLF split in August 1990, and a new faction was created called the Independent National Patriotic Front for Liberia (INPFL) led by Prince Johnson. The same month, at a meeting in Gambia, the Economic Community of West African States established a cease-fire monitoring group known as ECOMOG.

From the start this was a Nigerian dominated body. Most of its troops came from Nigeria, and after a month the Ghanaian commander of the force, General Arnold Quainoo, was replaced by a Nigerian. Other states who contributed contingents for the initial deployment were Guinea, Ghana, Sierra Leone and Gambia. Mali and Senegal also provided contingents after the force was in place. By October 1990 the force was 9,000 strong and was funded by the United States. It was deployed without the parties to the conflict accepting a cease-fire and against the wishes of Charles Taylor, who saw it as an attempt to boost the Doe presidency. In a display of their displeasure Taylor's troops sacked the Nigerian Embassy in Monrovia shortly before ECOMOG was deployed and Taylor referred to President Babangida of Nigeria as a 'mad military dictator'.

ECOMOG took over control of Monrovia and helped with the evacuation of foreign nationals, but its relative powerlessness was demonstrated in September 1990. In that month Doe surrendered to the force but was abducted from them by soldiers belonging to the Johnson faction. He was then murdered. ECOWAS then supported Amos Sawyer as interim president of Liberia. He was appointed by a meeting of Liberians in Banjul, though in practice he controlled little of the territory of the country.

Fighting continued between the various factions throughout early 1991 and 1992. A major escalation of the violence occurred in October 1992, when Taylor's forces besieged Monrovia and forced the closure of the airport. This prompted ECOMOG to adopt tougher tactics. The force was authorised to shoot members of the armed factions breaking a 6 pm to 8 am curfew in Monrovia and Nigerian aircraft and gunboats were used to bomb and shell 'rebel bases' around Monrovia and Taylor's 'capital' at Gbarnga. In November the West African states asked the United Nations Security Council to play the leading role in Liberia, but there was no real desire in New York to take up this burden. The UN still regarded it as a regional problem. By then the West African states were themselves divided with the French speaking countries such as Senegal and the Ivory Coast supporting Taylor and the NPLF and the English speaking countries backing Sawyer. The more Nigeria sided with Sawyer, the less happy the French speaking states were with the actions of ECOMOG, and so at the end of 1992, following the withdrawal of Francophone contingents, the force was composed of English speaking contingents only. By then over 60,000 people had been killed in the fighting.

In May 1993 ECOMOG launched a major offensive against the Taylor forces, and the escalation in fighting that this caused added significantly to these casualty figures. It also put added pressure on Taylor to compromise. Two months later the parties were at last willing to sign a peace accord. This was the Cotonou Peace Agreement, which set out a move, in stages, from cease fire to national elections. Sawyer would hand over power to a five-member council of state and 35 member transitional parliament would be composed of nominees from all the parties. One part of the accord involved changes to the composition of ECOMOG in order to dilute the Nigerian influence.

It is possible that the deployment of ECOMOG in Monrovia in 1990 did help to avert a blood-bath, but O'Neill's overall assessment of ECOWAS is not a flattering one. He claims that a well-intentioned effort has 'gone badly wrong' because of ECOMOG's lack of experience in peace-keeping, its association with human rights abuses, poor discipline and the use of Krahn soldiers as guides for the force (O'Neill, 1993, p. 217).

In September 1993 UN Security Council resolution 866 established the United Nations Observer Mission in Liberia (UNOMIL) to work with ECOWAS. It was to be composed of 303 military observers, 45 military engineers, 58 UN volunteers and 89 international personnel. Resolution 788 of 19 November 1992 had already imposed an arms embargo on Liberia except for weapons or military supplies destined for the sole use of ECOWAS peace-keeping troops. The main function of the force is to cooperate with ECOMOG and representatives of the warring factions in a Joint Cease-fire Monitoring Committee, which would help implement the July 1993 Cotonou Peace Agreement.

UNOMIL and ECOMOG work closely together, but have separate chains of command. The two missions verify compliance with the cease-fire and the arms embargo and monitor the disarmament and demobilization of combatants. UNOMIL also trains ECOMOG in mine clearance work. It may be that this close cooperation between the UN and a regional organization will be the first of several such initiatives in the coming years. Already we are witnessing the UN and NATO working together in Bosnia and Hercegovina.

The available evidence shows, therefore, that international peace-keeping can do good work and that none of the alternatives to UN forces have proven to be any more successful than UN operations themselves in the area of ethnic conflict. On the contrary, the OAU initiative in Chad was nothing short of a fiasco, and the creation of the Indian force in Sri Lanka was thought by many to be a foreign policy blunder by India. The MNF in Lebanon is also generally regarded as a failure and had to withdraw after bomb attacks on the American and French contingents in which approximately 300 US and French soldiers were killed. The very fact that this withdrawal was seen as a failure of US policy alerts us to the fact that this was not a peace-keeping operation in the traditional sense. The heavy-handed actions of ECOMOG have also pointed out the limitations of non-UN forces. We shall have to see if other new developments in peace-keeping prove to be any more successful. NATO, for example, is now interested in playing such a role, and has already acted to support UN peace-keeping in Bosnia and Hercegovina. Recent NATO declarations have put a lot of emphasis on its future peace-keeping role and on 18 December 1992 the North Atlantic Cooperation Council established an Ad Hoc Group on Cooperation in Peacekeeping. There has been talk of deploying a joint Turkish-Russian 'peace corps' in the Armenian-Azerbaijan conflict (*Moscow Times*, 10 September 1993, p. 5)

This rather negative assessment of non-UN operations is supported by Diehl (1987, p. 218-9), who writes

> The experience of regional peacekeeping does not inspire great confidence in this particular institutional alternative....All this is not to say that regional peacekeeping forces cannot be effective, but rather, that UN peacekeeping will have a comparative advantage in most circumstances. Thus, regional peacekeeping operations cannot be considered viable substitutes for current UN arrangements.

Nor is it too difficult to determine why the UN has this 'comparative advantage'. It has much more experience than other organizations in the peace-keeping field. It has financial and administrative support that is lacking in many regional and ad hoc operations. It is also more likely to be perceived as a neutral body, given that non-UN peace-keeping operations will often involve states with some vested interest in a particular outcome.

Even though no better alternative to UN peace-keeping exists in most cases, this is not to suggest that these peace-keeping forces do not have their problems or their critics. Because they are not enforcement forces, and because they are small and lightly armed operations, they rely on the general co-operation of the parties to a conflict in order to be effective. If one or more parties decides it will escalate the violence, there is little that the UN forces can do to stop them. UNFICYP could not stop the Turkish invasion of Cyprus in 1974, nor could UNIFIL stop the Israeli invasion of Lebanon in 1982 after its commander, General Callaghan of Ireland, was given a half hour's advance notice of Israeli intentions by the commander of the Israeli Defence Force, Lieutenant-General Eitan. Certain of the UNIFIL contingents did put up a token resistance, which delayed the Israeli advance for a short time, but the UN force was effectively powerless to do anything more. The work of UNPROFOR and UNAVEM has also been thwarted by uncooperative parties. Such cases alert us to the fact that although these peace-keeping forces can do very good work stopping unintended escalations of violence, they are ineffectual when the escalation is intended by one or more of the parties.

Three other problems with UN peace-keeping forces have received attention. These are the issues of preparation, finance and training. United Nations peace-keeping forces are created on an ad hoc basis by the Secretary General on the authorisation of (usually) the Security Council. In several cases it has not been possible to deploy these missions quickly in order to support a cease-fire agreement or to provide humanitarian assistance. There is, therefore, growing interest in measures that could be taken to speed up the organising and deployment of peace-keeping forces. This could involve, for example, the stockpiling of essential equipment or the standardization of components. These supplies could, as Norway has suggested, be located in potential crisis areas.

A reliable and efficient system of finance for UN forces is needed. Both the Cyprus and Lebanese operations, although funded in different ways, are in deficit. In mid-1992 UNFICYP, which depends on voluntary contributions, was over $192 million in deficit. (UN Doc. S/24050) In July 1992 UNIFIL, which relies on assessed contributions from member states, was $231.2 million in deficit (UN Doc. S/24341). This can undermine the will of contributing states, who are not reimbursed fully for work undertaken for the UN. In 1986, for example, Sweden agreed to replace a French infantry battalion that had been withdrawn from UNIFIL. The reason for this withdrawal, it is claimed, is that the French government were afraid that a high French profile in Lebanon would threaten the lives of French hostages in Beirut, than a major priority for the French government. However, in undertaking this extra peace-keeping burden the Swedish government were forced to withdraw most of its contingent from UNFICYP, citing the economic burden and the lack of any movement towards a political solution as two major reasons for their action. The financial situation of UNFICYP had become so desperate by 1993 that the UN Security Council, no longer able to ignore the complaints from the Secretariat and contributing states about the chronic financial crisis, passed a resolution on 27 May by which the costs of the force not met by voluntary contributions would be treated as expenses of the Organization under Article 17 (2) of the UN Charter. At the same time Greece and Cyprus agreed to pay more than half of UNFICYP's annual expenses in order to reduce demands that the force be wound up. This reform came too late to stop the withdrawal of Canadian and Danish contingents. As the peace-keeping forces fall deeper into debt, it is possible that other states may find the extra financial burden harder to bear, and they may be forced to reassess their commitment to a UN role. The case of Cyprus shows that the patience of troop-contributing countries can run out if they are not reimbursed for their peace-keeping tasks. Action directed at addressing this problem should therefore be one of the priorities at the UN (Saito, 1993, p. 107-110).

It is rather surprising, also, that the UN offers no formal training for soldiers involved in peace-keeping. When one considers that the peace-keeping soldier has to adopt a different style of operation from what he will have been trained for, some sort of instruction in peace-keeping techniques would surely be useful. At present this is left in the hands of contributing governments, some of whom do provide special training, whereas others do not. Training may also be provided, in part, by the New York based International Peace Academy; whose president is General Rikhye, an ex-soldier with considerable experience of UN peace-keeping operations. This non-governmental organization was founded to link academics interested in peace with the world of peace action, and every year the institute offers a two week seminar in Vienna for senior military officers and diplomats on the theme of negotiation and peace-keeping. This is, no doubt, a valuable experience for those who participate, but resources are limited, time is short, and there is no compulsion on governments to allow their personnel to attend. Better preparation of UN personnel also seems to be needed in a number of areas apart from peace-keeping techniques. In Sarajevo, for example, the French, Egyptian and Ukrainian contingents were often unable to communicate with one another (Fisk, 1992a).

A criticism sometimes made of UN peace-keeping is that it leads to the 'pacific perpetuation' of disputes. That is, by reducing the losses associated with overt violence it removes the main incentive for the parties to negotiate an end of their conflict. There is a hidden compliment contained in such a criticism, of course, which is that UN forces do play a major role in stopping overt violence. Doob (1986, p.

385) seems to support this view and argues that 'peace-keeping that benefits the two communities in conflict may hinder peace-making'. However, surely pacific perpetuation is to be preferred to the violent perpetuation of a dispute. The latter may encourage a greater effort to resolve the conflict. On the other hand no-one can be certain that this will be the case. Violence is as likely to create a momentum of its own as it is to bring the sides 'to their senses'. As we have already noted, peace-keeping forces cannot resolve conflicts, that is not their purpose. All they can do is manage the conflict for a period of time to allow the people who can resolve it to negotiate a resolution of their differences in an atmosphere not poisoned by death and destruction. There is no guarantee that such an opportunity will be used constructively. If it is not, one should not blame the peace-keepers. UN peace-keeping forces do save lives and do promote a minimum degree of temporary stability, and no better alternative has yet been found by the inter-state system for the work they perform. Surely we should be worried that there is not enough successful international peace-keeping, not that there is too much of it.

Peace-making and the United Nations

This leads us on to the next category of UN involvement in ethnic conflict. This is peace-making, which is the attempt to help the parties to a conflict to negotiate a peaceful solution to their problems. This may take several forms. The Secretary-General might be instructed by the Security Council to undertake a mission of good offices or mediation. Resolution 186, for example, which established UNFICYP also instructed the Secretary-General to appoint a mediator to negotiate with the interested parties. Alternatively, the Secretary General, as in the Congo crisis, may use his unrivalled network of international contacts to work behind the scenes with warring parties (e.g. Skjelsbaek, 1991). Or the General Assembly or the Security Council may pass resolutions which address specific conflicts and which may even try to set the agenda by which conflicts can be solved. Resolution 242 is the best example of this, with its 'land for recognition' approach to the Jewish-Palestinian conflict. Finally, the concentration of diplomats in New York provides ample opportunities for behind the scenes meetings by delegations themselves. Such a meeting between the Greek and Turkish governments in 1958 paved the way for the London-Zurich settlement of the Cyprus issue.

Ernst Haas (1986, 1987a), has attempted to quantify the relative success of the UN in the collective management of conflict. He has analysed 319 disputes which included two or more states between July

1945 and September 1984. Thirty-one per cent of these conflicts were 'civil wars'. Of these 319 disputes only 137 reached the UN agenda - though others did reach the agenda of regional organizations. Haas's conclusions are revealing. He claims to have found that the UN's effectiveness in managing conflict is declining and since the early 1960s there has been no overall consistency in stopping hostilities. The UN record in settling disputes is 'nearly always dismal'. But the organization has been more effective in isolating conflict and has been even more successful in abating (i.e. scaling down) hostilities. Overall, then, he concludes, UN impact on the conflicts considered was 'marginal but not absent'. It should be stressed here that Haas is concerned with conflicts which have an inter-state dimension and his study was concerned primarily with the UN role in managing inter-state relations. Nevertheless, they are of interest for our more limited study into the UN role in ethnic conflict, since many of the cases studied did have an ethnic element and because any such general study can allow us to reach some tentative conclusions about the worth of the organization as a conflict resolver.

If the record of the UN is rather dismal in responding positively to all types of international conflict it is likely that the record in responding to ethnic violence will be even worse. Haas (1987b) has stated in his own work that internal conflicts tend to be the most intractable. He offers no definitive conclusions about why this is the case, but perhaps part of the reason is that the Security Council and the General Assembly are inappropriate arenas for the settlement of ethnic conflict because they are composed of states and exclude ethnic groups that do not represent sovereign states. For as Bailey (1982, p. 469) notes

> The UN is not very well equipped to deal with non-state actors. The Charter was drafted on the assumption that disputes arise between states...there is no provision in the Charter by which the Security Council or General Assembly may relate to non-state agencies such as liberation movements, communal minorities, or political parties.

In order to transmit their views to the UN non-dominant ethnic groups have to rely on members of the organization. The Turkish Cypriots, for example, have consistently relied on Ankara to raise their grievances. However, there will be some ethnic groups who will not be able to find a state sponsor. The Kurds, who are a significant minority in several Middle Eastern states being the best example. In such circumstances the UN will be regarded as biased and its capacity to resolve disputes will suffer.

There are also more general problems associated with UN peace-making by the General Assembly and the Security Council. Even when they do pass resolutions relating to ethnic conflict there will be no enforcement mechanism to ensure that they are put into practice. So the present Secretary General had to admit in his 1982 annual report that the UN 'often finds itself unable to take decisive action to resolve conflicts and its resolutions are increasingly ignored by those who feel themselves strong enough to do so' (quoted in Haas, 1983, p. 189). Another problem with Security Council and General Assembly peace-making has been identified by Claude, who has been critical of the whole enterprise of trying to resolve conflicts by passing resolutions. He argues that such a process may not involve an attempt to get the parties to negotiate about the issues which divide them. Rather

> In the present moral context, voting tends to produce a specious sense of moral superiority among the majority, which exacerbates irritation, encourages uncompromising attitudes, and tempts the majority to stress outvoting members of the minority rather than reaching agreement with them. In the present power context, it promotes decision-making without sensitivity to the realistic limits of policy (Claude, 1971, p. 179).

The temptation at the UN, then, is to approach problems in a parliamentary style, rather than adopt an approach based on negotiation. In other words, an attempt is made to out-vote the opponent rather than to sit with him to discuss conflicting interests. Luard (1988, 537f) has also argued, in support of Claude, that there is a need for fewer resolutions and more negotiations at the United Nations.

The UN, as noted in the previous chapter, also tends to approach mediation in an unimaginative way. This is a point made by Azar (1990, p. 31), who writes that

> Formal 'third party' mediation (e.g., by the United Nations) is rarely effective because it inhibits frankness by placing a premium on concluding agreements rather than searching for options and non-binding outcomes. The UN, a perfectly logical body to provide third party mediation, finds it difficult to act outside the 'limelight', and also suffers from constraints stemming from its permissible role in internal and regional politics. The UN tends to appoint mediators who relay proposals and counter-proposals between opposing sides, thus maintaining the bargaining framework.

Burton (1988, p. 202) agrees with this assessment and argues that the

Secretary-General's initiatives tend to be 'the traditional mediatory ones in which the mediator makes proposals, which are then bargained over, rather than an analytic process through which new and acceptable options can be discovered'.

Yet, despite these criticisms one should not imagine that there is not a constructive role for the UN in peace-making in ethnic conflict. Skjelsbaek (1991) has pointed out some of the assets which the Secretary-General, in particular, possesses because of his place in diplomatic and organizational networks and because of his claim to impartiality. He can also call on a staff that are experienced in international politics and in mediation work.

There are ways to improve the capability of the UN in the area of mediation. More training could be given in the skills of conflict resolution and more use could be made of outside specialists. A paper by the United States United Nations Association (1969), for example, recommended that the 'United Nations' peaceful settlement capabilities be strengthened by additional advance identification of exceptional talent and experience to assist the United Nations in its conciliation and mediation work'. It has even been suggested that a United Nations based Mediation Centre could be established, which could undertake research and training activities (Mapes, 1985, p. 141).

Ury (1987), has recently called for the creation of greater co-ordination of mediation at the global level. Ury has in mind an informal support network of specialists in mediation which could: act as a sounding board; interchange practical knowledge; spotlight danger areas; identify sources of information; provide a referral service; supply support staff; and offer pre-negotiation involvement. Although he does not mention the UN, indeed his emphasis on an informal network would seem to rule out the involvement of an international organization, it would be interesting to see this organization showing some interest in such a development. Curle (in Woodhouse, 1991, p. 56) has proposed the establishment of an International Mediation Centre, having voluntary status with the UN as a non-governmental organization.

Peace-building and the United Nations

Whereas much has been written about the peace-keeping and peace-making functions of the UN there is very little available information on the organization's record in peace-building, which involves working with ordinary people from all sides to a conflict to reduce mutual antagonism and promote 'peace from below' through attitudinal change and socio-economic reconstruction. In chapter five we identified the different types of peace-building activity. They included development, education for mutual understanding, the pursuit of superordinate goals and confidence building.

This is an area where it might be thought that the UN specialised agencies could play a major role (UNESCO in the field of education, UNDP, the FAO and others in development, the UNEP and other bodies in pursuing superordinate goals relating to the environment and health). But the record of such bodies in the area of ethnic conflict is disappointing for a very simple reason. This is that it is too politically sensitive to try and work with governments and groups who may be opposed to existing governments at the same time. UN specialised agencies are meant to be non-political and cannot be seen to be interfering in the internal affairs of sovereign states. The only way to be seen to be avoiding infringing Article 2 (7) of the UN Charter is to avoid politically sensitive work that would be opposed by the government concerned.

Nevertheless it is possible to find some examples of work by the specialised agencies in inter-communal peace-building. One such case is the Nicosia Master Plan project. This is a United Nations Development Programme led project which is concerned with the redevelopment of the capital city of Cyprus, presently divided, like the island, into Greek Cypriot and Turkish Cypriot controlled zones. To quote from a UN publicity document, the Nicosia Master Plan

> ...was to aim at transcending immediate political differences through technical collaboration designed to find solutions to common socio-economic, physical and environmental problems affecting the city. The underlying belief was that out of the routine co-operation between the technical specialists of the two communities... would emerge new bonds of understanding. (UNDP Publicity Leaflet, January 1987)

Ever since 1980 teams of specialists from both communities have met routinely in the UN controlled buffer zone to discuss the various aspects of the plan, which was to chart the future of the city to the year 2000, regarding the city as a single entity and linking socio-economic growth with traffic management, conservation and recreation.

The first phase was completed in 1984. This involved preparing physical plans for the city to the year 2000. Phase two, which lasted from 1984-6, examined in detail how the plans could be implemented, with special emphasis being given to the walled city. Phase three now involves attempts to get the plans implemented. It already seems that the UNDP will fund a project to halt damage to the Selimiye-St. Sophia national monument, and a joint West German/UNHCR project will undertake work on the old walled city. West German money has been allocated to converting a run down building into a community centre on the Greek Cypriot side and to restore a sixteenth century Ottoman inn on the Turkish Cypriot side (Jensen, 1988, p.18). Crucial to the success of the project has been the cooperation of the mayors of the Greek and Turkish parts of the capital.

UNESCO has also recently started an initiative in Sri Lanka which appears to have similar aims to the Nicosia Master Plan project. This is based at the Marga Institute, and involves a study of conditions

> Conducive to the implementation of development projects likely to ensure mutual understanding and cultural consensus through consultation between all the social partners, and through consideration by the decision-makers of the interests and aspirations of those population groups that are most vulnerable to the adverse effects of social change (UNESCO Budget Proposal for 1988, UN Doc. 24/C/5, Paris. Project number 08104).

The overall aim of the project seems to be to link development with projects for mutual understanding, and this project is itself lined to a wider UNESCO project on the cultural dimension of development.

As well as these examples, which have the specific aim of bringing warring communities closer together, the UN specialised agencies can contribute more indirectly to peace by helping the victims of conflict achieve a minimum standard of physical and mental well-being. The UNHCR, for example, has done much good work in assisting refugees in the Horn of Africa, Cyprus and Nicaragua (the Meskito Indians), providing them with basic care and working for their peaceful return to their former homes. UNWRA has done equally good work with refugees in the Middle East. Another attempt to help the victims of violence is the UNDP programme of assistance to the Palestinian people in the occupied territories, which is based on General Assembly Resolution 33/147 of December 1978. Programmes include work in the areas of health and sanitation and education and vocational training. The Israeli government does not oppose this work, and the UNDP has been able to continue implementing these programmes despite the recent uprisings in the occupied territories.

However, the most notable and encouraging move by the UN to embrace the concept of peace-building is in the Boutros-Ghali (1992) *An Agenda for Peace* document. Chapter six of this report deals with 'post-conflict peacebuilding', and recognises that in the aftermath of war there is a need for 'concrete cooperative projects which link two or more countries in a mutually beneficial undertaking that can not only contribute to economic and social development but also enhance the confidence that is so fundamental to peace' (Boutros-Ghali, 1992, p. 32). There is only a half-hearted attempt to extend this idea to intercommunal conflict and the proposal to restrict peace-building to post-conflict situations is also far too limiting. Nevertheless, a generation after Galtung first suggested the importance of peace-building it is good to see the idea finally enshrined in UN thinking about its role in the new world order.

Conclusions: An integrated UN strategy?

There has been a growing awareness of the need to link up the work of the UN in the areas of peace-keeping, peace-building and peace-making. This is not an original insight, however. The links between peace-making and peace-building were pointed out in a memo submitted by the UN Secretary General to the UN Sub-Commission on the Prevention of Discrimination and the Protection of Minorities in June 1949 (UN Doc. E/CN.4/Sub. 2/40). This was entitled *The Main Types and Causes of Discrimination,* and pointed out the links between group conflict and prejudice, stereotyping and scapegoating. One of the important arguments of the report was that successful conflict resolution required both mediation and initiatives to deal with stereotyping, false propaganda and the lack of understanding of other cultures.

There have also been proposals in recent years to link the peace-keeping and peace-building aspects of UN involvement in violent conflict. Often these take the form of suggestions that a 'civilian relief unit' or 'humanitarian support organization' be attached to a UN peace-keeping force. Several commentators have also recognised that effective peace-keeping requires the support of peace-making (e.g. Holst, 1990). Without such complementary action the UN might, on occasions, be able to neutralise ethnic conflicts, but it will not be able to resolve them; and this lack of progress towards resolution will eventually undermine its ability to neutralise.

Within the last few years changes at the global level of power politics did seem to create a situation that would allow for a stronger, integrated UN role in responding to conflicts in the 'new world order'. Within the Organization the high point of this optimistic interpretation of global trends was the Secretary-General's *An Agenda For Peace* document of 1992. This was the response to a Security Council invitation to prepare an analysis and to make recommendations on ways of strengthening the capacity of the UN for peace-making, peace-keeping and preventive diplomacy. The report begins with an analysis of the changing context of international relations and it is interesting that it mentions ethnic conflict and human rights 'with a special sensitivity to those of minorities'. On the other hand paragraph 17 states that the 'foundation-stone' of the work of the UN must remain the state.

In the section on definitions of key ideas the Secretary-General points out how the terms preventive diplomacy, peace-making and peace-keeping are 'integrally related', and adds to these three strategies the idea of post-conflict peace-building. These four areas for action, it is claimed, offer a 'coherent contribution towards securing peace in the spirit of the Charter' (par. 22). The idea of an integrated strategy is also addressed in other parts of the document. Paragraph 45 goes on to state that 'there may not be a dividing line between peace-making and peacekeeping' and the deployment of a UN presence in the field may 'expand possibilities for the prevention of conflict, facilitate the work of peacemaking and in many cases serve as a prerequisite for peace-building. Paragraph 55, which is in the section on peace-building, points out that 'peacemaking and peacekeeping operations, to be truly successful, must come to include comprehensive efforts to identify and support structures which will tend to consolidate peace and advance a sense of confidence and well-being among people'.

There are certain criticisms that can be made of the *Agenda's* peace strategy. Its approach to conflict prevention is rather limited and tends to rely on early warning and military deployment rather than social change. The peace-making section also places too much emphasis on law, sanctions and military force rather than on exploring innovating conflict resolution strategies proposed by Burton, Azar and others. Also the strategy of peace-building, for some unexplained reason, is limited to 'post-conflict' situations. The idea that peace-building can also be a conflict resolution strategy in its own right is therefore not addressed. The UN experience since 1992 in Somalia, Bosnia, Haiti and Angola has also shown that there are very real limits to what the organization can do in situations of internal conflict. Yet, despite these criticisms, the *Agenda* is an important step towards expanding the role of the UN in conflict resolution and prevention. Whatever its flaws, it now exists and can be built on.

In the discussions on conflict prevention the *Agenda* mentions the importance of respecting the rights of minorities. Paragraph eighty-one states that respect for human rights and fundamental freedoms requires a 'deeper understanding and respect for the rights of minorities'. There are some who might regard this as an ironic statement, given the United Nation's own record in the field of minority rights. In the next chapter we shall explore this record in some detail.

Notes

1. In June 1992, for example, western diplomats were reported to be annoyed when the Secretary-General challenged the view that the Serbs were primarily to blame for the violence in Bosnia and Hercegovina two days after the Security Council had authorised sanctions against the remnants of the Yugoslavian state (see Guardian, 5 June, 1992).
2. The figures used here are taken from Sabaratnam (1987). There is a more detailed analysis of the population breakdown based on the 1981 census in Schwarz, (1986).

7 The international protection of ethnic minorities

It is difficult to know what contribution has been made to the amelioration of offensive rule by this vast outpouring of ethical norms and the ratification of numerous covenants. But some of the negative consequences are very clear. For many years, the preoccupation with ethical norms was associated with, or perhaps even a cover for, the neglect of practical measures against gross violations of human rights. And now these norms and ratified covenants seem to be honoured more in the breach than the observance. Nevertheless, the debates in the Commission on Human Rights are informed by the exalted rhetoric of high ethical norms, which serve to camouflage the often naked pursuit of national self-interest (Kuper, 1992, p. 137).

Introduction

The attempt to implement the principle of the self-determination of nations following the first world war was clearly a failure. Alfred Cobban was surely right to note that what was taken for self-determination was to a large extent not self-determination at all. Gellner has pointed out that the new states created after 1918 had all the defects of the old empires they replaced, plus new ones of their own. So 'they were just as minority-haunted, but they were smaller, unhallowed by age and often without experienced leaders, while the minorities whose irredentism they had to face included members of previously dominant cultural groups, unused to subordination and well-placed to resist it' (Gellner, 1992, p. 288). Instead of the pure simplicity of true nation-states, what emerged out of the collapse of the three great monarchies of Germany, Austria-Hungary and the Ottoman Empire, was a hotchpotch of multi-ethnic states and multi-state nations. This, according to Hobsbawm (1990, p. 132), reveals the 'utter impracticability of the Wilsonian principle'.

In order to try to impose some degree of stability on this potentially volatile situation, these new states were forced to accept that their treatment of their religious, linguistic, national and racial minorities would be subject to external scrutiny. The precise basis of this obligation differed from country to country (Thornberry, 1980 and 1991). Five states (Poland, Yugoslavia, Rumania, Greece and Czechoslovakia) signed special minority treaties. Four (Austria, Bulgaria, Hungary and Turkey) had special clauses relating to minorities included in their post war peace treaties.[1] Five (Albania, Lithuania, Latvia, Estonia and Iraq) issued general declarations on their admission to the League of Nations. There were also special treaties relating to territories that were not sovereign states (Danzig, Memel and Upper Silesia). In all cases the states concerned guaranteed to respect certain special rights of individuals belonging to minorities. These included the right to be treated in a non-discriminatory manner; the right to use their own language; the right to establish, at their own expense, religious, social and charitable institutions; the right to practise their own religion; and in areas where the minorities were a 'considerable' proportion of the population the state had an obligation to ensure adequate facilities for primary education in the minority language and to allocate an 'equitable share' of public subventions for educational, religious and charitable purposes (Claude, 1969, pp. 18-19).

The idea of international supervision of a state's treatment of minorities was not a new idea (see Thornberry, 1991). Capotorti (UN Doc. E/CN.4/Sub 2/384), has traced the history of minority protection as far back as the Treaty of Vienna of 1606, which had provisions relating to the treatment of the Protestant minority in Hungary. Several treaties since then included provisions that were concerned with the safety of religious minorities. They include the Treaty of Westphalia (1648), the Treaty of Oliva (1660), the Treaty of Nijmegen (1678), the Treaty of Paris (1763), the Treaty of Vienna (1815), the Treaty of Paris (1856) and the Treaty of Berlin (1878).

The minority protection regime implemented after the Great War, however, was different from these treaties in at least four respects. Firstly, the definition of a minority was broader than was hitherto the case. Religious minorities were still included, but so were linguistic and national minorities. Secondly, the role of guarantor passed from certain sovereign states to the League of Nations. Minority protection therefore became much more of an issue of general international concern and it became much harder to use the issue of the treatment of minorities to mask self-interested intervention by other states. Thirdly, the League established a minorities section, which could, for the first time, provide permanent supervision of the treatment of minorities in the designated states. Finally, a judicial element was introduced into the process of protection by the role that was envisaged for the Permanent Court of International Justice.

We shall begin this chapter by exploring the history of the League system of minority protection. Then we shall set out the reasons why the UN decided not to adopt a similar system when it superseded the League. Finally, although the UN has not been active in promoting the rights of ethnic groups, it has not been able to avoid this issue altogether. We shall therefore examine the work of the UN in four areas: genocide, the Sub-committee for the Prevention of Discrimination and the Protection of Minorities, the 1992 Declaration on the Rights of Persons Belonging to National or Ethnic, Religious and Linguistic Minorities, and the right of national self-determination.

The League of Nations minority protection regime

The League of Nations regime for the protection of minorities did not spring ready made into life. It developed over time. Its overall aim, according to an advisory opinion of the permanent Court of International Justice in 1935, in a decision relating to minority schools in Albania was to

> Secure for certain elements incorporated in a state...the possibility of living peaceably alongside the majority population and co-operating amicably with it, while at the same time preserving those characteristics which distinguish them from the majority, and satisfying the ensuing needs.

When it was operating fully, from about 1923, the system of protection involved seven main stages (Fawcett, 1979, p. 10).

Stage one was the right of individuals belonging to minorities to petition the League of Nations if they felt that their rights were not being respected by governments. Such petitions, which had no status in the League system other than being a source of information, had to fulfil certain conditions before they were regarded as admissible. A petition could be declared inadmissible if: it had not exhausted local remedies; if it came from an anonymous or unauthenticated source; or if it requested the severance of political relations between the minority group and the state.

Stage two was the acceptance of the petition by the League Minorities Section. This was composed of about a half-dozen international civil servants who could not be a national of a state subject to League supervision or a national of a 'kindred state'. As well as deciding on the permissibility of individual petitions, the Minorities Section was responsible for executing decisions of the League Council and the Minority Committees and for preparing data. If the petition was accepted by the League it went on to stage three, when the League requested that the government concerned comment on the petition. This would normally have to be completed within two months, though there was a possibility that a longer period could be granted. The accused state also had a right to appeal against the acceptance of the petition by the League.

Stage four was the passing of the petition and the comments of the government to the League Council. The Council then initiated stage five, which was the creation of an *ad hoc* Committee (usually of three Council members) to consider the documents in more detail. These committees met about 1000 times to consider about 400 petitions (Sierpowski, 1990). They were composed of the president of the Council and two others appointed for each specific case, and they were empowered to reject a petition, or to try to work behind the scenes for an amicable settlement. This work, therefore, involved talks with governments, the examination of treaty provisions and the verification of information contained in the petition. On completion of its work, the Committee of Three passed on a recommendation to the Council, together with all the paperwork collected during its work. This was stage six, and up to this point the investigation of a complaint was based on an automatic procedure.

There was nothing automatic, however, about the seventh and final stage. For once the report of the Committee of Three was with the Council there was no guarantee that it would be raised during a formal League session, which was the only way it could become a public document. These matters could only be taken up if a member of the Council decided to raise them. There were attempts to make stage seven automatic as well, but they met with no success. Although the Permanent Court of International Justice could be used to give non-binding advisory opinions at the request of the Council on the interpretation of the Minority treaties, and did so on several occasions, the League secretariat preferred to work in a non-legalistic, behind-the-scenes manner. Azcarate (1945, p. 47), a former director of the Minorities Section, explains that this was because minority issues were so complex 'politically, legally, socially, and psychologically, that to seek to resolve them by strictly legal criteria can only lead to equivocal and contradictory situations'.

A full analysis of the League's involvement may never be possible, since much of the work was done in secret and no minutes of the meetings of the Committee of Three were ever kept. It must also be borne in mind that the system is being judged on its work over a short, twenty year period, at a time of enormous political upheaval in Europe. Nevertheless, the overall record of the League in the area of minority protection is a disappointing one. Indeed it was difficult to find more than a handful of governments, minority groups or League officials who were happy with the system.

Minorities criticised the system because of its secrecy and its bias in favour of governments. Azcarate (1945, p. 52), has argued that this charge of state bias can be overstated. He has claimed that the representatives who served on the Committee of Three were usually reasonably objective. However, it cannot be denied that the petitioners were not regarded as equals to states by the League, which was also reluctant to treat members as accused parties. Indeed, until 1929 the petitioners were not even informed if their petition had been accepted. Nor were they informed, officially, of the replies made by governments to their petitions. Minorities could also point to the poor punishment record of the League, and this would support the claim that the system could provide them with neither a prompt nor an effective hearing (Claude, 1955). They complained that the system had given them false hopes; or pointed out that the cultural groups they belonged to had no rights *per se,* since the protection was offered to *individuals* belonging to religious, linguistic, national and racial minorities, not to the groups themselves. Perhaps for these reasons Sipos (1991, p. 106) has claimed that the League system proved to be a 'fiasco' which 'in practice provided no protection whatever for the nationalities'.

This is a little unfair. The League regime did have some successes (Alexander, 1947; Claude, 1955; Mair, 1928; Robinson, 1943). In Poland it was able to stop the eviction of German farmers and upheld a complaint that Jewish entry into the learned professions was being unfairly restricted. It also was able to reverse an attempt by Rumania to take over control of the local administration in the Magyar district of Szekler. It was also able to obtain compensation for Russians on Mount Athos after the Greek Government expropriated some land there.

The states who were subjected to minority protection provisions were also unhappy with the system. Only one-third of League members and about a half of all European states were subjected to minority protection obligations (Sierpowski, 1990). They pointed out that the minority treaties infringed the principle of sovereign equality, since only a minority of states had been forced to accept restrictions on how they dealt with minorities. Several states also complained that the system encouraged minorities to dissent, that it hindered assimilation, or that it encouraged abuses of the system by hostile neighbours. In fact, with one or two exceptions (especially Czechoslovakia and Estonia), the 'record of the minority states was discreditable' (Claude, 1955, p. 40). They resorted to evasions and flagrant violations. They tried to nullify the international guarantee they were subjected to and sought to undermine an effective League procedure.

Important League Council members had their own reasons for not supporting the minority protection regime. France, following the failure of the US to join the League, decided that its security interests were best served by entering into alliances with several states in Central Europe who were subject to League supervision. In order not to anger these allies, the French had an interest in not pushing too strongly for them to abide by their obligations to their minorities. The British were also less than enthusiastic about the regime. Austen Chamberlain, for example, illustrating the ambiguous nature of the provisions, believed that the system of protection should be a temporary measure, which might ease the path towards the assimilation of minorities (Calderwood, 1931). Germany, often a keen champion of minority rights, adhered to this principle, not out of commitment to the international protection of minorities, but because of affective links with specific German minorities in specific states. Indeed, under Hitler, it became clear that Germany was fundamentally opposed to the assumption that German minorities should live under 'foreign' governments and undermined the League system by encouraging German minorities to act in a disloyal and provocative manner (Claude, 1955, p. 47). So Robinson (1943, p. 240) has noted that

> The entire history of the League of Nations does not furnish a single instance of a collective *demarche* or action on their part in order to protect the structure...The absence of coordinated action on their part was evident from the very start with regard to the primary question of the League's assumption of the international guarantor for minorities. Moreover, the Great Powers were extremely reluctant to exercise their prerogatives as members of the Council, even for the purpose of calling public attention to treaty infractions.

A Royal Institute of International Affairs (1939, ch.xvi) analysis of the

League record also pointed out that one of its 'deep defects' was the impossibility of eliminating political considerations from the treatment of minority issues, which meant that the most powerful members of the organization were often reluctant to alienate other states. Or as Janowsky (1945, p. 125) put it, the feeling by League members was that the less the minorities issue was discussed the better. If these issues were discussed the aim seemed to be peaceful settlement at all costs, even if justice for minorities had to be sacrificed.

Although the League system of minority protection was not officially dissolved until December 1939, its authority was severely dented in 1934, when Poland announced it would no longer deem itself to be bound by the provisions of its minority treaty. In 1939 only a paltry four petitions were received by the League, and three of these were rejected (Thornberry, 1990, p. 46). By this stage there seemed to be little will amongst League members to uphold the treaty and to force states to abide by their legal responsibilities. In April 1950 a memorandum by the UN Secretary-General (Doc. E/CN.4/Sub.2/85) declared that all obligations under the League of Nations treaties were terminated except for those states (Albania, Iraq and Finland) who had incurred such obligations under the Treaty of Lausanne, which remained in force. But even here the provisions were suspended. More remarkably, the study declared that

> In modern times, most nations have their own State, and most States represent the juridicial organization of a single nation. This is true even in the case of States formed by groups having widely varying cultural traditions (par. 30).

Although the report does examine various aspects of minority protection, this statement reveals an attitude which was hardly going to encourage strong interest in the problems of multi-ethnic and multi-national societies in the organization that replaced the League of Nations.

The UN rejection of a minority protection regime

There were discussions during the formative years of the UN about whether it should adopt a new system of minority protection, and even after the decision was made not to re-create such a regime, there were some attempts to get this body to pay some attention to the issue of minority rights and minority protection. Most of these attempts were unsuccessful. Indeed, the UN has retained to this day a policy which, in the words of Claude (1951, p. 310), means that they have 'definitely de-emphasised' the minority protection issue. This was despite the fact that in its infant years many of the most serious problems that the UN became involved in were rooted in ethnic conflicts. These included Kashmir, Palestine, and the Iran/Azerbaijan issue.

There were several reasons why this policy was adopted. Firstly, the experience of the inter-war years had shown how a state such as Hitler's Germany could abuse the minority issue for its own territorial aggrandisement. Here, the German minorities in Poland and Czechoslovakia were used to justify expansionist policies in central Europe and, in addition, ethnic divisions in Yugoslavia and between Hungary and Rumania were fostered to divide opponents (see Jaworski, 1990; Sipos, 1991, p. 107). After the war, this increased the fears of certain states that the preservation of a minority identity would increase their own insecurity. As an Iranian delegate put it, the acceptance of special minority rights would 'lead to abuses, encourage political provocation and collusion with foreign states and result in violations of Article 2 of the Charter' (UN Doc.E/CN.4/Sub. 2/SR. 47, p. 10). Iran had, of course, been a victim of Soviet intervention in support of independence for the Azerbaijani area of the country at the end of the war.

As well as this danger of external intervention, it was felt that the granting of minority rights would merely freeze a situation of majority/minority antagonism. This is still an argument used today. A Nigerian academic, for example, claims that strict adherence to group rights will certainly accentuate sectional feelings, militate against the development of transcendental loyalty to the centre, and lead to the triumph of atavistic parochialism (Okoli, 1982, p. 218). In 1991 an Egyptian member of the Sub-commission for the Prevention of Discrimination and the Protection of Minorities declared that 'emphasizing and enlarging upon minority status was bound to worsen already existing racial feelings and lead to the atomization of nations or to a regression to quasi-tribalism' (UN Doc E/CN.4/Sub.2/ 1991/ SR.16). At a UN meeting the following year a Rumanian observer complained that concepts such as the self-determination of minorities and collective rights were being 'invoked from time to time in order to envenom relations among the populations of certain states and also inter-state relations' (UN Doc. E/CN.4/Sub.2/1992/SR.33).

By 1945 the American position on the ethnic issue had changed significantly since Wilson had championed minority rights at Versailles. Now the US position reflected its supposed melting pot heritage of assimilation of different groups on the basis of equal treatment before the law. Even at the time observers such as Janowsky (1945) pointed out that the US experience was not typical of multi-ethnic states. The people who emigrated to the US chose to do so, they went as families

206

and did not form united, ethnic based political groups. But, not surprisingly, many governments were prepared to support the US position. This preference for a universal bill of human rights, which found expression in the 1948 Universal Declaration of Human Rights, can clearly be seen in the attitude of Eleanor Roosevelt, the first US representative on the Human Rights Commission, and its first chairperson. Arguing from the US experience, and claiming that her country had no minorities problem, she consistently opposed the idea of special group rights for ethnic groups. In this attitude she received strong support from the Latin American states, who also argued that they had no indigenous minority problem and feared that the acceptance of minority rights would make it harder for them to assimilate immigrant groups. An Equadorian delegate to the UN, Meneses Pallares, went as far as to claim that 'the object should be to encourage assimilation and not to promote the creation of minority groups' (UN Doc. E/CN.4/Sub 2/ SR 11 p. 20).

Another argument against a system of minority protection was that the conditions in multi-ethnic states varied so much that it was not possible to provide a clear cut, across the board system that would suit all occasions. Rather, it was felt that dealing with each case on an *ad hoc* basis was to be preferred. This comes out clearly in the 1950 memorandum by the Secretary-General which stated

> The validity of the claim of specific minorities to additional protective measures is, however, a political question normally to be decided on the basis of the conditions and arrangements under which the minority was included in the State, and of all other relevant circumstances. Hence it would seem that each such claim must be examined and passed upon separately. (UN Doc. E/CN.4/Sub.2/85, par. 59)

The mixed record of the League system of minority protection may also have influenced some in opposing a similar system for the UN. It was generally regarded as a failure, perhaps a little unfairly. But certainly, many of the states who had been forced to agree to League supervision of their treatment of minority groups were some of the most vocal opponents of a UN system of minority protection. Even many supporters of minority protection were not enthusiastic about the recreation of a minority protection regime. Claude writes that

> Many champions of the rights of minorities had been so little impressed by the actual and potential benefits of the League system that they had come to believe that the game was hardly worth the candle. Some minorities were no longer inclined to

base their hopes for liberal treatment on a system which, from their point of view, had promised too little and delivered even less (Claude, 1969, p. 58).

The hope was that a system of individual human rights protection based on non-discrimination would be enough. Interestingly, though, the emphasis on non-discrimination and individualism in the Charter has not always been pursued faithfully by the UN itself. In its appointment of members of the Secretariat, or in the composition of various UN bodies, the international organization has usually employed the device of regional quotas.

Supporters of an international system of minority protection have always pointed out that the minority issue would not disappear because the UN refused to deal with it properly, and a system of human rights protection was, on its own, not adequate to protect ethnic minorities.[2] For in addition to non-discriminatory treatment cultural minorities also may need the right to use their language or practise their religion, access to separate educational institutions, and even a degree of self-government in order to survive (Stavenhagen, 1991, p. 142). In the words of one specialist on the international protection of minorities

> Prohibition against discrimination is nonetheless not good enough. National minorities should receive positive safe-guards. They should be given the opportunity to continue their existence as nationalities... It is not enough that minority members should have protection as individuals for their linguistic and cultural rights. A national minority is a collective and its interests in education and other establishments of its own serving groups of minority members are the interests of a group and not of an individual. Minority protection should therefore be directed towards the collective population (Modeen, 1969, p. 144).

However, the Charter and the Universal Declaration of Human Rights show quite clearly that the principle of individual rights and non-discrimination have eased out an approach based on group rights and minority protection within the organization. Both documents refer several times to the principle of non-discrimination, but do not mention minorities once.

An even stronger charge can be made against the UN, however. For not only has it tended to downplay the issue of minority rights, in some cases it has blatantly ignored the wishes of ethnic groups in its own decisions about sovereignty and recognition. In the Congo, for example, the UN used peace-keeping forces to put down a secession attempt by Katanga (see Durch, 1993; James, 1990, part V: C; Luard, 1988, p. 306f). Although this was a contentious decision at least in this case there were some grounds for regarding this action as justified because Katangan secession was being actively promoted by western financial interests against the wishes of the government of the Congo. There is much less justification for the UN's role in the process which placed Eritrea under Ethiopian sovereignty and made West New Guinea a part of Indonesia.

Because Ethiopia was an important US ally the UN decided in December 1950 that the mainly Moslem area of Eritrea should be incorporated into the Ethiopian state under a federal arrangement (Hannum, 1990, p. 337f). Eritrea had been an Italian colony, which had been ruled temporarily by the UK from 1941 to 1950. It is an ethnically diverse region, and its population was itself divided in its attitude to the link with Ethiopia, who wanted control of the area for strategic reasons. It prevented the country becoming land-locked. The UN made no attempt to assess the wishes of the people of Eritrea in making this arrangement. In 1962 the government in Addis Ababa dissolved the federal arrangement and Eritrea was declared a province of Ethiopia. Years of repression followed, which eventually led to a bitter war between the Ethiopian government and the Eritreans. In the face of this blatant abandonment of the UN backed federal plan the organization remained unmoved and took no action against the government of Ethiopia.

The people of West New Guinea, a former Dutch colony, were culturally distinct from Indonesians and had expressed no desire to become part of this state. The western powers, however, were anxious not to offend Indonesia, who claimed the island, and the US in particular strongly supported Jakarta. The UN was used to smooth the transition from Dutch to Indonesian rule and the territory was placed under international administration between October 1962 and May 1963, when it was taken over by Indonesia. The wishes of the local people were regarded as irrelevant. As Luard (1988, p. 346) notes during the period of UN administration the organization 'made no serious attempt in the way it administered the territory to allow those people any genuine measure of choice'. In fact, administration officials discouraged expressions of anti-Indonesian or pro-independence views (Luard, 1988, p. 342). After its incorporation into Indonesia a guerrilla war began in West New Guinea in order to gain self-determination.

Yet despite the disinterest or even the hostility towards ethnic difference the UN has not been able to avoid issues relating to minority protection and group rights altogether. Four examples of this involvement can now be examined to illustrate how the UN has responded to such issues.

The United Nations and Genocide

The UN first took up the issue of genocide in earnest in November, 1946 when a draft resolution was submitted to the General Assembly largely due to the initiatives of India, Cuba and Panama. The result of this action was General Assembly Resolution 96 (1) of December 11th 1946, which described genocide as a crime and called on ECOSOC to produce studies to allow member states to enact the necessary legislation to prevent and punish such actions. After a lengthy process of consultation and deliberation this climaxed in the Convention on the Prevention and Punishment of the Crime of Genocide, which was passed unanimously by the General Assembly on 9 December 1948 (Resolution 260 A [III]).

In fact the document has much more to say about prevention than punishment, and legal specialists at the time pointed out that the Convention added nothing to existing provisions under the Charter, Resolution 96 (1) and the decisions of the Nuremburg Tribunal (Robinson, 1949). It has not been easy to define clearly the term genocide (Fein, 1993), and the Convention's definition has been criticised by many. It did, however, state quite clearly that it was a crime to undertake actions with the intent to destroy, in whole or in part, a 'national, ethnical, racial or religious group'. Actions which would constitute a crime include killing members of a group; causing serious bodily or mental harm to a group; deliberately inflicting conditions of life calculated to result in the physical destruction of the group; and actions to prevent births within the group or the physical transfer of children out of the group.

The Convention is meant to protect groups, not individuals, and so can be seen as a softening in this case of the general UN reluctance to consider group rights. As a Lebanese delegate to the UN at the time noted, 'for the first time in an international or constitutional document, mention was made... of the protection of the human group as such and not only of the individual' (ORGA 3 Session Part 1 66 Meeting 6th Committee 1948). However, there are omission and ambiguities in the UN approach. A article in the original draft, which referred to cultural genocide and would have made it a crime to destroy the language, religion or culture of a national, religious or racial group was dropped when being considered by the Sixth Committee of the General Assembly. Also the Convention has nothing to say about the mass murder of one's own cultural group, sometimes called political genocide. This was also criminalized in the first draft of the

Convention, but was subsequently omitted. As a result the Convention offers only limited protection from genocide (Jonassohn, 1992), and even for proscribed acts terms like 'intent to destroy a group...as such' are so imprecise they could hinder attempts to implement the Convention (Fein, 1993, p. xvi).

Under Article VI of this convention it was proposed that an international tribunal could be established that would have jurisdiction with respect to states who had accepted the tribunal's authority. This has never happened. Article VIII allows contracting parties to call upon the competent organs of the UN to take action under the Charter to prevent or suppress acts of genocide. Yet since its adoption the Convention has hardly been invoked at all, despite several cases of genocidal activity since 1948. These include the murder of Hutus in Burundi, the Ibo in Nigeria and Southern Sudanese in Sudan; the persecution of Bah'is in Iran, the Tibetans in China and the Kurds of Iraq; the destruction of the Ache Indians in Paraguay and the Ixil in North West Guatemala; and the massacres of Bangladeshis in East Pakistan, and ethnic Chinese in Indonesia. (Fein, 1992 and 1993; Horowitz, 1980; Kuper, 1981 and 1985; McGarry and O'Leary, 1993, p 6f; van den Burghe, 1990). The one significant attempt to apply the Genocide Convention to state conduct has occurred in the former Yugoslavia. Here UN Security Council resolution 780 (1992) has established a Commission of Experts to monitor breaches of humanitarian law, including the Genocide Convention (Higgins, 1993). The International Court of Justice has also ruled that the events in Bosnia and Hercegovina can be classified as genocide as defined by the 1948 Convention.

A 1985 report by Ben Whitaker on Genocide called for improvements to be made to the United Nations Genocide Convention (UN Doc. E/CN. 4/Sub 2/1985/6). He wanted to see protection broadened to include political groups, cultural genocide and ecocide. In the rain forests of Latin America, for example, we are witnessing the 'genocide through ecocide' of what van den Burghe has called 'micro-ethnies'. Whitaker felt that an international, independent 'Committee on Genocide' should be established, along with an international penal tribunal to investigate and prosecute offences under the Convention. He also thought more could be done to prevent genocide through the establishment of an early warning system, early mediation, education and the publicising of outrages. Finally, he pleaded for more states to ratify the Convention, and pointed out that countries that had still not ratified the Convention included South Africa, Paraguay, Bangladesh, Uganda, Indonesia and Sudan. All are facing, or have recently experienced, serious ethnic conflict. The UN made no moves to implement the Whitaker proposals, and perhaps this was to be expected. An earlier report on genocide by Nicodeme

Ruhasyankiko in June 1973 encountered similar disinterest (UN Doc. E/CN.4/Sub. 2/L597). When it was forwarded to the 30th session of the Commission on Human Rights the deletion of all references to specific historical cases was requested.

All told, therefore, the UN's work in the area of genocide has not been impressive. In one of the best studies on the prevention of genocide, Kuper has been extremely critical of the international organization. He claims that UN members tend to put political interests above human rights and argues that 'clearly, the UN cannot now be relied upon to initiate and carry out preventive action against genocide' (Kuper, 1985, p.19). He goes on to state that 'the impact on the outside observer, in such organs of the United Nations as the Commission on Human Rights, is of overwhelming hypocrisy' (Kuper, 1985, p. 89). It is, he claims, characterised by cliche-ridden statements, an unctuous style of debate and a repetitive ritual of elaborate congratulations. In fact, the UN 'condones genocide by delay, evasion and subterfuge' (Kuper, 1981, p. 183).

The Sub-commission on the Prevention of Discrimination and the Protection of Minorities

A second way in which the UN has been forced to consider issues relating to ethnic minorities is through the work of the Sub-commission on the Prevention of Discrimination and the Protection of Minorities, which is an offspring of the UN Human Rights Commission (HRC). The Sub-commission was established in 1946 by ECOSOC during its second session, held in Hunter College in the Bronx. In the first instance the role of the Sub-commission was to 'examine what provisions should be adopted in the definition of the principles which are to be applied in the field of the protection of minorities, and to deal with the urgent problems in this field by making recommendations to the Commission' (Resolution 2/11, par. 9b). Initially the Sub-commission was composed of twelve members who were nominated by governments, but who were supposed to serve as independent experts. This is a principle which some delegates have taken more seriously than others. Today the Sub-commission is composed of 26 members, appointed so as to ensure an acceptable regional distribution. So the Sub-commission is made up of seven Africans, five Asians, six West Europeans (a category that includes North America as well), five Latin Americans and three East Europeans (a category which may now have lost its meaning).

It is certainly true, as some critics have pointed out, that the Sub-commission occupies a very lowly place in the UN hierarchy and that it spends too much time discussing procedural rather than substantive issues. It is also true that the Sub-commission seems to lack a clear idea of its role and so lacks a sense of direction. It cannot be denied either that the Sub-commission has rarely been able to press successfully for positive measures to protect minority groups. Perhaps its only real success was the inclusion of Article 27 in the International Covenant of Civil and Political Rights of 1966 (General Assembly Resolution 2200 A (XX)). This was drafted by the Sub-commission and states

> In those states in which ethnic, religious or linguistic minorities exist, persons belonging to such minorities shall not be denied the right, in community with the other members of their group, to enjoy their own culture, to profess and practise their own religion, or to use their own language.

Yet, even here, the protection granted to minorities is rather limited. It applies to 'persons belonging to such minorities' and so no concession is made to the idea of group rights except in the weak phrase 'in community with other members of their group'. States are not required to take measures to promote the rights of such persons, they are merely obliged not to deny these rights. There is, therefore, no requirement for states to provide resources for minority groups. The phrase 'in those states in which...minorities exist' could allow states to deny that they have minorities. Finally, the state is only obliged to respect the rights of persons belonging to minorities in the areas of language, culture and religion.

One of the main reasons for this poor record is the rather strained relationship the Sub-commission has often had with its parent body, the Human Rights Commission (HRC). The Commission can effectively determine the fate of Sub-commission resolutions because the latter body can only make requests or recommendations through the Commission, which remains free to determine what to do with them. Sometimes this involves the Commission simply deferring a decision on an issue raised by the Sub-commission. Indeed, when in 1951 ECOSOC proposed that the Sub-commission be abolished, the HRC did little to protect it, and salvation only came when ECOSOC was asked by the General Assembly to reconsider its decision. However, perhaps chastened by this assault on its very existence, from 1952 the work of the Sub-commission tended to concentrate much more on the issue of non-discrimination than on the more sensitive issue of minority protection. When it did address the latter issue, it received little encouragement from the HRC. A 1954 request by the Sub- Commission, for example, that the HRC approve the appointment of an expert to work on a report of the present position of minorities in the world was refused by the parent body (Humphrey, 1968). Indeed, a former director of the UN's Human Rights Division has stated that the HRC 'has never shown the slightest interest in what may be called the positive protection of minorities...every effort which the Sub-commission made to protect minorities in a positive way was frustrated by the Human Rights Commission and higher bodies' (Humphrey, 1984, p. 20).

Claude has pointed out that there were two general directions which the Sub-commission could have taken (Claude, 1951). It could have remained a body of experts, whose sole function was to produce reports and definitions at the request of the HRC - what Claude refers to as the scholarly approach. Or it could have adopted a more activist role, pressing to improve the legal and factual position of minorities in the inter-state system. This would have involved drafting articles and acting on petitions of complaint from minority groups. However, whenever the Sub-commission tried to adopt the later role, the HRC made its disapproval very clear.

One good example of this was the debate over whether there should have been an article on minority rights in the Universal Declaration on Human Rights. The first draft of the Bill of Rights (as the Universal Declaration was then called) contained an Article sponsored by Dr. Malik of the Lebanon which stated that in areas where a minority group made up a substantial proportion of the population they should have the right to their own schools, religious institutions, and a media in their own language. The business of public assemblies and courts should also be conducted in the minority language. This draft article was submitted to the Sub-commission by the Commission and after debate the article was re-drafted in such a way that its scope was broadened. This version stated

> In states inhabited by well-defined ethnic, linguistic or religious groups which are clearly distinguished from the rest of the population, and which want to be accorded differential treatment, persons belonging to such groups shall have the right, as far as is compatible with public order and security, to establish and maintain their schools and cultural or religious institutions, and to use their own language and script in the Press, in public assembly, and before the courts and other authorities of the State, if they so choose. (UN Doc. E/600 Annex A Art. 31)

However when this particular draft reached the Commission on Human Rights it was decided to omit all reference to minorities from the Universal Declaration, despite some support for such a clause from the Lebanese, Soviet and Yugoslavian delegates. When the draft declaration reached the Third Committee of the General Assembly the Soviet,

Yugoslavian and Danish delegates did attempt to re-insert a minority rights clause, but they were not successful.[3] The US and Australian delegates thought such a clause would inhibit assimilation, and the French and certain Latin American representatives argued that it would increase instability within states. As Haksar has pointed out, here we find a curious reversal. Instead of protecting minorities from state power, the UN seems to be protecting states from minorities (Haksar, 1974, p 86).

There was another unsuccessful attempt by the Soviet Union, Yugoslavia and Denmark to include the mention of minority rights in the Universal Declaration during discussions in the General Assembly plenary session, but this too failed. However, on the same day that the Universal Declaration was approved the General Assembly passed Resolution 217 C (III) on the 'Fate of Minorities'. This stated that the General Assembly considered that the UN could not remain indifferent to the fate of minorities. Since it was difficult to adopt a uniform solution of this complex issue, however, the Commission on Human Rights and the Sub-commission were requested to make a thorough study of the problem of minorities in order that the UN could take effective protective measures. This was forty years ago. Three years after this decision Claude (1951, p. 311) could not refrain from suggesting that member states of the UN were 'more concerned to keep the problem of minority rights bottled up in an impotent and infrequently convening Sub-commission than to let it be brought out for genuine consideration'.

Three years after this, Max Sorensen (1956, p. 324), who had served as Chairman of the Sub-commission, argued that it

> Did not meet with the approval of the Commission on Human Rights. The reason was primarily that a number of countries were fundamentally opposed to the idea of protecting minority groups and claimed that their assimilation with the rest of the population was a necessity (Sorensen, 1956, p. 324).

Therefore, he goes on, the work of the Sub-commission was regarded with suspicion and distrust. Twenty years later, another student of the work of the UN in this area was equally critical. Lowe (1976, p. 40) argued that the Sub-commission was 'probably designed as a shelf upon which to place any minority questions that inconveniently came to the United Nation's attention'. She also points out that in general, the Commission on Human Rights delayed, ignored, or modified considerably draft reports by the Sub-commission, with the result that the Sub-commission had done very little to better the lot of minorities throughout the world (Lowe, 1976, p. 125). This was especially true of the period from the mid-50s to the late 60s when hardly any work of note was done at all on the issue of minority protection. In a more recent study Maher and Weissbrodt (1990, p. 312) have argued that the Sub-commission has found the issue of minority protection 'particularly problematic due to its complex and political nature' and has 'generally avoided the question altogether'.

Despite these various limitations the Sub-commission has undertaken some interesting work, though Humphrey (1968) is probably correct to state that this has been mainly in the area of the prevention of discrimination rather than the protection of minorities. Nevertheless, even in this area some valuable reports on the definition and protection of minorities have been produced.[4] The best recent example of this is the report being prepared by Asbjorn Eide on the protection of minorities. This is an investigation, authorised by the HRC in March 1990, into national experiences with minority rights. It is intended that this will aid the construction of models for peaceful solutions of minority issues. It is, therefore. less concerned with normative frameworks and is more interested in the practical experiences of states, especially the scope of minority rights and the institutions and procedures that have been created to deal with ethnic relations.[5] One of the assumptions of the exercise is that there is no single, universal remedy to this problem, but there is a belief in the 'paramount importance of non-discrimination'. The report has very little to say about the right of self-determination. In fact Eide is opposed to the idea of a unilateral right of self-determination and believes in the necessity of promoting the rights of minorities in a manner consistent with the unity and stability of states. A major weakness is that, despite the aims of the study, it seems that Eide will not be formally consulting minorities themselves about their experiences. The assessment will be based on reports by states already submitted to UN agencies on this issue and a special questionnaire that was sent to governments and non-governmental organizations. To date, there have been difficulties in getting a wide range of states to respond to this questionnaire. Because the Eide report will make no attempt to define the term minority, or to answer questions such as whether indigenous peoples or religious groups are to be included, it will be left to each state to provide its own implicit or explicit definition in the questionnaire returns.

The Sub-commission has created working groups to investigate issues such as indigenous peoples, slavery, states of emergency and prisoners and detainees. These also produce reports which can form the basis of international action against abuses. The Sub-commission has played a leading role in organising seminars on minority issues. These include a meeting in Ljubljana in 1965 on the multinational society and another in Ohrid in 1974 on the theme of the promotion and protection of the human rights of national, ethnic and other minorities.[6] Furthermore, debates during sessions of the Sub-commission do provide an opportunity to publicise human rights violations and to hear evidence from non-governmental organizations that can be the catalyst for international action. The Sub-commission also has a working group that is charged with examining allegations of human rights abuse that are received by the UN and bringing to the attention of the international organization any pattern of gross violation of human rights that such an examination reveals.

In the 1980s the Sub-commission requested a more active role for itself.[7] During its 1980 session, for example, there were calls for the Sub-commission to be given an investigatory and fact finding capability. During the 1988 session Van Boven complained about the 'pace at which standard-setting in respect of the protection of minorities was proceeding was not satisfactory and the alternative models and mechanisms must be developed' (UN Doc. E/CN.4/Sub. 2/1988/SR. 32). As a result of criticism such as this Claire Palley was asked to prepare a working paper on possible ways and means by which the Sub-commission might facilitate the peaceful and constructive resolution of situations involving racial, national, religious and linguistic minorities. The Secretary-General was also requested to provide all the assistance necessary for the completion of this task (UN Doc. E/CN.4/Sub. 2/1988/L.62). This paper led to the decision to begin the Eide report, which we have just discussed. It was also suggested that it should be able to bring situations of serious human rights abuse directly to the attention of the General Assembly instead of relying on the existing system of reporting to the Commission on Human Rights, which then reports to ECOSOC, which then reports to the General Assembly. At best this results in serious delays. So far, however, such calls have not been favourably received. On the contrary, at its forty-third session in 1987 the Commission on Human Rights stated that although it valued the work of the Sub-commission, it also pointed out that it should adopt an expert advisory role and should remain politically aloof (UN Doc. E/CN.4/Sub 2/1987/2 par. 9). In another sign of growing assertiveness the Sub-commission, for the first time, adopted a resolution on the situation in Tibet during its forty-third session in 1991. This was despite strong Chinese lobbying and the opposition of the Chinese member of the Sub-commission (Reinerson and Weissbrodt, 1992).

A tension is still evident between the HRC and the Sub-commission. During the Sub-commission's 1988 session, for example, there was talk by some about breaking links with what was regarded as a paternalistic and unresponsive HRC. The HRC is correct to accuse the Sub-commission of taking on too much work, of duplicating work done elsewhere at the UN, and of not allowing enough time for in-depth

217

discussions of issues. At its forty-third session in 1991, for example, the Sub-commission dealt with the following agenda items: the elimination of racial discrimination, the elimination of all forms of intolerance and discrimination based on religion or belief, violations of human rights and fundamental freedoms, human rights and disability, the protection of children and women, human rights and states of emergency, the right to a fair trial and the right of detainees, minority protection, discrimination against indigenous peoples and the New International Economic Order and the promotion of human rights. The Sub-commission also found the time, in a new development, to organise a joint session with the Committee for the Elimination of Discrimination. All of this took place between the 5th and 30th of August. However there is a feeling that the HRC is using these legitimate concerns about over-work as an excuse to limit the Sub-commission's role and to avoid difficult political issues.

At the forty-fifth session of the HRC, in early 1989, amid growing feeling that the Sub-commission was straying too far from its original mandate, the subordinate body was asked to 'restrict its requests to the Secretary-General...to requests relating to those studies which have received prior explicit approval from the Commission' (Resolution 1989/36, par. 7). It was also asked (paragraph 3) to give priority to topics 'on which standards are being prepared, in accordance with decisions taken by the Commission'. It was also proposed that the Sub-commission should not begin new studies until ones authorised previously had been completed. In a discussion about reform at the forty-fourth session of the Sub-commission in 1992, which was largely held in private without an opportunity for NGOs to have an input, it was agreed that the number of studies undertaken would be limited to thirteen at any one time and that there would be a three year time limit for completing these reports. At this forty-fourth session, for the first time, third world experts trying to attend the meetings had problems entering Switzerland (Kayal, Parker and Weissbrodt, 1993). A reminder, perhaps, of the increased significance of ethnic and racial issues in the 'new Europe'.

The Declaration on the Rights of Persons Belonging to National or Ethnic, Religious and Linguistic Minorities

In 1978 the Human Rights Commission established a working group to study a Yugoslavian draft on the rights of minorities. This body worked closely with the Sub-commission. It is interesting to note that one of the first acts of the HRC was to alter the Yugoslavian emphasis on minority groups *per se* to the rights of persons belonging to national, ethnic, religious and linguistic minorities. Even though this work began in 1978, it was not until 18 December 1992 that the Declaration on the Rights of Persons Belonging to National or Ethnic, Religious and Linguistic Minorities was adopted by General Assembly resolution 47/135.

The declaration has been viewed as an important step in the international protection of minority rights (Thornberry, 1993, p. 12). The preamble to the declaration acknowledges that the UN 'has an important role to play regarding the protection of minorities' and places the issue of minority rights a bit higher up the UN's agenda. General Assembly resolution 47/135, for example, has invited UN agencies and intergovernmental and non-governmental organizations to intensify efforts to disseminate information on the declaration; UN bodies have been invited to give due regard to the declaration within their mandates; and the Secretary-General has been requested to consider appropriate ways to effectively promote the declaration and to report to the General Assembly at its forty-eighth session on the implementation of resolution 47/135.

In several areas the 1992 declaration goes further in its promotion of minority rights than Article 27 of the 1966 Covenant on Civil and Political Rights. The declaration refers to 'national' minorities as well as the ethnic, religious and linguistic minorities mentioned in the Covenant. States are now expected to take positive actions to protect persons belonging to these minorities. Article 1 (1) proclaims that 'states shall protect the existence and the national or ethnic, cultural, religious and linguistic identity of minorities within their respective territories, and shall encourage conditions for the promotion of that identity'. Article 1(2) goes on to say that states 'shall adopt appropriate legislative and other measures to achieve those ends'. Article 4 develops the obligations of states as regards their minorities. It requires them to 'take measures where required' to ensure that persons belonging to minorities may exercise their human rights without discrimination. They also have to take measures to create favourable conditions to enable such persons to express their characteristics and to develop their culture, language, religion, traditions and customs where this would not violate national law or international standards. Wherever possible, states should take appropriate measures so that persons belonging to minorities have adequate opportunities to learn their mother tongue or to be instructed in their mother tongue. States are also expected. 'where appropriate' to take measures to encourage knowledge of the history, traditions, language and culture of minorities in the states territory and to consider appropriate measures so that persons belonging to minorities may participate fully in economic progress and development. Article 2 recognises the right of persons belonging to minorities to participate effectively in decisions which affect them and to establish and maintain free and peaceful contacts with other members of their group and with persons belonging to other minorities. This also includes the right to contacts across frontiers with citizens of other states to whom they are related by national or ethnic, religious or linguistic ties.

Yet despite these advances, several commentators have pointed out the limitations of the declaration (e.g. Pitts and Weissbrodt, 1993). There is no attempt to define what is to count as a minority, which makes it easier for states to evade implementation. Once again there is no attempt to enshrine group rights, since the declaration refers only to persons belonging to national or ethnic, religious and linguistic minorities. There is a lack of precision in phrases such as 'appropriate measures' or 'create favourable conditions' and many of the burdens placed on states are heavily qualified by conditions such as 'where required' or 'wherever possible'. No mechanism for monitoring implementation is created and the Declaration is not legally binding and carries only moral force. We have to wait to see what impact the declaration has on policy. As with other human rights instruments adoption by the UN is no guarantee of implementation in the real world.

National self-determination

The fourth area where the UN has been drawn into the issue of minority rights and minority protection is the question of the right of self-determination, which is a collective right. Although this idea has a long history, it was not until the present century that it became a widely accepted principle in international relations (see e.g. Neuberger, 1986; Ronen, 1979). Towards the end of the First World War it was an idea propounded by both Wilson in the US and Lenin in post-revolutionary Russia. Despite this, there was no mention of the principle in the League Covenant. But it was to be enshrined in the Atlantic Charter of 14 August 1941, and Articles 1 (2) and 55 of the UN Charter refer to the principle of the self-determination of peoples. They do not refer to national or ethnic groups, though one could reasonably argue that such groups do constitute a 'people'. After the influx of newly independent third world states into the UN in the late fifties and early sixties this principle of self-determination came to be regarded as a right. Thus the famous 1960 General Assembly Resolution 1514 (XV) on the Granting of Independence to Colonial Peoples states that 'all peoples have the right to self-determination' (Art. 2). However, the Declaration goes on to restrict the application of this right by stating that 'any attempt aimed at the partial or total disruption of the national unity and territorial integrity of a country is incompatible with the principles of the Charter'

(Art. 6). The two 1966 International Covenants on Human Rights also refer to the right of self- determination, but it is generally accepted that this right cannot be claimed by all minority groups.

Reference to this right at the UN is now found most frequently in resolutions on Palestine. There has been a plethora of General Assembly Resolutions since 1974 which proclaim the right of the Palestinian people to self-determination.[8] The UN has even established a Committee on the Exercise of the Inalienable Rights of the Palestinian People. In addition to resolutions on specific countries, nearly every year the General Assembly also overwhelmingly supports a Resolution on the 'Importance of the universal realisation of the right of peoples to self-determination and of the speedy granting of independence to colonial countries and peoples for the effective guarantee and observance of human rights'.[9]

The best known attempt by the UN to clarify the right to self-determination is the Cristescu report of 1981, which was the result of an initiative by Sub-Commission for the Prevention of Discrimination and the Protection of Minorities. It stated that in 1981 'it is generally recognised that the concept of self-determination entails legal rights and obligations and that a right of self-determination definitely exists' (UN Doc E/CN.4/Sub.2/404/Rev.1 par. 95). It does not apply to every ethnic group, however. Although this report has little to say about the rights of minorities and concentrates on the right of self-determination as applied to inter-state relations, it points out that the right of peoples to self-determination was written into international legal instruments not to encourage secession or irrendentism. In fact the report seems to indicate that a proper interpretation of the right would rule out any act likely to prejudice the national unity and territorial integrity of the state outside of the colonial context (par. 228). This study of self-determination has concluded that

> While there is no doubt that there is an international legal right of self-determination in the context of decolonization, the extension of that right to non-colonial situations was not clear as the Cold War came to an end Most scholars and governments had concluded that the principle of political unity prevailed over any expression of self-determination within a state. (Halperin, Scheffer and Small, 1992, p. 24)

Despite attempts to qualify such calls to peoples who are victims of colonialism and racism, support for the right seems have spread wider than the UN would have wanted. Mazrui (1969), for example, has argued that it is not accidental that the ethnic revival in the west occurred shortly after the attention given to the issue of self-determination during the post-war era of decolonization. It must also be said that a status of self-determination has been muddied by state practice. Moynihan (1993, chapters 2-3) has pointed out how attempts to implement the right to self-determination have given rise to ironies, contradictions and problems. It certainly seems to make hypocrites out of most governments. Serbia, for example, is supporting the right of self-determination of Serbs in Croatia and Bosnia and Hercegovina, but is denying it to Albanians in Kossovo. Turkey has invaded Cyprus in support of the right of the Turkish Cypriots to self-determination, but is fighting a war against the Kurds who are claiming a similar right. Israel's pursuit of its right to self-determination has involved a denial of the right of self-determination to the Palestinians. And so on.

Conclusions

This examination of the role of the UN in the area of minority protection and minority rights is by no means complete. In order to be comprehensive it would also have to consider the work of the UN specialised agencies. UNESCO, for example, in its 1960 Convention Against Discrimination in Education included Article 5 (1c) which stated that it was 'essential to recognise the right of members of national minorities to carry on their own educational activities, including the maintenance of schools and, depending on the education policy of each state, the use or the teaching of their own language'. It has also sponsored a series of meetings on the concept of peoples rights, with a special focus on cultural identity. The 1989 UN Convention on the Rights of the Child, drawing on the wording of Article 27 of the 1966 Covenant on Civil and Political Rights, states in Article 30 that a child belonging to an ethnic, religious or linguistic minority 'shall not be denied the right, in community with other members of his or her group, to enjoy his or her own culture, to profess and practise his or her own religion, or to use his or her own language'. The 1965 International Convention on the Elimination of All Forms of Racial Discrimination, which came into force in 1969, defines racial discrimination to include a distinction based on national or ethnic origin' (Hannum, 1990, p. 64). A comprehensive examination would also have to examine the work of the United Nations University, which has recently begun a project on ethnic minorities, and the work of the Committee on the Elimination of Racial Discrimination and the Human Rights Committee established by the International Covenant on Civil and Political Rights. This, however, is beyond the scope of the present study.

From the brief analysis offered in chapters six and seven it should be clear that the record of the UN in the area of ethnic issues is mixed.

On the one hand the UN Charter does not mention peace-keeping, peace-building, peace-making; nor does it refer to minority rights or minority protection. On the other hand, the Charter does give the UN a responsibility for ensuring international peace and security. This may effectively exclude many ethnic conflicts which are contained within the borders of individual states, but it would also include other ethnic conflicts that spill over into inter-state relations and are then included on the UN agenda. There is undoubtedly a reluctance to get involved in conflicts between ethnic groups and states within the international organization. Even those associated with peace-keeping operations will express unease at the prospect of having to conduct negotiations with parties who may be able to promise certain things, but then cannot deliver because they do not control their constituents. As a result the UN can become bogged down in a messy situation from which it may be difficult to extricate itself.

The UN has also undertaken a responsibility for ensuring human rights protection and the equal treatment of individuals on the basis of non-discrimination. Many ethnic conflicts involve the violation of these standards, which again means that the organization cannot remain indifferent to ethnic conflict. As the previous discussion has shown, it has also been unable to avoid completely discussions on minority rights and minority protection. So, since violent and protracted ethnic conflicts seem to be a permanent feature of the modern world the UN is unlikely to avoid involvement in ethnic issues altogether.

If such involvement remains true to its past record we would expect that the UN would have some success in managing conflict through peace-keeping, as long as such operations retain the support of the parties to a conflict. But although the UN may be able to keep the warring sides apart it is likely to be less successful in bringing them together again either to negotiate an end to their differences (peace-making) or to involve ordinary people in reconstruction and reconciliation projects that might create a momentum for peace (peace-building). The 1992 Declaration on the Rights of Persons Belonging to National or Ethnic, Religious or Linguistic Minorities may be as far as the UN is prepared to go in addressing minority rights.

It is sometimes said that the UN can be no more than a mirror of the world in which it operates. This is not strictly true. Rather, it would be more accurate to claim that the UN mirrors the state-centric view of the world held by its member governments. A part of this view is that a clear distinction can be drawn between the internal and external affairs of state and that the UN has no right to concern itself with the former. Van Boven has shown us how difficult it can be to attempt to break down the importance states place on maintaining this boundary. When he was Director of the UN Human Rights Division he attempted to intervene more robustly in what states regarded as their internal affairs. However, when he named in public several states with a poor human rights record he came into conflict with member governments and with senior UN figures, which included the Secretary-General. He was then removed from office. Another example was Iraq's membership of the Human Rights Commission at a time when it was gassing Kurds. Iraq was able to use this position to thwart attempts to investigate its human rights abuses (Middle East Watch, 1990, p. 121).

Yet as long as the majority of states continue to adopt such an attitude to outside involvement in how they treat (and mistreat) their populations it is unlikely that there will be much progress made in attempts to create an international system of ethnic group protection. This need not necessarily be the case. Governments might decide that outright opposition to such a move may not be the best course of action and it is in their enlightened self-interest to introduce a system that could reduce the incidents of ethnic violence. However, there is nothing to suggest that this will be the case. This may have a paradoxical impact though. For if member governments stop UN action to maintain peace in multi-ethnic states through a minority protection regime there may be even more outbreaks of inter-communal violence. As some of these outbreaks will threaten international peace and security and international standards to restrict arbitrary killing the UN will be forced to react with peace-keeping and peace-making initiatives.

So whatever road the UN takes it will not be able to avoid the problems associated with ethnic violence altogether. However any successful attempt to reduce ethnic violence will probably involve a mixture of all four strategies. Political initiatives may not be successful if groups are not adequately protected in law, and legal protection may be inadequate if violent conflict cannot be managed or resolved.

Notes

1. In the case of Austria see Treaty of St. Germain (1919) Articles 62-9; for Bulgaria, the Treaty of Neuilly (1919) Articles 49-57; for Hungary the Treaty of Trianon (1920) Articles 54-60; and for Turkey The Treaty of Lausanne (1923) Articles 37-45 (Sierpowski, 1990).
2. Support for the idea of minority protection in the immediate post-war world can be found in Colban (1944); Layburn (1947); Vishniak (1945); Wirth (1945).
3. The texts of these proposed amendments can be found in UN Doc. E/CN.4/Sub. 2/85.
4. Recent examples of such reports include one by Capotorti on the *Study of Persons Belonging to Ethnic, Religious and Linguistic Minorities* (UN Doc. E/CN. 4/ Sub. 2/384), and another by Deschene *Concerning the Definition of the Term Minority* (UN Doc. E/CN. 4/ Sub. 2/ 1985/3).
5. See Progress report submitted to Sub-commission in 1990, UN Doc.

E/CN.4/Sub.2/1992/37/Add.1 and 2.

6. See UN Doc. ST/TAO/HR/49.

7. For analyses of specific Sub-commission sessions see Hannum (1981a and 1981b); Gardeniers, Hannum and Kruger (1982); Garber and O'Connor (1985); Maher and Weissbrodt (1990) and Reinerson and Weissbrodt (1992); Kayal, Parker and Weissbrodt (1993).

8. For a collection of UN resolutions and documents on Palestine from 1980 to 1988 see UN Doc. A/AC. 183/L.2/Add 1-8.

9. See chapter two, note 1.

Conclusions

There is a quality even meaner than outright ugliness or disorder, and this meaner quality is the dishonest mask of a pretended order (Jerome Charyn).

Always, in every situation, it is possible to do something (Martin Buber).

Any realistic analysis of ethnic conflict and international relations has to start with the realisation that inter-ethnic conflicts are likely to be a continuing feature of politics both within and between sovereign states. Cultural groups are not going to be assimilated, as the nation-building optimists predicted. Nor are there any indications that nationalism is going to loosen its grip on the popular consciousness. Smith (1993, p. 8) has gone as far as to argue that 'for all the ills it has been used to inflict, the nation and nationalism remain the cornerstones of any new global order'. On the other hand, states are not going to readily accept secession by their ethnic minorities, nor are they going to dissolve themselves in a manner suggested by supporters of a Europe of the regions. To use Stanley Hoffmann's phrase, states are more obstinate than they are obsolete. As a consequence we are still going to have demands for recognition judged through the prism of *realpolitik* and power politics. This, alas, will mean that there will be no inherent fairness about which minorities gain international support and which do not. We will, therefore, have to live in an uneasy world characterised by the competing claims of state interest and nationalist demands, and as Mayall (1992, p. 35) has noted, 'however the political map is redrawn, the issue of minority rights will dominate the international agenda for the remainder of the century'.

However, the fact that states and nations are going to be with us for some time is no reason to accept either statist solutions suggested by supporters of the status quo or calls for separation by nationalist groups, that can, as in the case of the former Yugoslavia, lead to the horror of ethnic cleansing. Both of these simplistic solutions usually involve a turning away from dialogue in favour of a unilateral solution. Over-optimism, of course, has to be resisted, and the plural society theory developed by Furnival and Smith warns us against this. However it would be quite wrong to regard violent ethnic conflicts as tragedies of inevitability. For consociationalism does point out the possibility of stable and democratic multi-ethnic states and also shows the mechanisms by which such societies can be created and maintained.

It appears that any successful multi-ethnic state will have to be based on a recognition, not a rejection, of cultural diversity. Liberal individualism, Marxist class analysis and nationalist exclusiveness have all tended to work against such an accommodation. A lifting of ideological blinkers may then lead to changes in political/constitutional, economic and cultural spheres. We need to be sensitive to each case seen in its particular context, but we can also point out some general issues that have been examined in this study that might illuminate the debate about how best to respond to the problem of ethnic conflict.

The impact of the international political system and the need for effective conflict resolution strategies

It was pointed out in chapter two that the nature of the international political system tends to load the dice against the successful workings of multi-ethnic societies. This is because consociational based solutions believe that certain institutional devices, based on enlightened self-interest, can be created to regulate and reduce ethnic tensions. These devices include the grand coalition, the mutual veto, proportional representation and regional autonomy. Unfortunately, consociationalism has to be worked for in an international environment which involves a decentralised system of power distribution and has the idea of national self-determination as one of its key legitimising principles. The former undermines the consociational approach by encouraging an exaggerated fear of minorities and by assuring that there will be an ever present risk of external intervention by other states. The latter, a manifestation of nationalist sentiment, makes it harder to reach a mutual accommodation within multi-ethnic states because ethnic groups are encouraged to become nations and to claim their own state and because dominant groups cannot recognise the claims of other cultures without undermining the legitimacy of their 'nation state'.

The international political system can therefore be a threat to stable and democratic multi-ethnic states, but it can also be a resource in the search for conflict resolution. In chapters three, four and five we examined the structure of ethnic conflict and identified the processes involved in conflict escalation and conflict reduction. We saw there that third party involvement is often a vital component of conflict reduction strategies, but only under certain circumstances. The two most important conditions are that it promotes the de-internationalization of a conflict so that indigenous solutions can emerge and that it contributes to one or more of our three conflict resolution strategies identified as peace-keeping, peace-making and peace-building. Under these conditions external involvement might feed constructive not destructive processes in intercommunal interaction.

There is something of a paradox in stating that third parties can be brought into a conflict in order to insulate a multi-ethnic state from the interstate system. However, this is often what conflict management through UN involvement entails. An important aim of the UN forces in Cyprus and Lebanon is to stop these conflicts escalating to the point where outside powers become involved. In this function peace-keeping forces have had only partial success. UNFICYP did not stop the Turkish invasion of Cyprus in 1974, and UNIFIL did not stop the Israeli invasion of Lebanon in 1982.

In chapter six we saw that UN peace-keeping forces can do valuable work, and that there appears to be no viable alternative at present to such a force, given the failures of the OAU in Chad, the IPKF in Sri Lanka and the MNF in Beirut. The problem with such UN involvements, however, is that the valuable peace-keeping work is not matched by progress in the peace-making and peace-building areas. Indeed, the UN has traditionally ignored the peace-building dimension almost entirely. Therefore, the periods of relative calm provided by the peace-keepers is often not used to establish a meaningful dialogue between the warring parties or to undertake initiatives to change the attitudes and socio-economic circumstances of the people involved. It has therefore been suggested that the work of the UN in these two areas needs to be examined carefully and that more attention could also be given to how to improve peace-keeping capabilities. Some suggestions were offered. UN forces could be better trained for their unique role and they should be better financed. In the area of peace-making a greater UN interest in contemporary conflict theory and a willingness to examine the deficiencies of traditional diplomatic methods might be fruitful. The establishment of a conflict resolution centre at the UN might also improve efforts to mediate in ethnic conflicts. Finally, much more work could be done in the peace-building area. This would involve work in the areas of reconciliation, the pursuit of superordinate goals (e.g. the Nicosia Master Plan Project), economic development, confidence building and education for mutual understanding.

In addition, the UN should look again at its attitude to the international protection of minorities, for an international regime to protect ethnic groups might make a significant contribution to the prevention of violent intercommunal conflict. The UN, as pointed out in chapter seven, has not been able to avoid involvement in this area entirely, despite what appear to some to be vigorous efforts not to look at group rights. The UN has enacted the Genocide Convention of 1948. It has established a Sub-commission for the Prevention of Discrimination and the Protection of Minorities, and in 1992 the Declaration on the Rights of Persons Belonging to National, or Ethnic, Religious and Linguistic Minorities was adopted. The foundation therefore exists to build a regime to protect minorities.

However, Kuper (1985) is right to point out that the record of the organization in responding to genocide has been quite dismal and the Sub-Commission has been effectively prevented by the Human Rights Commission from taking an active role in the area of minority rights. The right of self-determination has been heavily qualified in what can seem a very unreasonable way when viewed from the perspective of oppressed ethnic groups. All of these weaknesses seem to be based on a short sighted approach however, even if one acknowledges the limitations on UN action in these areas (the pro-state bias and the prohibition against intervention in the internal affairs of member states set out in Article 2(7) of the Charter). For by turning away from attempts to prevent the outbreaks of violent ethnic conflict, the UN only makes it more likely that it will become involved in the much more dangerous and probably more costly task of ethnic conflict resolution.

The Prevention of Ethnic Conflict

The prevention of ethnic conflict will not be an easy task. For it seems to demand that there be a modification of statist and nationalist approaches to ethnic issues in a world that is still dominated by an uneasy relationship between states and nations. If real progress is to be made then the international community in general, and the UN in particular, needs to address at least three areas: the de-nationalization

230

of the state, the creation of a stable inter-state environment and appropriate economic development strategies.

(a) De-nationalizing the state.

It is vital that the state should not be made the instrument of a dominant cultural group, but promotes tolerance and diversity. What is needed is a civil society to counter ethno-nationalist statism; but one that is sensitive to ethnic difference. The aim should not be to replace a system of individual human rights with a system of group rights, but to find a way of combining both that does not do severe damage to either. Much of the classic liberal literature on the civil society is not much help here since it does not address the issue of cultural pluralism but is built around the individual's relationship with the state. Perhaps what we really need is thinking about how to establish what Martin Buber called a 'community of communities'. Here the UN, which is in a unique position to establish new international norms, could play a significant role in helping to promote both the rights of minorities and new international mechanisms for the protection of minorities. There already exists a greater willingness to address such issues, as the recent adoption by the General Assembly of the Declaration of the Rights of Persons Belonging to National or Ethnic, Religious or Linguistic Minorities indicates.

Successful multi-ethnic states respect the right of open cultural expression. This will often involve a degree of cultural autonomy for schools and religious institutions, the recognition of minority languages as official languages and the use of these languages in the media, official transactions and the courts. The 1967 Welsh Language Act gives the Welsh language equal status with English in the administration of the province. The Welsh also have their own television channel and bilingual road signs are now the norm. Canada created a Minister of State for Multiculturalism in 1971, and a Consultative Council for multiculturalism in 1973. In 1971 the state also adopted the policy of bilingualism and biculturalism (which hostile cynics with separatist leanings branded the bye and bye strategy). The management of the ethnic conflict in Corsica has been more successful since the adoption by the French government of the 1982 Special Statute which devolved powers over local taxation, economic planning, education and culture to a local executive and regional assembly. The Nicaraguan Constitution of 1987 also recognised that the Indian communities had the right to preserve and develop their own identities (Prigent, 1990).

Hannum (1990, p. 473) argues that there is a new principle in international law emerging which will 'support creative attempts to deal with conflicts over minority and majority rights before they escalate into civil wars and demands for secession'. This is the right to 'autonomy or internal self-determination', which allows for a flexible and pragmatic response to ethnic issues. The autonomy solution has also been championed by Clare Palley, who argues that it is one of the key factors in controlling ethnic conflict and is especially good at stemming separatist tendencies (Minority Rights Group, 1986, p. 3). This view receives support from Connor (1990, p. 27), who points out that most members of national minorities are prepared to accept a solution less than total separation if they are allowed an acceptable degree of autonomy. Decentralization was a key feature of the 1972 settlement which brought ten years of relative peace to the Sudan (Mitchell, 1989). It has been a major success in Spain, where it contributed to political stability in the post-Franco transition, especially in Catalonia and the Basque country.

Walzer (1982, pp. 4-5) has stated that 'whether composite states can survive as federations is by no means certain, but it is unlikely that they can survive in any other way'. Certainly Switzerland (with 26 cantons), Canada, Austria and Belgium are all states with a considerable degree of political decentralization and where there is a combination of 'self-rule and shared rule' (Elazar, 1984). All are also liberal-democratic states. This is important, especially when we note how federalism in more authoritarian states such as the former USSR, the former Yugoslavia and the former Czechoslovakia, did not stop the build of serious latent conflict that led eventually to political disintegration.

Burton (1984, ch. 9) has claimed that successful conflict resolution may depend on the establishment of a 'zonal functional system', where there are geographically separated groups linked in matters of common concern by functional agencies. The geographic separation is important because it provides a sense of security; allows for the creation of political institutions on a regional basis that will be more sensitive to cultural difference; and gives different groups the space to express their own distinctiveness. Lijphart (1977, pp. 41-47) has also promoted this approach with his idea of segmented autonomy. He points out that this could take both a territorial and a non-territorial form, since not all cultural minorities are concentrated in a specific region. The non-territorial form can draw on the experience of the Ottoman empire's *millet* system and the writings of the Austro-Marxists Renner and Bauer (Ra'anan et al., 1991). The basis of such a system would be an autonomous organization, such as a communal council or chamber, which could unite a dispersed community to decide policy in areas such as education, religion or cultural affairs.

One should also note the greater interest in minority issues in the 'new' Europe, where there have been significant developments since the end of the cold war, especially through the Conference on Security and Cooperation in Europe (CSCE). Beginning with a meeting in Vienna in January 1989, this organization has quickly developed several significant declarations relating to minorities. The Copenhagen (1990) and Moscow (1991) Human Dimension conferences both addressed this issue, as did a meeting on minorities held in Geneva in July 1991 (Beddard and Hill, 1992; Mastny, 1992). The Charter of Paris for a New Europe (1990), signed by the 34 participating states, affirms that 'friendly relations among our peoples,as well as peace, justice, stability and democracy, require that the ethnic, cultural, linguistic and religious identity of national minorities be protected and conditions for the promotion of that identity be created'. [1] The CSCE has also developed a monitoring capability, and has dispatched observers to various ethnic trouble spots in recent years to examine human rights situations. Places visited include Estonia, Moldova, Croatia and Bosnia and Hercegovina (see, for example, Bloed, 1993). Resident missions have been established places such as Georgia, Estonia, Kossovo, Vojvodina, Moldova and Macedonia. These missions can offer advice, gather information and facilitate dialogue (Mastny, 1992).

The other main initiative of the CSCE is the creation of the High Commissioner on National Minorities, which began operating in January 1993 following the appointment of the Dutchman Max van der Stoel, who is answerable to the CSCE's Committee of Senior Officials.[2] He also has a monitoring role and it is intended that one of his key functions should be to provide early warning of ethnic tensions. His work is clearly focused on central and eastern Europe and official business has taken him to the Baltic states, Albania, Rumania, Macedonia and Slovakia. Some concern has been expressed about the High Commissioner's lack of resources. For example, he only has a staff of four.

To date, advances in Europe have not been matched in other regions. The Organization of African Unity seems opposed to the concept of minority rights in general, and the right of national self-determination in particular. For as Mayall (1983, p. 77) has noted, 'it is an organization which claims to support the self-determination of all African peoples, but which in practice is committed to the existing state order'. This commitment has been challenged occasionally. Tanzania, Zambia, Ivory Coast and Gabon, for example, supported the Biafran right to secede from Nigeria. But even in this case most African states supported the 1967 Kinshasa Declaration which reaffirmed the adherence of the OAU to the territorial integrity of its members, and stated that Biafra was an internal problem for Nigeria. Legum (1983, p. 11) has also noted that 'in its approach to the Eritrean question, the OAU has rigidly upheld its Charter which opposes all separatist and secessionist movements. Nor does the African Charter on Human and Peoples' Rights, adopted in Banjul at a meeting of the OAU in 1981, have much to say about minorities. Thornberry (1991, p. 20) points out that the term peoples is left undefined, and there is no indication that peoples 'means anything more than the whole peoples of the States, and not ethnic or other groups'.

Stavenhagen (1990) has examined the Latin American approach to ethnic questions and points out that the 'no minorities homogeneity principle' has guided legal approaches to minority issues. So, the 1948 American Declaration of the Rights and Duties of Man forbids discrimination but contains no reference to minorities. The same is true of the 1969 American Convention on Human Rights. However, Stavenhagen does note that, as far as indigenous Indian peoples are concerned, there has been some recognition of their need for special status.

In the third world as the strong nationalist passions aroused by independence subside and as the costs of continuing ethnic violence are assessed, it might be that a re-evaluation will take place of the rigid adherence to boundaries that were bequeathed by colonial powers, particularly as the old 'inheritance elite' disappear from the political stage. This could result in an international climate more amenable to non-statist solutions that are based on a greater sensitivity about the ethnic factor in politics. This, of course, is highly speculative.

Humanitarian intervention to stop gross violations of human rights is another area where the international community has developed an interest in ethnic conflict, and where there may be emerging some international legal limitations to state sovereignty. Two cases, in particular, have revealed the growing willingness to intervene in the internal affairs of states in order to protect the victims of armed conflict. These are the protection offered to the Kurds and the 'marsh Arabs' in Iraq and the Moslems in Bosnia and Hercegovina. In both states the international community has created air-exclusion zones, designed to reduce the vulnerability of people under threat of attack. In the Iraqi part of Kurdistan thousands of coalition troops were deployed in operation Provide Comfort as a symbol of the international commitment to protect Kurds and to assist the delivery of relief supplies. In Bosnia and Hercegovina the UN has also established 'safe areas' in an attempt to limit Serbian attacks on Moslem areas. The attempt to implement a safe-havens policy in Iraq, first suggested by President Ozal of Turkey, came to nothing because of doubts about its legality and because of opposition from China and the USSR (Gunter, 1993). All of these actions have been given international legitimacy by the UN Security Council.

The problem with such humanitarian interventions are already clear from an analysis of the Bosnian and Kurdish examples. They do not offer a long term solution to the problem since they focus on the symptoms of conflict rather than its causes; and sometimes humanitarian interventions could escalate the violence. Nor can humanitarian intervention produce political settlements. Also, international opinion is rather fickle, and as the 'CNN factor' moves global attention to other issues it may be that the commitment of governments to protect specific groups will wane and indifference will undermine humanitarian missions. Furthermore, governments, anxious to protect their own sovereignty, may be reluctant to accept a breach of the non-intervention principle in all but the most exceptional cases. Intervention in Iraq was made easier because it had become an international pariah as a result of its invasion of Kuwait, whilst Bosnia was a new state born amidst the confusion of the break-up of Yugoslavia. Both were, therefore, exceptional cases. A final problem is that there are limits to what a policy of safe areas and air exclusion zones can provide to populations in danger. In Bosnia the safe havens have been violated by Serbian forces on many occasions and in Iraq international concern has not prevented an economic embargo imposed on Kurdistan by Baghdad or the draining of the marshlands where the southern Shi'ites live.

Another controversial area is the right of self-determination. The state-centric response of the international community to this idea has been criticised by many commentators, who question the way the right has been restricted to colonial or racist situations. There have even been calls for the UN to establish a Commission on Self-Determination to investigate the validity of self-determination claims (e.g. International Alert, 1993a, 1993b).

Christie (1992) has argued that we need to adopt a more flexible approach to separation in the new international system. Another recent study has attempted to set out more precise guidelines to determine how states (especially the US) might judge self-determination claims. Halperin, Scheffer and Small (1990) believe that five factors, in particular, are crucial: the conduct of the ruling group, the choice of the people, the conduct of the self-determination movement, the potential for violent consequences and the historical background (is there, for example, a history of independence for the group seeking self-determination?). However, resistance to the right of secession remains strong, and Mayall (1991) reminds us that it would be dangerous to believe in an emerging norm supportive of unilateral self-determination claims from an analysis of what has happened in the Baltic states and a few other recent examples.

(b) A stable inter-state environment.

The second issue that conflict prevention has to address is the inter-state dimension of many ethnic conflicts. Perhaps the only truly effective way to do this is to settle the constitutional status, or what Alcock has called the territorial destiny, of disputed regions. This is, clearly, not an easy task. Nevertheless, we can learn a great deal about this approach from the study of the South Tyrol and the Aland Islands. In both cases local minorities have foregone the option of secession to join with their co-nationals (Austria and Sweden) in return for a large degree of autonomy which allows them to run their own affairs (Isaksson and Johansson, 1988; Minority Rights Group 1986; Modeen, 1991). Also, the general international environment today is not as threatening as it was during the cold war, and the general relaxation in superpower politics undoubtedly contributed to the peace process in Israel, South Africa, Angola and Ethiopia.

Even in central and eastern Europe and the former Soviet Union, where the euphoric passions of independence or regional decentralization may mean that a heightened nationalist sentiment will take some time to play itself out, the international environment is probably more supportive of inter-ethnic accommodation than at any other time in the twentieth century. One of the interesting features of Europe of the 1990s, as opposed to Europe of the 1930s, is that the present interstate system in Europe seems to be more supportive of a workable compromise. Kuper (1969, p. 486) has noted that 'the peaceful resolution of internal conflict may very well be contingent on the reduction of international tensions and the move toward a world community of nations'. We are a long way from this on a global scale. In Europe, however, we may be moving towards a closer European community, and at the very least it cannot be denied that international tensions have been reduced within the continent. Given the formal end of the cold war, moves towards liberalization in eastern Europe, the signing of significant arms control treaties, a growing economic interdependence, talk of an expanded European Community and a Council of Europe to include Eastern European States, and the reduction of perceived external threats, it might be that a successful accommodation of ethnic differences will be possible without widespread violence and repression.

(c) Economic development appropriate for multi-ethnic states.

A third focus for conflict prevention should be action to address the economic inequalities that seem to be a factor in many violent ethnic conflicts. The economic dimension is important because a multi-ethnic

236

state that is characterised by an uneven distribution of wealth is a state where ethnic antagonisms are likely to grow. Economic well being also contributes to a sense of security, and gives ethnic minorities a stake in the system. Horowitz (1985) has called this the distributive approach to ethnic conflict resolution, as opposed to structural approaches based on creating a political framework. He points out that such an approach can include preferential policies aimed at raising certain groups to a position of equality through investment, employment practices, access to education and land distribution. However, he also points out that this can be a high risk strategy because it can alienate those groups who are doing well out of the status quo and do not want to see a redistribution of wealth and opportunity.

Especially important here is Stavenhagen's idea of 'ethno-development'. This involves 'redefining the nature of nation-building and enriching the complex, multicultural fabric of many modern states, by recognising the legitimate aspirations of the culturally distinct ethnies that make up the national whole' (Stavenhagen, 1990, p. 90-91). If adopted this approach would require international financial institutions such as the World Bank to link their development strategies to respect for cultural diversity. It is interesting to observe that Article 4 (5) of the 1992 Declaration on the Rights of Persons Belonging to National or Ethnic, Religious and Linguistic Minorities says that states 'should consider appropriate measures so that persons belonging to minorities may participate fully in the economic progress and development in their country'. Article 5 (2) also states that 'programmes of cooperation and assistance among States should be planned and implemented with due regard for the legitimate interests of persons belonging to minorities'. Appropriate development strategies may also involve giving minority regions control over natural resources and land. As we noted in chapter four, South Africa and Palestine will provide two crucial tests of the link between development and peace.

Conclusions

Walzer (1982, p. 27) is right to insist that 'ethnic citizens can be remarkably loyal to a state that protects and fosters private communal life, if that is seen to be equitably done'. Horowitz (1985) is also correct to point out that it is possible to make moderation pay for all parties if the right incentives can be found. All of this, however, will mean a move away from the concept of the *nation*-state in favour of the separation of the nation and the state and an effort to live with cultural pluralism (Claude, 1969, p. 86). This will not, of course, be easy, but a combination of the de-nationalization and democratization of the state, the de-internationalization of ethnic conflict and ethnodevelopment do seem to offer the best hope for the creation of peaceful and democratic multi-ethnic societies, and therefore a more stable and just international system. They need to be supplemented by effective peace-keeping and peace-making strategies, which seem lacking at the moment. Much more attention should also be given to grass-roots peace-building work by non-governmental agencies and UN specialised agencies. A major worry, however, is that the present international system has a tendency to work against these developments. It seems to lack the sturctures to prevent costly and destructive ethnic conflict, and is poorly equipped to respond positively to serious ethnic violence when it does break out. The heartbreaking consequences of these failures are all to obvious today.

Notes

1. The full text of the Charter of Paris can be found in Mastny (1992 p. 219f) or *NATO Today*, December 1990.
2. A partial bibliography of HCNM-related materials is available from the office of the High Commissioner in the Hague.

Bibliography

Adelphi Papers 82 and 83 (1971), *Civil Violence and the International System*, International Institute of Strategic Studies: London.

Agnew, J. (1989), 'Beyond reason: Spatial and temporal sources of ethnic conflicts' in Kriesberg, L., Northrup, T.A. and Thorson, S.J., eds, *Intractable Conflicts and Their Transformation*, Syracuse University Press: Syracuse.

Alam, G.M.S. (1982), 'Peace-keeping without conflict resolution: the Kashmir dispute' , *Fletcher Forum*, vol. 8, no. 1.

Alcock, A. (1986), Contributions on South Tyrol and Asland Islands to Minority Rights Group, *Coexistence in Some Plural European Societies*, Minority Rights Group: London.

Alger, C. (1984),'Effective Participation in Western Society: Some Implications of the Columbus Study' in Banks, M., ed, *Conflict in World Society*, Wheatsheaf: Brighton.

Alger, C. (1991), 'Creating a global vision for peace movements' in Boulding, E., Brigagao, C. and Clements, K., eds, *Peace, Culture and Society*, Westview: Boulder.

Ali, S. Husin (1991), 'Development, social stratifications and ethnic relations' in Samarsinghe, S.W.R. de A. and Coughlan, R., eds, *The Economic Dimensions of Ethnic Conflict*, Pinter: London.

Ali, R. and Lifschultz, L. (1993), *Why Bosnia*, Pamphleteer's Press: Stony Creek, CT.

Allen, I.L. (1983), *The Language of Ethnic Conflict,* Columbia University Press: New York.

Allport, G. W. (1954), *The Nature of Prejudice*, Beacon Press: New York.

Amir, Y., Ben-Ari, R. and Bizman, A. (1986), 'Prospects of Intergroup Relations in an Intense Conflict Situation: Jews and Arabs in Israel' in Paranjpe, A.C., ed, *Ethnic Identities and Prejudices: Perspectives From the Third World*, E.J. Brill: Leiden.

Amnesty International (1984), *Sri Lanka: Current Human Rights Concerns and Evidence of Extra-Judicial Killings by the Security Forces*, Amnesty International: London.

Amnesty International (1989), *Turkey: Brutal and Systematic Abuse of Human Rights*, Amnesty International: London.

Amnesty International (1992), *Annual Report 1990*, Amnesty International: London.

Anderson, B. (1983), *Imagined Communities*, Verso: London.

Anderson, J. (1973), *The Anderson Papers*, Random House: New York.

Apter, D. (1990), 'A view from the Bogside' in Giliomee, H. and Gagiano, J., eds, *The Elusive Search for Peace*, Oxford U.P: Cape Town.

Arasaratnam, S. (1987), 'Sinhala-Tamil Relations in Modern Sri Lanka' in Boucher, J., Landis, D. and Clarke, K.A., eds, *Ethnic Conflict: International Perspectives*, Sage: London.

Arendt, H. (1973), *On Revolution*, Penguin: Harmondsworth.

Arthur, P. (1990), 'Negotiating the Northern Ireland problem: track one or track two diplomacy?', *Government and Opposition*, vol. 25, no. 4.

Arthur, P. and Jeffery, K. (1988), *Northern Ireland Since 1968*, Blackwell: London.

Assefa, H. (1987), *Mediation of Civil War: Approaches and Strategies-The Sudan Conflict*, Westview: Boulder.

Avruch, K., Black, P. and Scimeca, J. (1991), eds, *Conflict Resolution: Cross-Cultural Perspectives*, Greenwood: Westport.

Azar, E.E. and Burton, J.W. (1986), eds, *International Conflict Resolution*, Wheatsheaf: Brighton.

Azar, E.E. and Moon, C.I. (1986), 'Managing protracted social conflicts in the third world', *Millenium*, vol. 15, no. 3.

Azar, E.E. and Marlin, R.E. (1987), 'The Costs of Protracted Social Conflict in the Middle East: The Case of Lebanon' in Ben-Dor, G. and Dewitt, D.B., eds, *Conflict Management in the Middle East*, Lexington Books: Lexington.

Azar. E.E. (1990), *The Management of Protracted Social Conflict,* Dartmouth: Aldershot.

Azcarate, P. de (1945), *The League of Nations and National Minorities,*

240

Carnegie Endowment for International Peace: Washington. Translated by E.E. Brooke.

Bailey, S. (1982), 'The UN and the termination of armed conflict-1946-64', *International Affairs* (London), vol. 58, no. 3

Ball, G. (1982), *The Past has Another Pattern*, W.W. Norton: New York.

Banac, I (1993), 'Separating history from myth: an interview with Ivo Banac, in R. Ali and L. Lifschultz, eds, *Why Bosnia*, Pamphleteer's Press: Stony Creek CT.

Banks, M. (1984), ed, *Conflict in World Society*, Wheatsheaf: Brighton.

Banton, M. (1977), *The Idea of Race*, Tavistock: London.

Banton, M. (1986), 'Ethnic Bargaining' in Thompson, D.L. and Ronen, D., eds, *Ethnicity, Politics and Development*, Lynne Rienner: Boulder.

Barth, F. (1969), ed, *Ethnic Groups and Boundaries*, Allen and Unwin: London.

Beddard, R. and Hill, D.M. (1992), eds, *Emerging Rights in the New Europe*, Southampton Studies in International Policy in association with Macmillan: University of Southampton.

Beitz, C.R. (1979), *Political Theory and International Relations*, Princeton University Press: Princeton.

Belfrage, S. (1988), *The Crack: A Belfast Year*, Deutsch: London.

Bell, D. (1990), *Acts of Union: Youth Culture and Sectarianism in Northern Ireland*, Macmillan: Basingstoke.

Bell, D. (1991), 'Cultural studies in Ireland and the postmodernist debate', *Irish Journal of Sociology*, vol. 1 no. 1.

Bell, W. and Freeman, W.F. (1974), eds, *Ethnicity and Nation Building*, Sage: Beverley Hills.

Ben-Ari, R. and Amir, Y. (1986), 'Contact between Arab and Jewish Youth in Israel' in Hewstone, M. and Brown, R., eds, *Contact and Conflict in Intergroup Encounters*, Blackwell: Oxford.

Bercovitch, J. and Rubin, J.Z. (1991), eds, *Mediation in International Relations*, Macmillan: Basingstoke.

Berg, R. and Rotfeld, A.D. (1986), *Building Security in Europe: Confidence Building Measures and the CSCE*, Westview: Boulder.

Bertelsen, J.S. (1977), *Non-State Actors in International Politics*, Praeger: New York.

Bloed, A. (1993), 'The CSCE and the protection of minorities' in A. Phillips and A. Rosas, eds, *The United Nations Minority Rights Declaration*, Abo Akademi: Abo.

Boulding, E. (1990), *Building a Global Civic Culture*, Syracuse University Press: Syracuse.

Boutros-Ghali, B. (1992), *An Agenda for Peace: Preventive Diplomacy, Peacemaking and Peacekeeping*, UN: New York.

Boyce, G. (1991), 'Northern Ireland: a place apart' in Hughes, E., ed, *Culture and Politics in Northern Ireland*, Open University Press: Milton Keynes.

Brass, P. (1985), 'Ethnic Groups and the State' in Brass, P., ed, *Ethnic Groups and the State*, Barnes and Noble, Tottawa: NJ.

Buber, M. (1992), *On Intersubjectivity and Cultural Creativity*, ed. with introduction by S.N. Eisenstadt, University Press of Chicago: Chicago.

Buckheit, L.C. (1978), *Secession: The Legitimacy of Self-Determination*, Yale University Press: New Haven.

Budiardjo, C. and Liong, L.S. (1984), *The War Against East Timor*, Zed Press: London.

Bull, H. (1977), *The Anarchical Society*, Macmillan: London.

Bull, H. (1984), ed, *Intervention in World Politics*, Clarendon: Oxford.

Bulletin of Peace Proposals, vol. 18, no. 4. Special issue on Ethnic Conflict and Human Rights.

Burton, F. (1978), *The Politics of Legitimacy*, Routledge and Kegan Paul: London.

Burton, J.W. (1979), *Deviance, Terrorism and War*, M. Robertson: Oxford.

Burton, J.W. (1982), *Dear Survivors*, Pinter: London.

Burton, J.W. (1983), 'The individual as a unit of explanation in International Relations, *International Studies Newsletter*, vol. 10, no. 2.

Burton, J.W. (1984), *Global Conflict*, Wheatsheaf: Brighton.

Burton, J.W. (1987), *Resolving Deep Rooted Conflict*, University Press of America: Lanham.

Burton, J.W. (1988), 'Conflict Resolution' in R.A. Coate and J.A. Rosati, eds, *The Power of Human Needs in World Society*, Lynne Rienner: Boulder.

Burton, J.W. (1990), *Conflict: Resolution and Provention*, Macmillan: Basingstoke.

Butterfield, H. (1951), *History and Human Relations*, Collins: London.

Byers, R.B., Larrabe, F.S. and Lynch, A. (1987), *Confidence Building and International Security*, Institute for East-West Security: New York.

Cairns, E. (1987), *Caught in Crossfire*, Appletree Press: Belfast.

Cairns, E. and Wilson, R. (1991), 'Psychological coping and political violence', in Alexander, Y. and O'Day, A., eds, *The Irish Terrorism Experience*, Dartmouth: Aldershot.

Calderwood, H.B. (1931), 'The protection of minorities by the League of Nations', *Geneva Special Studies*, vol. 2, no. 9.

Calliess, J. and Merkel, C. (1993), eds, *Peaceful Settlement of Conflict: A Task for Civil Society*, Loccumer Protokolle 7/93, Evangelische

Akademie: Loccum.

Calvocoressi, P. (1981), 'The future of international conflict', *International Relations*, vol. 7, no. 2.

Campaign for Social Democracy (1989), 'Sri Lanka: the choice of two terrors', *Race and Class*, vol. 30, no. 3.

Carment, D.B. (1993),'The international dimensions of ethnic conflict: concepts, indicators and theory', *Journal of Peace Research*, vol. 30, no. 2.

Carter Centre (1993), *Resolving Intra-National Conflicts: A Strengthened Role for Intergovernmental Organizations*, Carter Centre of Emory University: Atlanta.

Ceadal, M. (1987), *Thinking About Peace and War*, Oxford University Press: Oxford.

Chaliand, G. (1980), ed, *People Without a Country: The Kurds in Kurdistan*, Zed Press: London.

Chaudhuri, B. (1991), 'Ethnic conflict in the Chittagong Hill Tracts' in Samarsinghe, S.W.R. de A. and Coughlan, R., eds, *The Economic Dimensions of Ethnic Conflict*, Pinter: London.

Chesterton, G.K. (undated), *What I Saw in America*, Hodder and Stoughton: London.

Childe, J. (1980), 'Peacekeeping and the inter-American system', *Military Review* , vol. 60, no. 10.

Chomsky, N. (1992), *Deterring Democracy*, Verso: London.

Christie, C.J. (1992), 'Partition, separation and national identity: A reassessment', *Political Quarterly*, vol. 63 no. 1.

Christision, K.M. (1987), 'Myths about Palestinians', *Foreign Policy*, vol. 87, no. 66.

Church, C.H. (1989), 'Behind the consociational screen: politics in contemporary Switzerland', *West European Politics*, vol. 12, no. 2.

Clammer, J. (1986), 'Ethnicity and the Classification of Social Differences in Plural Societies' in Paranjpe, A.C., ed, *Ethnic Identities and Prejudice: Perspectives from the Third World,* E. Brill: Leiden.

Claude, I.L. (1951), 'The nature and status of the Sub-commission on the Prevention of Discrimination and the Protection of Minorities', *International Organisation*, vol. 5, no. 2.

Claude, I.L. (1955), *National Minorities: An International Problem,* Harvard University Press: Cambridge Mass.

Claude, I.L. (1969), *National Minorities: An International Problem,* Greenwood: Westport. Reprint of 1955 edition.

Claude, I.L. (1971), *Swords Into Plowshares*, 4th ed, Random House: New York.

Clausewitz, C. von (1968), *On War*, Penguin: Harmondsworth. Edited by A. Rapaport.

Cobban, H. (1985), *The Making of Modern Lebanon*, Hutchinson: London.

Cohen, P. (1968), *Modern Social Theory*, Heinemann: London.

Colban, E.(1944), 'The minorities problem',*Norseman*, vol.2, no. 5.

Cole, S. (1990), 'Cultural technological futures', *Alternatives*, vol. XV, no. 4.

Condor, S. and Brown, R. (1988), 'Psychological processes in intergroup conflict' in Stroebe, W. et al., eds, *The Social Psychology of Intergroup Conflict*, Springer-Verlag: London.

Connor, W. (1972), 'Nation-building or nation destroying', *World Politics,* vol. 24, no. 3.

Connor, W. (1978), 'A nation is a nation, is a state, is an ethnic group is a ...', *Ethnic and Racial Studies*, vol. 1, no. 4.

Connor, W. (1980), 'Ethno-political Change and Government Responses' in Sugar, P.E., ed., *Ethnic Diversity and Conflict in Eastern Europe*, ABC-Clio: Santa Barbara.

Connor, W. (1990), 'Ethno-nationalism and political instability: An overview' in H. Giliomee, H. and Gagiano, J. eds, *The Elusive Search for Peace*, Oxford University Press: Cape Town.

Conroy, M. (1988), *War as a Way of Life: A Belfast Diary*, Heinemann: London.

Coser, L. (1956), *The Functions of Social Conflict*, Routledge: London.

Coulon, C. (1978), 'French political science and regional diversity: A strategy of silence', *Ethnic and Racial Studies*, vol. 1, no. 1.

Crick, B. (1964), *In Defence of Politics*, Penguin: Harmondsworth.

Cross, M. (1977), 'On Conflict, Race Relations, and the Theory of the Plural Society' in Stone, J., ed, *Race, Ethnicity and Social Change*, Duxbury: London.

Cross, M. (1978), 'Colonisation and ethnicity: A theory and comparative case study', *Ethnic and Racial Studies*, vol. 1, no. 1.

Curle, A. (1976), 'Peace Studies', *Yearbook of International Affairs*, London.

Curle, A. (1990), *Tools for Transformation*, Hawthorn: Stroud.

Dalberg-Acton, J.E.E. (1909), *The History of Freedom and Other Essays*, Macmillan: London.

Darby, J. (1986), *Intimidation and Control of the Conflict in Northern Ireland*, Gill and Macmillan: Dublin.

Day, A.R. (1986), 'Conclusions' in Day, A.R. and Doyle, M.W., eds, *Escalation and Intervention*, Westview: Boulder.

de Cuellar,J. P. (1990), *Report of the Secretary-General on the Work of the Organization 1990*, United Nations: New York.

de Silva, K.M. (1986), *Managing Ethnic Tensions in Multi-Ethnic Societies: Sri Lanka 1880-1985*, University Press of America: Lanham.

244

de Silva, K.M. (1991),'Indo-Sri Lankan relations, 1975-89' in de Silva, K.M. and May, R.J., eds, *Internationalization of Ethnic Conflict*, Pinter: London.

de Silva, K. M. and Samarasinghe, S.W.R. de A. (1993), eds, *Peace Accords and Ethnic Conflict*, Pinter: London.

de Waal, A. and Omaar, R. (1993), 'Doing harm by doing good? The international relief effort in Somalia', *Current History*, vol. 92, no. 574.

Deane, S. (1992). 'Cannon fodder' in Lundy, J. and MacPoilin, A., eds, *Styles of Belonging*, Lagan Press: Belfast.

Deletant, D. (1992), 'The rights of ethnic minorities in eastern Europe: Some considerations' in Beddard, R. and Hill, D.M., eds, *Emerging Rights in the New Europe*, Southampton Studies in International Policy in association with Macmillan: University of Southampton.

Deng, F.M. and Zartman, I.W. (1991), eds, *Conflict Resolution in Africa,* Brookings: Washington.

Der Derian, J. (1987), *On Diplomacy: A Genealogy of Western Estrangement*, Blackwell: Oxford.

Der Derian, J. (1992), *Antidiplomacy*, Blackwell: Oxford.

Deutsch, M. (1964),'Producing change in an adversary' in Fisher, R., ed, *International Conflict and Behavioural Science*, Basic Books: New York.

Deutsch, M. (1973), *The Resolution of Conflict*, Yale University Press: New Haven.

Deutsch, M. (1991), 'Subjective features of conflict resolution' in Vayrynen, R., ed, *New Directions in Conflict Theory*, Sage: London.

Diehl, P.F. (1987), 'When does peacekeeping not lead to peace?', *Bulletin of Peace Proposals*, vol. 18, no. 1.

Dixon, N.F. (1987), *Our Own Worst Enemy*, J. Cape: London.

Doob, L. (1986), 'Cypriot patriotism and nationalism', *Journal of Conflict Resolution*, vol. 30 no. 2.

Drakulic, S. (1993), *Balkan Express*, Hutchinson: London.

Dunn, S. (1993), *The Common School*, Centre for the Study of Conflict: Coleraine.

Durch, W.J. (1993),'The UN Operation in the Congo' in Durch, W.J., ed, *The Evolution of United Nations Peacekeeping*, St. Martin's Press: New York.

Eastby, J. (1985), *Functionalism and Interdependence*, University Press of America: Lanham.

Efthymiadou, E. (1979), The Role of the United Nations as Regards Cyprus,1964-74, undergraduate dissertation, University of Keele, unpublished.

Ellis, I.M. (1986), *Peace and Reconciliation Projects in Ireland*, Irish Council of Churches: Belfast.

Elshtain, J.B. (1987), *Women and War*, Harvester: Brighton.

Enloe, C. (1973), *Ethnic Conflict and Political Development*, Little Brown: Boston.

Enloe, C. (1980), *Ethnic Soldiers*, Penguin: Harmondsworth.

Ertekun, N.M. (1981), *The Cyprus Dispute*, K. Rustem: Nicosia.

Esman, M.J. (1990), 'Political and Psychological Factors in Ethnic Conflict' in Montville, J., ed, *Conflict and Peacemaking in Multiethnic Societies*, Lexington Books: Lexington

Falconer, A. (1990), ed, *Reconciling Memories*, Columba: Blackrock.

Farley, L.T. (1986), *Plebiscites and Sovereignty*, Westview: Boulder.

Farrell, M. (1980), *Northern Ireland: The Orange State*, Pluto Press: London.

Fawcett, J. (1979), *The International Protection of Minorities*, Minority Rights Group: London.

Fein, H. (1992), ed, *Genocide Watch*, Yale University Press: New Haven.

Fein, H. (1993), *Genocide: A Sociological Perspective*, Sage: London.

Fisher, R. and Ury, W. (1987), *Getting to Yes*, Arrow Books: London.

Fisher, R.J. (1983), 'Third party communication as a method of intergroup conflict resolution', *Journal of Conflict Resolution*, vol.27, no. 2.

Fisher, R.J. (1989), 'Pre-negotiation and problem-solving discussions: Enhancing the potential for successful negotiation', *International Journal*, vol. 44 no. 2.

Fishman, J.A. (1980), 'Social Theory and Ethnography' in Sugar, P.F., ed, *Ethnic Diversity and Conflict in Eastern Europe*, ABC-Clio: Santa Barbara.

Fisk, R. (1975), *The Point of No Return*, Times Books: London.

Fisk, R. (1990), *Pity the Nation*, Oxford University Press: Oxford.

Fisk, R. (1992a), 'Bungling threatens failure for UN force', *The Independent*, 21 September, London.

Fisk, R. (1992b), 'Lie that leaves Bosnia in the lurch', *The Independent on Sunday*, 6 December, London.

Fitzduff, M. (1991), 'Towards a new paradigm', *Dawn Train*, No. 10.

Flowers, M.K. (1984), 'Canada and Quebec' in Shiels, F.L., ed, *Ethnic Separatism and World Politics*, University Press of America: Lanham.

Fortna, V.P. (1993), 'The United Nations Angola Verification Mission I' and 'The United Nations Angola Verification Mission II' in W.J. Durch, ed, *The Evolution of United Nations Peacekeeping*, St. Martin's Press: New York.

Foster, D. and Finchilescu, G. (1986), 'Contact in a Non-Contact Society' in Hewstone, M. and Brown, R., eds, *Contact and Conflict in Intergroup Encounters*, Blackwell: Oxford.

Fraser, T.G. (1984), *Partition in Ireland, India and Palestine: Theory and Practice*, Macmillan: London.

Frazer, H. and Fitzduff, M. (1991), *Improving Community Relations*, Community Relations Council: Belfast.

Fromm, E. (1974), *The Anatomy of Human Destructiveness*, Cape: London.

Fukuyama, F. (1992), *The End of History and the Last Man*, H. Hamilton: London.

Furnival, J.S. (1977), 'Colonial Policy and Practice' in Stone, J., ed, *Race, Ethnicity and Social Change*, Duxbury: London.

Furnival, J.S. (1986), *Netherlands India: A Study of Plural Economy*, B.M. Israel: Amsterdam.

Gallagher, E. and Worrall, S. (1982), *Christians in Ulster, 1968-1980*, Oxford University Press: Oxford.

Galtung, J. (1976), 'Three approaches to peace; peacekeeping, peacemaking and peacebuilding' in *Essays in Peace Research, Volume II*, Christian Ejlers: Copenhagen.

Galtung, J. (1981), *The True Worlds*, Free Press: New York.

Galtung, J. (1985), 'Twenty five years of peace research', *Journal of Peace Research* vol. 25, no. 2.

Garber, L. and O'Connor, C.M. (1985), 'The 1984 UN Sub-commission on the Prevention of Discrimination and the Protection of Minorities', *American Journal of International Law*, vol. 79, no.1.

Garcia, E. and Hernandez, C. (1989), *Waging Peace in the Philippines*, Centre for Social Policy and Public Affairs, University of Philippines: Manila.

Gardeniers, T., Hannum, H. and Kruger, J. (1982), 'The UN Sub-commission on the Prevention of Discrimination and the Protection of Minorities', *Human Rights Quarterly*, vol. 4, no. 3.

Gellner, E. (1983), *Nations and Nationalism*, Blackwell: Oxford.

Gellner, E. (1988), *Plough, Sword and Book*, Collins Harvill: London.

Gellner, E. (1992), 'Nationalism reconsidered and E.H. Carr', *Review of International Studies*, vol. 18 no. 4.

Georghallides, G.S. (1979), *The Political and Administrative History of Cyprus, 1918-1926*, Cyprus Research Centre: Nicosia.

Giddens,A. (1976), *New Rules of Sociological Method*, Hutchinson: London.

Giddens, A. (1984), *The Constitution of Society*, Polity Press: Cambridge.

Giddens, A. (1985), *The Nation State and Violence*, Polity Press: Cambridge.

Giddens, A. (1990), *The Consequesnces of Modernity*, Polity Press: Cambridge.

Glazer, N. (1983), *Ethnic Dilemmas1964-82*, Harvard University Press:

Cambridge, MA.

Glenny, M. (1992), *The Fall of Yugoslavia*, Penguin: Harmondsworth.

Groom, A.J.R. and Taylor, P. (1975), eds, *Functionalism: Theory and Practice in International Relations*, University of London Press: London.

Groom, A.J.R. (1986), 'Problem Solving and International Relations, in Azar. E. and Burton, J.W., eds, *International Conflict Resolution*, Wheatsheaf: Brighton.

Guelke, A. (1988), *Northern Ireland: The International Perspective*, Gill and Macmillan: Dublin.

Gunter, M.M. (1993), *The Kurds of Iraq*, St. Martin's Press: New York

Gupta, M.G. (1985), *Indian Foreign Policy: Theory and Practice*, Y.K. Publications: Agra.

Gurion, D.B. (1970), *Recollections*, Macdonald: London.

Gurr, T.R. (1989), 'Minorities rights at risk: A global survey', *Human Rights Quarterly*, vol. 11, pp. 375-405.

Haas, E.B. (1964), *Beyond the Nation State*, Stanford University Press: Stanford.

Haas, E.B. (1983), 'Regime decay: Conflict management and International Organisations 1945-81', *International Organisation*, vol. 37, no. 2.

Haas, E.B. (1986), *Why We Still Need the UN Collective Management of International Conflict*, Institute of International Studies Policy Paper in International Studies No. 26, University of California.

Haas, E.B. (1987a), 'War, Interdependence and Functionalism' in Vayrynen, R., ed, *The Quest for Peace*, Sage: London.

Haas, E.B. (1987b), 'The collective management of international conflict, 1945-1984' in UNITAR, *The United Nations and the Maintenance of International Peace and Security*, Nijhoff: Dordrecht.

Haddad, W.D. (1985), *Lebanon: The Politics of Revolving Doors*, Washington Center for Strategic and International Studies, Georgetown University Washington Papers No. 114, Praeger: New York.

Hadden, T. and Boyle, K. (1987), 'Northern Ireland: Conflict and Conflict Resolution', *Bulletin of Peace Proposals*, vol. 18, no. 4.

Haff, B. (1986), 'Genocide as State Terrorism' in Stohl, M. and Lopez, G.A. eds, *Government, Violence and Repression*, Greenwood: Westport.

Haff, B. (1987), 'The Etiology of Genocide' in Wallimann, I. and Dobkowski, M.N. eds, *Genocide in the Modern Age*, Greenwood: Westport.

Haksar, U. (1974), *Minority Protection and International Bill of Human Rights*, Allied Publishers: Bombay.

Halperin, M.H, Scheffer, D.J. and Small, P. (1990) *Self-Determination in the New World Order*, Carnegie Endowment for International Peace: Washington.

Hamilton, A. et al. (1990), *Violence and the Communities*, Centre for the Study of Conflict: Coleraine.

Hannum, H. (1981a), 'Human Rights and the United Nations: Progress at the 1980 session of the Sub-Commission on the Prevention of Dicrimination and the Protection of Minorities', *Human Rights Quarterly*, vol. 3, no. 1.

Hannum, H. (1981b), 'The thirty-third session of the United Nations Sub-Commission on the Prevention of Discrimination and the Protection of Minorities', *American Journal of International Law*, vol. 62, no. 4.

Hannum, H. (1990), *Autonomy, Sovereignty and Self-Determination*, University of Pennsylvania Press: Philadelphia.

Hansen, E. (1987), ed, *Africa: Perspectives on Peace and Development*, Zed: London.

Harbottle, M. (1971), *The Blue Berets*, Lee Cooper: London.

Harbottle, M. (1979a), 'Cyprus: An analysis of the United Nation's third party role in a "small war"', in P. Worsley and P. Kitromilides, eds, *Small States in the Modern World: The Conditions of Survival*, Nicosia.

Harbottle, M. (1979b), 'The strategy of third party intervention in conflict resolution', *International Journal*, vol. 25, no. 1.

Harbottle, M. (1986), 'Confidence building and international security' in Laszlo, E. and Yoo, J.Y. (eds), *World Encyclopedia of Peace*, Vol. 1, Pergamon: Oxford.

Hare, A.P. (1985), *Social Interaction as Drama,* Sage: Beverly Hills California.

Hart, P.T. (1990), *Two NATO Allies at the Threshold of War*, Duke University Press: Durham.

Havel, V. (1991), 'Address to the NATO Council, 21 March 1991', *NATO Review*, April 1991.

Hayes, M. (1991), *Whither Cultural Diversity?*, Community Relations Council: Belfast.

Heaney, S. (1975), *North*, Faber: London.

Heberer, T. (1989), *China and Its National Minorities*, M.E. Sharpe: Armonk NY.

Hechter, M. (1975), *Internal Colonialism: The Celtic Fringe in British National Development 1536-1966*, Routledge and Keagan Paul: London.

Hechter, M. (1988), 'Rational Choice Theory and the Study of Race Relations' in Rex, J. and Mason, D., eds, *Theories of Race and Ethnic Relations*, Cambridge University Press: Cambridge.

Heiberg, M. and Holst, J.J. (1986) 'Peacekeeping in Lebanon: Comparing UNIFIL and the MNF', *Survival*, vol. 28 , no. 5.

Helsinki Watch (1987), *Destroying Ethnic Identity: The Turks of Bulgaria*, Helsinki Watch: New York.

Helsinki Watch (1988), *Destroying Ethnic Identity: The Kurds of Turkey*, Helsinki Watch: New York.

Heraclides, A. (1990), *The Self-Determination of Minorities in International Politics*, Frank Cass: London.

Heradstveit, D. (1974), *The Outline of a Cumulative Research Strategy for the Study of Conflict Resolution in the Middle East*, NUPI-Rapport: Oslo.

Hersch, S. (1983), *The Price of Power: Kissinger in the White House*, Summit Books: New York.

Hewstone, M. (1986), *Understanding Attitudes to the European Community*, Cambridge University Press: Cambridge.

Hewstone, M. and Brown, R.(1986), eds, *Contact and Conflict in Intergroup Encounters*, Blackwell: Oxford.

Hewstone. M. (1988), 'Attributional bases of intergroup conflict' in Stroebe, W. et al., eds, *The Social Psychology of Intergroup Conflict*, Springer-Verlag: London.

Higgins, R. (1993), 'The new UN and the former Yugoslavia', *International Affairs*, vol. 69, no.3.

Hirabayashi, L.R. and Hirabayashi, J.A. (1984), 'A Reconsideration of the US Military's Role in the Violation of Japanese-American Citizenship Rights' in van Horne, W.A., ed, *Ethnicity and War*, University of Wisconsin: Milwaukee.

Hobsbawm, E.J. (1990), *Nations and Nationalism Since 1780*, Cambridge University Press: Cambridge.

Hoffmann, S. (1981), *Duties Beyond Borders*, Syracuse Univeristy Press: Syracuse.

Hoffmann, S. (1983), *Dead Ends*, Ballinger: Cambridge MA.

Hoffmann, S. (1984),'The Problem of Intervention' in Bull, H. (ed), *Intervention in World Politics*, Clarendon: Oxford.

Hofman, J.E. (1988), 'Social identity and intergroup conflict' in Stroebe, W. et al., eds, *The Social Psychology of Intergroup Conflict*, Springer-Verlag: London.

Hoslt, J.J. (1990), 'Enhancing peace-keeping operations', *Survival*, vol. 32, no. 3.

Horowitz, D. (1985), *Ethnic Groups in Conflict,* University of California Press: Berkeley.

Horowitz, I.L. (1980), *Taking Lives:Genocide and State Power,* Transaction Books: New Brunswick.

Howard, M. (1988), 'Ideology and international relations', *Review of International Studies*, vol. 15, no. 4.

Human Rights Watch (1993), *Human Rights and United Nations Field Operations: The Lost Agenda*, Human Rights Watch: New York.

Humphrey, J.P. (1968), 'The United Nations Sub-commission on the Prevention of Discrimination and the Protection of Minorities', *American Journal of International Law*, vol. 62, no. 4.

Humphrey, J.P. (1984), *Human Rights and the United Nations: The Great Adventure*, Transnational Publications: Dobbs Ferry NY.

Hurrell, A. (1990), 'Kant and the Kantian paradigm in international relations', *Review of International Studies*, vol. 16, no. 3.

Hyndman, P. (1988), *Sri Lanka: Serendipity Under Siege*, Spokesman: Nottingham.

Ignatieff, M. (1993), *Blood and Belonging: Journeys into the New Nationalism*, BBC Books and Chatto and Windus: London.

International Alert (1991), *International Conference on the Consequences of Organised Violence in Southern Africa*, International Alert: London.

International Alert (1993a), Position paper presented to UN World Conference on Human Rights, Vienna.

International Alert (1993b), *Self-Determination: Statement and recommendations arising from the Martin Ennals Memorial Symposium on Self-Determination, Saskatoon, Canada*.

International Negotiations Network (1993), *State of the World Conflict Report 1991-1992*, Carter Centre: Atlanta.

Irwin, Z.T. (1984), 'Yugoslavia and Ethno-regionalism' in Shiels, F.L., ed, *Ethnic Separatism and World Politics*, University Press of America: Lanham.

Isaksson, M. and Johansson, L.I. (1988), *The Aland Islands: Autonomous Demilitarized Region*, Alands Fredsforening r.f.

Israeli, R. (1980), 'Muslim minorities under non-Islamic rule', *Current History*, vol. 78, no. 456.

James, A. (1969), *The Politics of Peacekeeping*, Praeger: New York.

James, A.(1973), ed, *The Bases of International Order*, Oxford University Press: Oxford.

James, A. (1984), 'Options for Peacekeeping' in Howe, J.O. (ed), *Armed Peace*, Macmillan: London.

James, A. (1989a), 'The realism of Realism: the state and the study of international relations', *Review of International Studies*, vol.15, no.3.

James, A. (1989b), 'Peacekeeping and keeping the peace', *Review of International Studies*, vol. 15, no. 4.

James, A. (1989c), 'The UN force in Cyprus', *International Affairs* (London), vol. 65, no. 3.

James, A. (1990), *Peacekeeping in International Politics*, Macmillan: Basingstoke.

Jandt, F.E. (1985), *Win/Win Negotiating*, Wiley: New York.

Janowsky, O.I. (1945), *Nationalism and National Minorities*, Macmillan: New York.

Jaworski, R. (1991), 'The German minorities in Poland and Czechoslovakia in the interwar period' in P. Smith, ed, *Ethnic Groups in International Relations*, Dartmouth: Aldershot.

Jayawardene, C.H.S. and Jayawardene, H. (1984), *Tea For Two*, Crimecare Inc: Ottowa.

Jean, F. (1992) ed, *Populations in Danger: Medicins Sans Frontieres*, John Libbey: London.

Jenkins, R. (1988), 'Social and Anthropological Models of Inter-Ethnic Relations' in Rex, J. and Mason, D. (eds), *Theories of Race and Ethnic Relations*, Cambridge University Press: Cambridge.

Jensen, L. (1988), 'Planning together for Nicosia's future', *World Development*, March 1988.

Jonassohn, K. and Chalk, F. (1987), 'A Typology of Genocide' in Wallimann, I. and Dobkowski, M.N., eds, *Genocide in the Modern Age*, Greenwood: New York.

Jonassohn, K. (1992), 'What is genocide?' in H. Fein, ed, *Genocide Watch*, Yale University Press: New Haven.

Jones, J.M. (1972), *Prejudice and Racism*, Newby Award Records Inc: New York.

Journal of International Affairs (1962), vol. 16, no. 2.

Kaloudis, S. (1982), The Role of the United Nations in Cyprus from 1964-1979, PhD thesis, University of Kansas, unpublished.

Kapuscinski, R. (1987), *Another Day of Life*, Picador: London.

Kayal,A.Z., Parker, P.L. and Weissbrodt, D. (1993) 'The forty-fourth session of the UN Sub-commission for the Prevention of Discrimination and the Protection of Minorities and the special session of the Commission on Human Rights on the situation in the former Yugoslavia', *Human Rights Quarterly*, vol. 15 no. 2.

Kearney, R. (1985), 'Myth and Motherland' in Fielday Theatre Company *Ireland's Field Day*, Hutchinson: London.

Kearney, R.N. (1985), 'Ethnic conflict and the Tamil separatist movement in Sri Lanka', *Asian Survey*, vol. 25, no. 9.

Keashley, L. and Fisher, R.J. (1990), 'Towards a contingency approach to third party intervention in regional conflict: a Cyprus illustration', *International Journal*, vol. 65, no. 2.

Kee, R. (1976), *The Green Flag. Volume Two: The Bold Fenian Men*, Quartet Books: London.

Kelley, M.P. (1986), *A State in Disarray: Conditions of Chad's Survival*, Westview: Boulder.

Kelman, H.C. (1985), 'Overcoming the psychological barrier: An analysis of the Egyptian-Israeli Peace Process', *Negotiation Journal*, vol. 1, no. 3.

Kelman, H.C. (1990), 'Interactive problem solving' in V. Volkan et al. (eds) *The Psychodynamics of International Relationships*, Lexington Press: Lexington MA.

Kelman, H.C. and Cohen, S. (1976), 'The problem-solving workshop', *Journal of Peace Research*, vol. 13, no. 2.

Khalidi, W. (1979), *Conflict and Violence in Lebanon*, Harvard Studies in International Affairs, No. 38, Harvard Center for International Affairs: Cambridge MA.

King, C.S. (1983), *The Words of Martin Luther King Jr.*, Collins: London.

Kodikara, S.U. (1987), 'International Dimensions of Ethnic Conflict in Sri Lanka', *Bulletin of Peace Proposals*, vol. 18, no. 4.

Koestler, A. (1974), *The Heel of Achilles*, Hutchinson: London.

Korzec, P. (1991), 'The Ukranian Problem in Interwar Poland' in Smith, P., ed, *Ethnic Groups in International Relations*, Dartmouth: Aldershot.

Kriesberg, L. (1982), *Social Conflict*, Prentice Hall: Englewood CA.

Kriesberg, L., Northrup, T.A. and Thorson, S.J. (1989), eds, Intractable Conflicts and Their Transformation, Syracuse University Press: Syracuse.

Kull, S. (1990), 'War and the attraction to destruction' in Glad, B., ed, *Psychological Dimensions of War*, Sage: London.

Kuper, L. (1969),'Conclusions' in Kuper, L. and Smith, M.G., eds, *Pluralism in Africa*, University of California Press: Berkeley.

Kuper, L. (1974a), *Race, Class and Power*, Duckworth: London.

Kuper, L. (1974b), 'On Theories of Race Relations' in Bell, W. and Freeman, W.F., eds, *Ethnicity and Nation Building*, Sage: Beverley Hills.

Kuper, L. (1977), *The Pity of it All*, Duckworth: London.

Kuper, L. (1981), *Genocide*, Penguin: Harmondsworth.

Kuper, L. (1985), *The Prevention of Genocide*, Yale University Press: New Haven.

Kuper, L. (1988), 'The plural society and civil war' in *UNESCO Yearbook on Peace and Conflict Studies 1986*, Greenwood Press: Westport.

Kuper, L. (1989), 'The prevention of genocide: Cultural and structural indicators of genocidal threat', *Ethnic and Racial Studies*, vol. 12, no.2.

Kuper, L. (1990), 'The Genocidal State: An Overview' in Van Den Burghe P.L., ed, *State Violence and Ethnicity*, University of Colorado Press: Colorado.

Kuper, L. (1992), 'Reflections on the prevention of genocide' in H. Fein, ed, *Genocide Watch*, Yale University Press: New Haven.

Lall, A.S. (1985), *Multilateral Negotiations and Mediation,* Pergamon:

New York.

Lampen, J. (1987), 'Dimensions of the search for reconciliation in Ireland', unpublished paper.

Laswell, H. (1964), The Garrison State' in Bramson, L. and Goethals, G.W., eds, *War*, Basic Books, New York.

Lawler, J.L. (1976), 'Conflict avoidance in Africa', *Peace Research Reviews*, vol. 7, no. 1.

Lawyers' Committee for Human Rights in Liberia (1986), *A Promise Betrayed*, Lawyers' Committee for Human Rights in Liberia: New York.

Layburn, J.G. (1947), *World Minority Problems*, Public Affairs Committee: New York.

Lee, J.J. (1989), *Ireland 1912-1985*, Cambridge University Press: Cambridge.

Legum, C. (1983), *Eritrea and Tigre*, Minority Rights Group: London.

Lemarchand, R. (1990), 'Burundi: Ethnicity and the genocidal state' in van den Berghe, P.L., ed, *State Violence and Ethnicity*, University Press of Colorado: Niwot.

Lijphart, A. (1977), *Democracy in Plural Societies*, Yale University Press: New Haven.

Lijphart, A. (1980), Preface to Ashworth, G. (ed), *World Minorities in the 1980s*, Quartermain: Sunbury.

Lijphart, A. (1984), *Democracies: patterns of Majoritarian and Consensus Government in Twenty-One Countries*, Yale University Press: New Haven.

Lijphart, A. (1989a), 'The Ethnic Factor and Democratic Constitution-making in South Africa' in Keller, E.J. and Picard, L.A., eds, *South Africa in Southern Africa: Domestic Change and International Conflict*, Lynne Rienner: Boulder.

Lijphart, A. (1989b), 'The Power-Sharing Approach' in Montville, J.V., ed, *Conflict and Peacemaking in Multiethnic Societies*, Lexington Books: Lexington.

Lippmann, W. (1962), *A Preface to Politics,* University of Michigan: Ann Arbor.

Loizos, P. (1975), *The Greek Gift*, Basil Blackwell: London.

Loizos, P. (1976), *Cyprus*, Minority Rights Group, London. Part 2.

Loizos, P. (1981), *The Heart Grown Bitter*, Cambridge University Press: Cambridge.

Loizos, P. (1989), 'Intercommunal killings in Cyprus', *Man*, vol. 23.

Lowe, M.F. (1976), International Organisation and the Protection of Minorities, unpublished thesis, Geneva Institute for International Studies.

Luard, E. (1988), *History of the United Nations. Volume 2: The Era of Decolonisation*, Macmillan: Basingstoke.

Lustick, I.S. (1979), 'Stability in deeply divided societies: consociationalism versus control', *World Politics*, vol. 21, no. 3.

Lustick, I.S. (1987), 'Israel's dangerous fundamentalists', *Foreign Policy* No. 68, Fall.

Lyons, F.S.L. (1979), *Culture and Anarchy in Ireland 1890-1939*, Oxford U.P.: Oxford.

Macartney, C.A. (1934), *The Nation State and National Minorities*, Oxford University Press: Oxford.

Mack, A. (1991), 'Objectives and methods of peace research' in Woodhouse, T., ed, *Peacemaking in a Troubled World*, Berg: New York.

MacKey, W.F. (1975), 'Trends in Multinationalism' in MacKey, W.F. and Verdoot, A., eds,*The Multinational Society: Papers of the Ljublijana Seminar,* Newbury House: London.

Mackinley, J. (1989), *The Peace-keepers*, Unwin Hyman: London.

Maher, R.M. and Weissbrodt, D. (1990), 'The forty-first session of the Sub-Commission on the Prevention of Discrimination and the Protection of Minorities', *Human Rights Quarterly*, vol. 12, no. 2.

Mair, L. P. (1928), *The Protection of Minorities: The Working and Scope of the Minorities Treaties under the League of Nations*, Christopher: London.

Mandelbaum, M. (1981), *The Nuclear Revolution*, Cambridge University Press: Cambridge.

Manning, C.A.W. (1975), *The Structure of International Society*, Macmillan: London.

Mapes, M.C. (1985), 'Why Establish a National Peace Academy?, in Smith, C.D., ed, *The One Hundred Percent Challenge*, Seven Locks Press: Bethesda MD.

Markides, R.C. (1977), *The Rise and Fall of the Cyprus Republic*, Yale University Press: New Haven.

Marlin, E. and Azar, E. (1981), 'The Costs of Protracted Social Conflict in the Middle East: The Case of Lebanon' in Ben-Dor, G. and Dewith, D.R., eds, *Conflict Management in the Middle East*, Lexington Books: Lexington.

Martin, G. (1991), 'Security and conflict management in Chad', *Bulletin of Peace Proposals*, vol. 21, no. 1.

Maslow, A.H. (1970), *Motivation and Personality*, Harper and Row: New York. Second edition.

Mastny, V. (1992), *The Helsinki Process and the Reintegration of Europe 1986-1991: Analysis and Documentation*, Pinter: London.

Mauzy, D. (1993), 'Malaysia: Malay political hegemony and coercive consociationalism' in McGarry, J. and O'Leary, B., eds, *The Politics of Ethnic Conflict Regulation*, Routledge: London.

Mayall, J. (1983), 'Self-determination and the OAU' in Lewis, I.M. ed,

Nationalism and Self-Determination in the Horn of Africa, Ithaca Press: London.

Mayall, J. (1991), 'Non-intervention, self-determination and the new world order', *International Affairs*, vol. 67, no. 3.

Mayall, J. (1992), 'Nationalism and international security after the cold war', *Survival*, vol. 34, no. 1.

Mazrui, A.A. (1969), *Post Imperial Fragmentation. The Legacy of Ethnic and Racial Conflict*, University of Denver: Colorado.

McAllister, I. and Rose, R. (1982), *Can Violent Political Conflict be Resolved by Social Change?*, Centre for the Study of Public Policy, University of Strathclyde: Glasgow.

McCreary, A. (1974), *Corrymeela: The Search for Peace*, Christian Journals Ltd: Belfast.

McDougal. D. (1984), *Harold D. Laswell and the Study of International Relations*, University Press of America: Lanham.

McFarlane, L. (1974), *Violence and the State*, T. Nelson, London.

McGarry, J. and O'Leary, B. (1990), eds, *The Future of Northern Ireland*, Clarendon Press: Oxford.

McGarry, J. and O'Leary, B. (1993), eds, *The Politics of Ethnic Conflict Regulation*, Routledge: London.

McGowan, W. (1992), *Only Man is Vile: The Tragedy of Sri Lanka*, Picador: London.

McRae, K.D. (1989), 'Power-Sharing and Conflict Management' in Montville, J.V., ed, *Conflict and Peacemaking in Multiethnic Societies*, Lexington Books: Lexington.

Mendle, W. (1974), *Prophets and Reconcilers: Reflections on the Quaker Peace Testimony*, Friends House Service Committee: London.

Merle, M. (1987), *The Sociology of International Relations*, Berg: Leamington Spa. Translated by D. Parkin.

Merrills, J.G. (1984), *International Dispute Settlement*, Sweet and Maxwell: London.

Miall, H. (1992), *The Peacemakers: Peaceful Settlement of Disputes Since 1945,* Macmillan: Basingstoke.

Middle East Watch (1990), *Human Rights in Iraq,* Yale U.P: New Haven.

Midlarski, M.I. (1992), ed, *The Internationalization of Communal Strife*, Routledge: London.

Miller, L.B. (1967), *World Order and Local Disorders: The UN and Internal Conflicts*, Princeton University Press: Princeton NJ.

Mill, J.S. (1972), *Utilitarianism, On Liberty and Considerations on Representative Government*, Dent: London. Ed. by H.B. Acton.

Mills, C.W. (1960), *The Causes of World War Three*, M.E. Sharpe Inc: Armonk NY.

Minns, A. (1990), *Citizens Apart: A Portrait of Palestinians in Israel*,

Tauris: London.

Minority Rights Group (1986), *Coexistence in Some Plural European Societies*, Minority Rights Group: London.

Mitchell, C.R. (1981a), *The Structure of International Conflict*, Macmillan: London.

Mitchell, C.R. (1981b), *Peacemaking and the Consultant's Role*, Gower: Aldershot.

Mitchell, C.R. (1986), 'GRIT and gradualism - twenty years on', *International Interactions*, vol. 3, no.1.

Mitchell, C.R. (1989), *Conflict Resolution and Civil War: Reflections on the Sudanese Settlement of 1972*, Center for Conflict Analysis and Resolution, George Mason University: Fairfax.

Mitchell, C.R. (1991), 'Ending conflict and wars:judgement, rationality and entrapment', *International Social Science Journal*, no. 127.

Mitchell, C.R. (1992), 'External peace-making initiatives and intra-national conflict' in Midlarsky, M., ed, *The Internationalisation of Communal Strife*, Routledge: London.

Mitchell, C.R. and Webb, K. (1988), eds, *New Approaches to International Mediation*, Greenwood Press: Westport.

Mitrany, D. (1966), *A Working Peace System*, Quadrangle Press: Chicago.

Mitrany, D. (1975), *The Functional Theory of Politics*, M. Robertson: Oxford.

Modeen, T. (1969), *The International Protection of National Minorities in Europe*, Abo Akademi: Abo.

Modeen, T. (1991), 'The Aland Island Question' in Smith, P., ed, *Ethnic Groups in International Relations*, Dartmouth: Aldershot.

Mohanty, S. (1992), *Political Development and Ethnic Identity in Africa: A Study of Angola Since 1960*, Sangam Books: London.

Monnet, J. (1978), *Memoirs,* Collins: London.

Montville, J. (1987), 'The Arrow and the Olive Branch: A Case for Track Two Diplomacy' in McDonald, J.W. and Bendahmane, D.B., eds, *Conflict Resolution - Track Two Diplomacy*, US State Department: Washington.

Montville, J. (1990), 'The psychological roots of ethnic and sectarian terrorism' in Volkan, V.D. et al., eds, *The Psychodynamics of International Relationships*, Lexington Books: Lexington.

Moore, C.W. (1986), *The Mediation Process*, Jossey-Bass: San Francisco.

Moran, S.F. (1991), 'Patrick Pearse and political soteriology: The Irish Republican tradition and the sanctification of political self-immolation' in Alexander, Y. and O'Day, A., eds, *Ireland's Terrorism Experience*, Dartmouth: Aldershot.

Morrow, D. (1991), 'Churches and the experience of violence', in

Alexander, Y. and O'Day, A., eds, *Ireland's Terrorism Experience*, Dartmouth: Aldershot.

Moses, R. (1990), 'Self, self-view, and identity' in Volkan, V.D. et al., eds, *The Psychodynamics of International Relationships*, Lexington Books: Lexington.

Moynihan, D.P. (1993), *Pandaemonium*, Oxford University Press: Oxford.

Mozaffar, S. (1986), *Leadership Process and the Management of Ethnic Conflict In Africa*, Boston University African Studies Center: Boston.

Munck, R. (1986), *The Difficult Dialogue: Marxism and Natonalism in the Third World*, Zed Press: London.

Murphy, D. (1979) *A Place Apart*, Penguin: Harmondsworth.

Nairn, T. (1977), *The Breakup of Britain: Crisis and Neo-Nationalism*, New Left Books: London.

Nardin, T. (1983), *Law, Morality and the Relations of States*, Princeton University Press: Princeton.

Ndovi, V. (1987), 'Chad: Nation-building, Security and OAU Peacekeeping' in Wright, S. and Brownfoot, J.N., eds , *Africa in World Politics*, Macmillan: London.

Neuberger, B. (1986), *National Self-Determination in Post Colonial Africa*, Lynne Rienner: Boulder.

Neuberger, B. (1990) 'Irredentism and Politics in Africa' in Chazan, N., ed, *Irredentism and International Politics*, Lynne Rienner: Boulder.

Neuman, S.G. (1976), ed, *Small States and Segmented Societies*, Praeger: New York.

Niederhauser, E. (1993), 'The National Question in Hungary' in M. Teich and R. Porter, eds, *The Nationalities Question in Europe in Historical Context*, Cambridge University Press: Cambridge.

Nielsson, G.P. (1985), 'States and Nation-Groups: A Global Taxonomy' in Tiryakian, E.A. and Ragowski, R., eds, *New Nationalisms of the Developed West*, Allen and Unwin: Boston.

Nordlinger, E.A. (1972), *Conflict Regulation in Divided Societies, Harvard Center for International Affairs*: Cambridge MA.

Northedge, F.S. and Donelan, M.D. (1971), *International Disputes: The Policial Aspects*, Europa: London.

Northern Ireland Council for Curriculum Development (1988), *Education for Mutual Understanding: A Guide*, NICED: Belfast.

Northrup, T.A. (1989), 'The dynamic of identity in personal and social conflict' in Kriesberg, L., Northrup, T.A. and Thorson, S.J., eds, *Intractable Conflicts and Their Transformation*, Syracuse University Press: Syracuse.

O'Connell, J. (1988), 'Conflict and conciliation: A comparative approach related to three case studies Belgium, Northern Ireland and

258

Nigeria' in Townshend, C., ed, *Consensus in Ireland*, Clarendon Press: Oxford.

O'Leary, B. and Arthur, P. (1990), 'Introduction' to J. McGarry and B. O'Leary, eds, *The Future of Northern Ireland*, Clarendon Press: Oxford.

O'Malley, P. (1983), *Uncivil War*: Blackstaff: Belfast.

O'Malley, P. (1990), *Biting at the Grave: The Irish Hunger Strike and the Politics of Despair*, Blackstaff, Belfast.

O'Neill, W. (1993), 'Liberia: and avoidable tragedy', *Current History*, vol. 92, no. 574.

Obaseki, N.O. (1983), *Africa and the Superpowers: External Intervention in Regional Disputes*, International Peace Academy: New York.

Oberg, J. (1990), "Coping with the loss of a close enemy: Perestroika as a challenge to the west', *Bulletin of Peace Proposals*, vol. 21, no.3

Okoli, E. (1982), 'Toward a Human Rights Framework in Nigeria' in Schwab, P. and Pollis, A., eds, *Towards a Human Rights Framework*, Praeger: New York.

Oppenheim, A.N. (1984), 'Psychological processes in world society' in Banks, M., ed, *Conflict in World Society*, Wheatsheaf: Brighton.

Opsahl Commission (1993), *A Citizens' Inquiry: The Opsahl Report on Northern Ireland*, Lilliput Press: Dublin.

Orwell, G. (1970), *Collected Essays etc.*, Vol. 4, Penguin: Harmondsworth.

Osgood, C. E. (1985), 'The GRIT Strategy' in Holroyd, F., ed, *Thinking About Nuclear Weapons*, Croom Helm: London.

Osgood, C.E. (1986), entry in Poulson, D., ed, *Strategies of Survival in the Nuclear Age*, Wisdom: London.

Parekh, B. (1986), 'The Concept of Multicultural Education' in Modgil, S. et al., eds, *Multicultural Education: The Interminable Debate*, Fulmer Press: London.

Parekh, B. (1988), 'Gandhi's concept of ahimsa', *Alternatives*, Vol. 13, no. 2.

Patrick, R. (1976), *Political Geography and the Cyprus Problem*, University of Waterloo: Waterloo.

Paul, D.W. (1985), 'Slovak Nationalism and the Hungarian State' in Brass, P., ed, *Ethnic Groups and the State*, Barnes and Noble: Tatawa NJ.

Pelcovits, C. (1983), 'Peacekeeping: the African Experience' in Wiseman, H., ed, *Peacekeeping: Appraisals and Approaches*, Pergamon: New York.

Phillips, A. and Rosas, A. (1993), eds, *The United Nations Minority Rights Declaration*, Abo Akademi: Abo.

Pitts, J.W. and Weissbrodt, D. (1993), 'Major developments at the

United Nations Commission on Human Rights', *Third World Quarterly*, vol. 15, no. 1.

Prigent, A. (1990),'The Atlantic coast and Indian minorities in Nicaragua' in Melasuo, T., ed, *National Movements and World Peace*, Avebury: Aldershot.

Pogany, I. (1987), *The Arab League and Peace-keeping in the Lebanon*, Avebury: Aldershot.

Popper, K.R. (1992), *In Search of a Better World*, Routledge: London.

Porter, J.N. (1982), ed, *Genocide and Human Rights*, University Press of America: Lanham.

Postman, N. (1989), *Conscientious Objections*, Heinemann: London.

Poulton, H. (1991), *The Balkans: Minorities and States in Conflict*, Minority Rights Publications: London.

Pringle, D. (1990), 'Separation and integration: The case of Ireland' in Chisholm, M. and Smith, D.M., eds, *Shared Space Divided Space*, Unwin Hyman: London.

Pruitt, D.G. (1981), *Negotiating Behaviour*, Academic Press: New York.

Pruitt, D.G. and Rubin, J.Z. (1986), *Social Conflict*, Random House: New York.

Ra'anan, U. et al. (1991), *State and Nation in Multi-ethnic Societies,* Manchester University Press: Manchester.

Rabushka, A. and Shepsle, K.A. (1972), eds, *Politics in Plural Societies: A Theory of Democratic Instability*, Charles E. Merrill: New York.

Rajanayagam-Hellmann, D. (1986), 'Educational Standards and Social Distance: Two Tamil Minorities in Sri Lanka' in Rothermund, D. and Simon, J. (eds) *Education and the Integration of Ethnic Minorities*, Pinter: London.

Ramcharan, B.G. (1983), *Humanitarian Good Offices in International Law*, M. Nijhoff: Dordrecht.

Ramcharan, B.G. (1987), *Keeping Faith With the United Nations*, UNITAR/M. Nijhoff: Dordrecht.

Ramet, S.P. (1992a), *Nationalism and Federalism in Yugoslavia, 1962-1991*, Indiana University Press: Bloomington.

Ramet, S.P. (1992b), 'War in the Balkans', *Foreign Affairs*, vol. 71, no. 4.

Rapaport, A. (1968), 'Concluding comments' in *Clausewitz On War*, Penguin: Harmondsworth. Edited by A. Rapaport.

Rees, M. (1985), *Northern Ireland: A Personal Perspective*, Methuen: London.

Reich, W. (1985), *A Stranger in My House*, Firethorn: London.

Reinerson, K. and Weissbrodt, D. (1992), 'The forty-third session of the Sub-Commission for the Prevention of Discrimination and the Protection of Minorities', *Human Rights Quarterly*, vol. 14, no. 2.

Reiss, H. (1991), ed, *Kant Political Writings*, Cambridge University Press: Cambridge.

Rex, J. and Mason, D. (1986), eds, *Theories of Race and Ethnic Relations*, Cambridge University Press: Cambridge.

Rhode, G.F. (1980), 'Koreans in Japan: Ethnic problems in a developed Asian state' in Ra'anan, U. and Roche, J.P. (eds), *Ethnic Resurgence in Modern Democratic States*, Pergamon: New York.

Richardson, J.M. and Samarasinghe, S.W.R. de A. (1991), 'Measuring the economic dimension of Sri Lanka's ethnic conflict' in Samarasinghe, S.W.R. de A. and Coughlin, R., eds, *Economic Dimensions of Ethnic Conflict*, Pinter: London.

Rikhye, I.J. (1983), 'Peacekeeping and Peacemaking' in Wiseman, H. (ed), *Peacekeeping: Appraisals and Prospects*, Pergamon: New York.

Riley, S.R. (1993), 'Intervention in Liberia: too little, too partisan', *World Today*, vol 49, no. 3.

Roberts, A. (1993) 'Humanitarian war: military intervention and human rights', *International Affairs*, vol. 69, no. 3.

Robinson, J. et al. (1943), *Were the Minority Treaties a Failure*, Institute of Jewish Affairs: New York.

Robinson, N. (1949), *The Genocide Convention: Its Origins and Interpretation*, Institute of Jewish Affairs: New York.

Rogers, R.R. (1990), 'Intergenerational transmission of historical enmity' in Volkan, V.D. et al., eds, *The Psychodynamics of International Relationships*, Lexington Books: Lexington.

Ronen, D. (1979), *The Quest for Self-Determination*, Yale University Press: New Haven.

Ronen, D. and Thompson, D.L., eds, (1985), *Ethnicity, Politics and Development*, Westview: Boulder.

Rorty, R. (1989), *Contingency, Irony and Solidarity*, Cambridge University Press: Cambridge.

Rosen, F. (1992), *Bentham, Byron and Greece*, Hurst: London.

Rothchild, D. (1970),'Ethnicity and conflict resolution', *World Politics*, vol. 22 no. 4.

Rothchild, D. (1986a), 'Inter-ethnic conflict and policy analysis in Africa', *Ethnic and Racial Studies*, vol. 2, no. 1.

Rothchild, D. (1986b), 'Hegemonic Exchange: An Alternative Model for Managing Conflict in Middle Africa' in Thompson, D.L. and Ronen, D., eds, *Ethnicity, Politics and Development*, Lynne Rienner: Boulder.

Rothchild, D. and Chazan, N. (1988), eds, *The Precarious Balance: State and Society in Africa*, Westview: Boulder.

Rothchild, D. (1991), 'An interactive model for state-ethnic relations' in Deng, F.M. and Zartman, I.W., eds, *Conflict Resolution in Africa*, Brookings Institute: Washington.

Rothman, J. (1992), *From Conflict to Cooperation*, Sage: London.

Royal Institute of International Affairs (1939), *Nationalism*, Oxford University Press: London.

Ruane, J. and Todd, J. (1991), '"Why can't you get along with each other?" Culture, structure and the Northern Ireland conflict' in E. Hughes ed. *Culture and Politics in Northern Ireland*, Open University Press: Buckingham.

Rubenstein, R.E. (1987), *Alchemists of Revolution*, Basic Books: New York.

Rupesinghe, K. (1987), 'Theories of conflict resolution and their applicability to protracted ethnic conflict', *Bulletin of Peace Proposals*, vol. 18, no. 4.

Rupesinghe, K. (1988), 'Ethnic conflict in South Asia: The case of Sri Lanka and the Indian peacekeeping force', *Journal of Peace Research*, vol. 25, no. 4.

Rupesinghe, K. (1989), 'Sri Lanka: Peacekeeping and peace-building', *Bulletin of Peace Proposals*, vol. 20, no. 3.

Rupesinghe, K. (1992), 'Conflict transformation in multi-ethnic societies', *Estudios Internacionales Revista del IRIPAZ*, vol. 3, no. 6.

Rupesinghe, K. and Kuroda, M. (1992), eds, *Early Warning and Conflict Resolution*, Macmillan: Basingstoke.

Rupesinghe, K. (forthcoming), *Conflict Transformation*, Macmillan: Basingstoke.

Russell, F.M. (1972), *Theories of International Relations*, Arno Press: New York.

Ryan, S. (1984), Ethnic Conflict and International Politics: External Involvement in the Cyprus Problem, 1974-83, PhD, University of London: unpublished.

Ryan, S. (1988), 'Explaining ethnic conflict: The neglected international dimension', *Review of International Studies*, vol. 14, no.3.

Ryan, S. (1990a), 'Ethnic conflict and the United Nations', *Ethnic and Racial Studies*, vol. 13, no. 1.

Ryan, S. (1990b), 'Conflict management and conflict resolution', *Terrorism and Political Violence*, vol. 2, no. 1.

Ryan, S. (1991), 'The intercommunal conflict in Cyprus' in Darby, J. and Gallagher, A.M., eds, *Comparative Approaches to Community Relations*, Centre for the Study of Conflict: Coleraine.

Ryan, S. (1992), 'The United Nations and the Resolution of Ethnic Conflict' in Rupesinghe, K. and Kuroda, M., eds, *Early Warning and Conflict Resolution*, Macmillan: Basingstoke.

Ryan, S. (1993), 'Grass-roots peacebuilding in violent ethnic conflict' in Calliess, J. and Merkel, C., eds, *Peaceful Settlement of Conflict: A task for Civil Society*, Loccumer Protokolle 7/93, Evangelische Akademie: Loccum.

Sabaratnam, L. (1987), 'The boundaries of the state and the state of ethnic boundaries: Sinhalese-Tamil relations in Sri Lankan history', *Ethnic and Racial Studies*, vol. 10, no. 3.

Said, A.A. and Simmons, L.H. (1976), ed, *Ethnicity in an International Context*, Transaction Inc: New Jersey.

Said, E.W. (1993), 'Nationalism, human rights and interpretation', *Raritan*, vol. XII no. 3.

Saito, N. (1993), 'The role of the UN in a post-cold war world' in S. Sato and T. Taylor, eds, *Prospects for Global Order*, Royal Institute for International Affairs: London.

Samarsinghe, S.W.R. de A. and Coughlan, R. (1991), eds, *The Economic Dimensions of Ethnic Conflict*, Pinter: London.

Sampson, A. (1968), *The New Europeans*, Hodder and Stoughton: London.

Saravanamuthi, P. (1990), *Instability in Sri Lanka,* Survival, vol. 22, no. 5.

Schachter, O. (1974), 'The UN and Internal Conflict' in Moore, J.N. (ed), *Law and Civil War in the Modern World*, John Hopkins University Press: Baltimore.

Schechterman, B. and Slann, M. (1993), eds, *The Ethnic Dimension in International Relations*, Westport: Boulder.

Schemerhorn, R.R. (1978), *Comparative Ethnic Relations*, University of Chicago Press: Chicago.

Schiff, Z. and Ya'ari, E. (1984), *Israel's Lebanon War*, Allen and Unwin: London. Translated by I. Friedman.

Schlesinger Jr., A.M. (1978), *Robert Kennedy and His Times*, Houghton Mifflin: Boston.

Schou, A. (1989), 'The breakdown of conflict management in Lebanon', *Bulletin of Peace Proposals*, vol. 20, no. 2.

Schwarz, W. (1986), *The Tamils of Sri Lanka*, Minority Rights Group: London.

Segal, D.R. and Gravino, K.S. (1985), 'Peacekeeping as a Military Mission' in Smith, C.D., ed, *The Hundred Percent Challenge:* Seven Locks Press: Washington D.C.

Sesay, A. (1989a), 'The OAU Peace-keeping force in Chad: What are the lessons for the future?', unpublished paper.

Sesay, A. (1989b), 'The OAU force in Chad: Some lessons for future operations', *Current Research on Peace and Violence*, vol. 12, no. 4.

Shamir, M. (1991), 'Political intolerance among masses and elites in Israel', *Journal of Politics*, vol. 53, no. 4.

Shanmugaratnam, H. (1989), 'Seven days in Jaffna: Life under Indian occupation', *Race and Class*, vol. 31, no. 2.

Sherif, M. (1967), *Group Conflict and Cooperation*, Routledge: London.

Sherif, M. (1969), 'Experiments in Group Conflict' in *Science, Conflict and Society*, a collection of readings from the *Scientific American*, W.H. Freeman: San Francisco.

Shiels, F.L. (1984), ed, *Ethnic Separatism and World Politics*, University Press of America: Lanham.

Sierpowski, S. (1990),'Minorities and the League of Nations' in P. Smith, ed, *Ethnic Groups in International Relations*, Dartmouth: Aldershot.

Simpson, J. (1990-91), 'The two Canadas', *Foreign Policy*, no. 81.

Sipos, P. (1991), Nationality conflicts and the democratic alternative in the Austro-Hungarian monarchy and its successors' in U. Ra'anan et al., eds, *State and Nation in Multi-ethnic Societies*, Manchester University Press: Manchester.

Skjelsbaek, K. (1991), 'The UN Secretary-General and the mediation of international disputes', Journal of Peace Research, vol. 28, no. 1.

Skogmo, B. (1988), *UNIFIL: International Peacekeeping in Lebanon, 1978-1988*, Lynne Rienner: Boulder.

Smith, A.D. (1971), *Theories of Nationalism*: Duckworth: London.

Smith, A.D. (1981), *The Ethnic Revival*, Cambridge University Press: Cambridge

Smith, A.D. (1982), 'Nationalism, Separatism and the Intelligentsia' in Williams, C.H., ed, *National Separatism*, University of Wales Press: Cardiff.

Smith, A.D. (1986a), *The Ethnic Origin of Nations*, Blackwell: Oxford.

Smith, A.D. (1986b), 'History and liberty: Dilemmas of loyalty in Western democracies', *Ethnic and Racial Studies*, vol. 9, no.1.

Smith, A.D. (1986c), 'Conflict and Collective Identity: Class, Ethnie and Nation' in Azar, E. and Burton, J.W., eds, *International Conflict Resolution*, Wheatsheaf: Brighton.

Smith, A.D. (1991), *National Identity*, Penguin: Harmondsworth.

Smith, A.D. (1993), 'Ties that bind', *LSE Review,* London School of Economics: London.

Smith, G., (1990) ed, *The Nationalities Question in the Soviet Union*, Longman: London.

Smith, M. (1991), *Burma: Insurgency and the Politics of Ethnicity*, Zed Press: London.

Smith, M.G. (1971), 'Some Developments in the Analytic Study of Pluralism', in Kuper, L. and Smith, M.G., eds, *Pluralism in Africa*, University of California Press: Berkeley.

Smith, M.G. (1986), 'Pluralism, Violence and the Modern State' in Kazancigil, A. (ed), *The State in Global Perspective*, Gower/UNESCO: Paris.

Smith, M.G. (1988), 'Pluralism, Race and Ethnicity in Selected African Countries' in Rex, J. and Mason, D., eds, *Theories of Race and Ethnic*

Relations, Cambridge University Press: Cambridge.

Smyth, J. (1991), 'Weasels in a hole: Ideologies of the Irish conflict' in Y. Alexander and A. O'Day, eds, *The Irish Terrorism Experience*, Dartmouth: Aldershot.

Smooha, S. (1987), 'Jewish and Arab ethnocentrism in Israel', *Ethnic and Racial Studies*, vol.10, no. 1.

Smooha, S. (1989), *Arabs and Jews in Israel. Volume One: Conflicting and Shared Attitudes in a Divided Society*, Westview: Boulder.

Smooha, S. (1990), 'Israeli options for handling the Palestinians in the West Bank and Gaza Strip' in van den Perghe, P.L.,ed, *State Violence and Ethnicity*, University Press of Colorado: Niwot.

Smooha, S. (1992), *Arabs and Jews in Israel. Volume Two: Change and Continuity in Mutual Intolerance*, Westview: Boulder.

Snyder, L.L. (1982), *Global Macro-Nationalisms*, Greenwood: Westport.

Snyder, L.L. (1990), *Encyclopedia of Nationalism*, St. James Press: Chicago.

Sohn, L.B. (1981), 'The Rights of Minorities' in Henkin, L., ed, *The International Bill of Rights*, Columbia University Press: New York.

Sohn, L.B. and Buergenthal, T. (1973), *International Protection of Human Rights*, Bobbs-Merrill Company: New York.

Sorensen, M. (1956), 'The quest for equality', *International Conciliation*, No. 507, March.

Souter, D. (1989), 'The Cyprus conundrum', *Third World Quarterly*, vol. 11, no. 2.

Spillmann, K.R. and Spillmann, K. (1991), 'On enemy images and conflict escalation', *International Social Science Journal*, no. 127.

Stavenhagen, R. (1990), *The Ethnic Question: Conflict, Development and Human Rights*, UN University Press: Tokyo.

Stavenhagen, R. (1991), 'Ethnic conflicts and their impact on international society', *International Social Science Journal*, No. 127.

Stedman, S.J. (1991), *Peacemaking in Civil War: International Mediation in Zimbabwe*, Lynne Rienner: Boulder.

Sterling, R.W. (1979), 'Ethnic Separation in the International System' in Hall, A.L., ed, *Ethnic Autonomy-Comparative Dynamics*: Pergamon: New York.

Stegenga, J.A. (1968), *The United Nations Force in Cyprus*, Ohio State University Press.

Stone, J. (1985), *Racial Conflict in Contemporary Society*, Fontana: London.

Sroebe, W. et al. (1988), 'Familiarity may breed contempt' in Stroebe, W. et al., eds, *The Social Psychology of Intergroup Conflict*, Springer-Verlag: London.

Suganami, H. (1983), 'The structure of institutionalism', *International*

Relations, vol. 9, no. 5.

Suhrke, A.S. and Noble, L.G.N. (1977), eds, *Ethnic Conflict in International Relations*, Praeger: New York.

Survival (1993), special edition on ethnic conflict and international security, vol. 35, no.1.

Survival International (1992), *Survival*, no. 30.

Suter, K. (1982), *East Timor and West Irian*, Minority Rights Group: London.

Tagil, S. (1984), ed, *Regions in Upheaval: Ethnic Conflict and Political Mobilization*, Scandinavian University Books.

Taylor, C. (1992), *Multiculturalism and the "Politics of Recognition"*, Princeton University Press: Princeton.

Teger, T.I. (1980), *Too Much Invested to Quit*, Pergamon: New York.

Thakur, R. (1987a), *International Peacekeeping in the Lebanon*, Westview: Boulder.

Thakur, R. (1987b), 'International peacekeeping, United Nations authority and United States power' in *Alternatives*, vol. 12, no. 4.

Thakur, R. (1988), 'International Peacekeeping' in Thakur, R. , ed, *International Conflict Resolution*, Westview: Boulder.

Thomas, F.A. (1985), *Race Relations and Ethnicity*, Ford Foundation.

Thornberry, P. (1980), 'Minority rights, human rights and international law', *Ethnic and Racial Studies,* vol. 3, no. 3

Thornberry, P. (1990), *International Law and the Rights of Minorities*, Clarendon Press: Oxford.

Thornberry, P. (1993), 'The United Nations declaration: background, analysis and observations' in Phillips, A. and Rosas, A., eds, *The United Nations Minority Rights Declaration*, Abo Akademie: Abo.

Toth, K. (1988), 'The Role of the Church in Conflict Resolution' in Thakur, R. (ed), *International Conflict Resolution*, Westview: Boulder.

Touval, S. and Zartman, I.W. (1985), eds, *International Mediation in Theory and Practice*, Westview: Boulder.

Tripathi, D. (1987), 'Sri Lanka's elusive peace', *World Today*, November.

Tripathi, D. (1988), 'India's foreign policy: The Rajiv factor', *World Today*, July.

Tully, M. and Jacob, S. (1986), *Amritsar,* Jonathan Cape: London.

U Thant (1977), *View From the United Nations*, David and Charles: Newton Abbot.

United States United Nations Association (1969), *Controlling Conflict in the 1970s*, United Nations Association: New York.

Urquhart, B. (1987), *A Life in Peace and War*, Weidenfeld and Nicolson: London.

Urquhart, B. (1988), 'A risky business...',*UN Chronicle*, vol. 25, no.4.

Ury, W. (1987), 'Strengthening international mediation', *Negotiation Journal*, vol. 3, no. 3.

van den Berghe, P.L. (1971), 'Pluralism and the Polity: A Theoretical Perspective' in Kuper, L. and Smith, M.G., eds, *Pluralism in Africa*, University of California Press: Berkeley.

van den Berghe, P.L. (1981a), *The Ethnic Phenomenon*, Elsevier: New York.

van den Berghe, P. L. (1981b), 'Protection of Ethnic Minorities: A Critical Appraisal' in Wirsing, R.G., ed, *Protection of Ethnic Minorities: Comparative Perspectives*, Pergamon: New York,

van den Berghe, P.L. (1990), ed, *State Violence and Ethnicity*, University Press of Colorado: Niwot.

van der Merwe, H. (1989), *Pursuing Justice and Peace in South Africa*, Routledge: London.

van Dyke, V. (1985), *Human Rights, Ethnicity and Discrimination*, Greenwood: Westport.

Vayrynen, R. (1991), ed, *New Developments in Conflict Theory: Conflict Resolution and Conflict Transformation,* Sage: London.

Vincent, R.J. (1974), *Non-Intervention and International Order*, Princeton University Press: Princeton.

Vincent, R.J. (1986), 'Introduction' in Freedman, L. et al., *Terrorism and International Order*, Routledge and Kegan Paul: London.

Vishinski,B. (1977), ed, *The Ohrid Seminar on Minorities*, Macedonian Review: Skopje.

Vishniak, M. (1945), 'The international protection of minorities and the international bill of rights', *International Postwar Problems*, vol. 2, no. 3.

Volkan, V.D. (1989), 'Psychoanalytic aspects of ethnic conflict' in Montville, J., ed, *Conflict and Peacemaking in Multiethnic Societies*, Lexington Books: Lexington.

Volkan, V.D. (1990), 'An overview of psychological concepts pertinent to interethnic and/or international relationships' in Volkan, V.D. et al., eds, *The Psychodynamics of International Relationships*, Lexington Books: Lexington.

Walker, R.B.J. (1988), *One World, Many Worlds*, Lynne Rienner: Boulder.

Wall, J.A. (1981), 'Mediation', *Journal of Conflict Resolution*, vol.25, no.1.

Waltz, K. (1959), *Man, the State and War*, Columbia University Press: New York.

Walzer, M. (1977), *Just and Unjust Wars*, Penguin: Harmondsworth.

Walzer, M. et al. (1982), *The Politics of Ethnicity*, Belknap Press: Cambridge MA.

Warren, R.L. (1987), 'American Friends' Service Committee Mediation

Efforts in Germany and Korea' in McDonald, J.W. and Bendahmane, D.B, eds, *Conflict Resolution - Track Two Diplomacy,* US State Department: Washington.

Warren, W. (1980), *Imperialism: Pioneer of Capitalism,* Verso: London.

Wedge, B. (1990), 'The individual, the group and war' in Burton, J.W. and Dukes, F., eds, *Conflict: Readings in Management and Resolution,* Macmillan: Basingstoke.

Wehr, P. (1979), *Conflict Regulation,* Westview: Boulder.

Weiner, (1974), 'Rumblings in the street', *Fortnight,* no. 76.

Whitaker, B. et al. (1982), *The Biharis of Bangladesh,* Minority Rights Group: London.

Whitaker, B. (1988), 'Genocide: The Ultimate Crime' in Davies, P., ed, *Human Rights,* Routledge: London.

Whitaker, M.P. (1990), 'A compound of many histories: the many of an east coast Tamil community' in J. Spencer, ed, *Sri Lanka: History and the Roots of Conflict,* Routledge: London.

White, S. (1990), *Gorbachev in Power,* Cambridge University Press: Cambridge.

Whyte, J. H. (1986), 'How is the boundary maintained between the two communities in Northern Ireland?', *Ethnic and Racial Studies,* vol. 9, no. 2.

Whyte, J.H. (1990), *Interpreting Northern Ireland.* Clarendon Press: Oxford.

Williams, R. (1989), *Resources of Hope,* Verso: London.

Wilson, A.J. (1988), *The Break-up of Sri Lanka,* C. Hurst: London.

Wirsing, R.G. (1981), ed, *Protection of Minorities: Comparative Perspectives,* Pergamon, New York.

Wirth, L. (1945), 'The Protection of Minority Groups' in Linton, P., ed, *The Science of Man in the World Crisis,* Columbia University Press: New York.

Wiseman, H. (1983), ed, *Peacekeeping: Appraisal and Proposals,* International Peace Academy: New York.

Woodhouse, T. (1991), 'Making peace: The work of Adam Curle' in Woodhouse, T., ed, *Peacemaking in a Troubled World,* Berg: New York.

Woodhouse, T. (1991), ed, *Peacemaking in a Troubled World,* Berg: New York.

Wu, D.Y.H. (1982), ed, *Ethnicity and Interpersonal Interaction,* Maruzen Asia: Singapore.

Young, C. (1985), 'Ethnicity and the Colonial and Post-colonial States in Africa' in Brass, P., ed, *Ethnic Groups and the State,* Barnes and Noble: Tatawa NJ.

Zariski, R. (1989), 'Ethnic extremism among ethnoterritorial minorities in Western Europe', *Comparative Politics*, vol. 21, no. 3.

Zartman, I.W. (1985), *Ripe for Resolution: Conflict and Intervention in Africa*, Oxford University Press: New York.

Zartman, I.W. (1986), 'Conflict in Chad' in Day, A.R. and Doyle, M.W., eds, *Escalation and Intervention*, Westview: Boulder.

Zartman, I.W. (1989), *Ripe for Resolution, Oxford University Press*: Oxford.

Ziedler, F.P. (1984), 'Hysteria in Wartime: Domestic Pressure on Ethnics and Aliens' in van Horne, W.A., ed, *Ethnicity and War*, University of Wisconsin: Milwaukee.

Index

Armenia
 ethnocentrism in 82
 irredentist policies of 7, 85, 90
 peace-keeping in 187
 Turkish genocide 13, 57, 62
armies *see* military
Arthur, P. 51 (n.2) 70, 149
Assefa, H. 109
assimmilation
 forced 9-11, 33, 55-9, 61, 215
 theory 16-18, 19, 20, 21, 29, 141,
  204, 206-7, 227
attitudes
 contact hypothesis and 133-4
 strategies to change 102-3, 115
  education 147-9, 194, 195, 230
  prejudice reduction 95, 149-51
 see also peace-building
Australia 34
Austria
 consociationalism in 43, 45, 232
 protection of minorities in 200,
  224 (n.1)
autonomy 231-2, 236
Avruch, K. 112
Azar, E.E. 6, 19, 67, 72, 92, 96,
 108, 113, 115, 118, 141, 143,
 144, 192, 197
Azcarate, P. de 203
Azerbaijan 2, 7, 85, 90, 187, 206

Bagley, J.H. 16
Bailey, S. 191
Baker, E. 31
Ball, G. 17
Banac, I. 32
Bangladesh
 decolonization of 2
 Indian intervention in 65
 instability in 6
 oppression of ethnic minorities in 13,
  38
 separation of 38, 39, 72, 156
 state of emergency in 104
 UN non-involvement in 156
Banks, M. 19, 110
Banton, M. 40
Barth, F. 21
Basques 2, 10, 36, 232
Beddard, R. 233
Beitz, C.R. 157
Belfrage, S. 81, 88, 100 (n.7)
Belgium
 consociationalism in 34, 42, 43, 45,
  232

Belgium (contd.)
 oppression of ethnic minorities in 61
 separation of 139
Bell, D. 86, 96, 150
Bell, W. 21
Bengalis 13, 38
Bercovitch, J. 107
Berg, R. 145
Bertelsen, J.S. 25 (n.3)
Biharis 38
Bizman, A. 133
Black, P. 112
Bloed, A. 233
Bosnia and Hercegovina
 intervention in 115-16
 oppression of ethnic minorities in 211
 peace-keeping by UN in 158, 168,
  169-70, 171-2, 198 (n.1), 234-5
 NATO support for 172, 186, 187
 refugees from 85
 self-determination in 222
 separation of 37, 39, 50, 51 (n.4)
Boulding, E. 91, 130
Boutros-Ghali, B. 172, 195-6
Boyce, G. 58
Bretons 2, 36
Brown, R. 131-2, 133
Buber, M. 135, 227, 231
Buckheit, L.C. 39, 71-2, 156
Buddhists 38, 59, 82, 90, 179
 see also Sinhalese
Budiardjo, C. 14
Buergenthal, T. 16
Bulgaria
 ineffective peace-building in 119-20
 irredentist policies of 7
 protection of ethnic minorities in 200,
  224 (n.1)
 Turkish minority in 2, 9, 10-11, 55,
  119-20, 200, 224 (n.4)
Bull, H. 18, 63
Bulletin of Peace Proposals 25 (n.3)
Burghers 179
Burma
 decolonization of 2
 isolationist policies of 66
 oppression of ethnic minorities in 9, 59
 refugees from 14
Burton, F. 78, 100 (n.7)
Burton, J.W. 19, 22, 72, 108, 192-3,
 197, 232
 human needs theory of 110-12, 115,
  120
 problem solving workshops (PSW)
  112-13, 114-15

Burundi 9, 13, 58-9, 211
Butterfield, H. 95, 122
Byers, R.B. 145

Cairns, E. 94, 136
Cairo Agreement 175
Calderwood, H.B. 204
Calvocoressi, P. 60
Campaign for Social Democracy 182
Canada
  consociationalism 42, 43, 66, 67,
    232
  economic development in 142
  multicultural policy of 231
  peace-building in 131, 142
Capotorti report 224 (n.4)
Carment, D.B. 25 (n.3)
Carter Center 109, 128 (n.3)
Catalans 2, 232
Ceadal. M. 61
Central African Federation 34
Chad
  intervention in 65, 173, 174
  oppression of ethnic minorities in 9
  peace-keeping by OAU in 105, 127,
    159, 173-5, 187, 229
Chaliand, G. 57
Chalk, F. 13
Charter of Paris for a New Europe
  (1990) 233, 238 (n.1)
Chaudhuri, B. 10, 38
Chazan, N. 47
Childe, J. 105, 173
China
  oppression of ethnic minorities in 10
    13, 58, 211
Chittagong Hill Tribes 38
Chomsky, N. 184
Christie, C.J. 235
Christision, K.M. 55
Church, C.H. 46, 50
Clammer, J. 46
class consciousness 17, 20
Claude, I.L. 31, 56, 59, 192, 200,
  203, 204, 205, 207-8, 214, 215
Clausewitz, C. von 101-2
Cobban, H. 163, 173
cognitive relativism 98
Cohen, P. 40
Cohen, S. 113
Colban, E. 224 (n.2)
Cole, S. 144
colonialism 2, 33, 54, 73 (n.1),
  220, 221-2
competition, economic 32-3

Condor, S. 132
Conference on Security and Cooperation in
  Europe (CSCE) 233
confidence building 145-7, 194, 230
Congo
  decolonization of 2
  peace-keeping in 158, 208-9
  peace-making in 190
separation of 38
Connor, W. 3, 5, 21, 63, 232
Conroy, M. 85, 88, 100 (n.7)
consociational democracy 22, 33-4, 42,
  43-6, 49-50, 52-3, 66-7, 163, 228,
  232
constitutions, written 43, 45-6, 56, 57,
  60, 61, 64, 107, 160
contacts, intercommunal
  contact hypothesis 131-4
  plus confidence building 145-7, 194,
    230
  plus economic development 130, 141-5,
    152 (n.2), 194-5, 230, 236-7
  plus education 147-9, 194, 195, 230
  plus forgiveness 134-7, 138-9, 152
    (n.1), 230
  plus prejudice reduction 95, 149-51
  plus superordinate goals 137-41, 143,
    194, 230
  restrictions on 123-5, 126
  right to maintain 220
containment of conflict 68-9
controls on conflict 96-7, 102
cornucopianism 141
Corrymeela 135, 136, 152 (n.1)
Corsica 2, 231
Coser, L. 60
costs of ethnic conflict 79, 92-3, 143
Cotonou Peace Agreement 186
Coulon, C. 56
Crick, B. 40
Crimea 37
Cristescu report 221
Croatia
  discrimination in 59
  ethnocentrism in 83-4
  peace-keeping by UN in 158, 168,
    171, 172
  refugees from 85
  self-determination in 222
  separation of 37, 39
  see also Croats
Croats 14, 57, 66, 77, 82, 83, 84,
  85, 168, 169, 170, 171
  see also Croatia
Cross, M. 40, 41

nationalism (contd.)
    identification with the state 3, 21, 52,
      55-9, 60, 65-6, 71, 155-6, 191,
      205, 223-4, 229, 231-5, 237
    neglect of in mainstream international
      relations 16-19
    see also ethnocentrism, increased
National Patriotic Front for Liberia
    (NPLF) 184-5
Noth Atlantic Treaty Organization (NATO)
    peace-keeping by 160, 172, 186, 187
NATO Today 238 (n.1)
Netherlands 43
Neuberger, B. 7, 17, 63, 220
Neuman, S.G. 25 (n.3)
neutrality 66
Neve Shalom 135, 136
Nicaragua 61, 195, 231
Nicosia Master Plan 194-5, 230
Niederhauser, E. 57
Nielsson, G.P. 3
Nigeria
    decolonization of 2
    domination of ECOMOG by 185, 186
    expulsion by 12
    hegemonic exchange in 48
    internal refugees (Ibos) 15
    oppression of ethnic minorities 211
    peace-making in 109
    separation of 38, 233
    UN non-involvement in 156
Noble, L.G.N. 25 (n.3), 67-9
Nordlinger, E.A. 44-5
Northedge, F.S. 65, 108
Northrup, T.A. 81
Norway 38
Nuremburg Tribunal 210

OAU *see* Organization of African Unity
Obaseki, N.O. 173
Oberg, J. 89
Occupied Territories *see* Gaza; West Bank
O'Connell, J. 123
O'Connor, C.M. 225 (n.7)
Okoli, E. 206
O'Leary, B. 37, 49, 51 (n.2), 211
Omaar, R. 25 (n.2)
O'Malley, P. 64, 80
O'Neill, W. 184, 186
Operation Iron Mind 177
Operation Liberation 180
Operation Litani 163
Oppenheim, A.N. 113
oppression of ethnic minorities
    A-B-C paradox and 37-8

oppression of ethnic minorities (contd.)
    economic development and 142-3
    ethical norms and 199
    fear of ethnic minorities and 60-62
    and national self-determination 54-9
    structural dominance and 35-6
    types of 9-14
    see also genocide; and *under names of
      individual countries*, e.g. Iraq
Opsahl Commission 94
optimistic approach *see* consociational
    democracy; hegemonic exchange
Organization of African Unity (OAU) 105,
    126, 159, 173-5, 187, 229, 233-4
Organization of American States 173
Orwell, G. 37
Osgood, C.E. 145
Ossetians 7
Oueddei, Goukouni 173-4, 175
Owen, David Anthony Llewellyn 50,
    51 (n.4), 170

Paisley, Rev. Ian 89-90
Pakistan
    Indian war with 65, 180
    irredentism in 7
    oppression of ethnic minorities in 13,
      211
    state of emergency in 104
    see also Bangladesh
Palestine
    Arab-Jewish relations in 2, 85, 133-4
    decolonization of 2
    peace-building in 133-4
    separation in 85
    see also Palestinians
Palestinians
    influx into Lebanon 163
    Jews and 2, 35, 48, 49, 55, 58, 60,
      62, 82, 87-8, 90, 109, 113, 123,
      124-5, 133-4, 135, 136, 137, 140,
      142-3, 144, 147, 148, 176-7, 190,
      222
    refugees 14, 15, 53, 62
    right to self-determination 54, 73 (n.2),
      124, 221, 222, 225 (n.8)
    UNDP assistance to 195
    see also Palestinians
Panic, Nenad 83
Paraguay 13, 211
Parekh, B. 135, 147, 148
Parker, P.L. 218, 225 (n.7)
Paul, D.W. 56
peace-building 23, 98, 127, Ch.5
    combining strategies for 151-2

proportional representation 43, 44, 45, 119, 228
Pruitt, D.G. 78, 79, 125, 139, 146
psychological distancing 78, 79, 87-9, 99 (n.2), 133, 134, 148, 149, 150, 196
Punjab 2, 9, 55, 87, 104

Ra'anan, U. 232
Rabushka, A. 34, 51 (n.1)
racial divisions 51 (n.3)
Rajanayagam-Hellman, D. 59
Ramcharan, B.G. 156
Ramet, S.P. 19, 36, 92, 99 (n.2)
Rapaport, A. 102
rational choice approach 40, 48, 97
reconciliation approach 134-7, 138-9, 152 (n.1), 230
re-entry problem 118, 133
Rees, M. 119
refugees 12-13, 14-15, 84-5, 92-3, 182, 195
Reich, W. 58
Reinerson, K. 217, 225 (n.7)
Reiss, H. 60, 97
rejectionist groups 5
religion, right to practise 208, 210, 213, 214, 218-20, 222, 223, 230, 231, 233, 237
reservationist groups 5
Rex, J. 22
Rhode, G.F. 149
Rikhye, I.J. 159
Riley, S.R. 184
Roberts, A. 25 (n.2)
Robinson, J. 203, 204
Robinson, N. 210
Rogers, R.R. 147
Ronen, D. 17, 220
Rorty, R. 151
Rose, R. 122, 141-2, 143
Rosen, F. 56
Rotfeld, A.D. 145
Rothchild, D. 36, 40, 43, 47
Rothman, J. 101, 116
Royal Institute of International Affairs 204
Ruane, J. 136
Rubenstein, R.E. 8
Rubin, J.Z. 78, 79, 107, 139, 146
Ruhasyankiko, N. 211-12
Rumania 61, 200, 203
Rumanians 57
Rupesinghe, K. 23, 116, 182
Russell, F.M. 30

Russia
peace-building in 144
Rwanda 121
Ryan, S. 25 (n.3), 98, 118, 152 (n.2), 160

Sabaratnam, L. 198 (n.2)
sacrifice trap 91-2
Said, A.A. 25 (n.3)
Said, E.W. 66, 147
Saito, N. 189
Samarsinghe, S.W.R. de A. 24
Sampson, A. 138
sanctification 79, 89-90
Saravanamuttu, P. 184
Sawyer, Amos 185-6
scapegoating 88-9, 134, 196
Schachter, O. 157-8
Schechterman, B. 25 (n.3)
Scheffer, D.J. 221, 235
Schermerhorn, R.R. 31
Schiff, Z. 134
Schlesinger, Jr. A.M. 135
Schou, A. 141, 163
Schwartz, W. 198 (n.2)
Scimecca, J. 112
Scotland
ethnic revival in 2
secession see separation
Segal, D.R. 105
self-determination 54-9, 63, 65-6, 71-2, 124, 199-200, 228, 229, 235
internal autonomy 231-2, 236
OAU attitude to 233-4
UN attitude to 73 (n.2), 124, 155-6, 191, 205, 208-9, 216, 220-22, 225 (n.8), 230
separation
argumenst for and against 32, 35, 36-9
and dynamics of ethnic conflict 78-9, 84-6
see also self-determination; and under names of individual states, e.g. Cyprus
Serbia
ethnocentrism in 83
irredentism by 7
peace-keeping by UN in 168, 169, 172
refugees from 85, 93
and right to self-determination 222
see also Serbs
Serbs 7, 14, 32, 37, 57, 59, 66, 82, 83, 85, 168, 170, 171, 198, 222, 234-5
see also Serbia
Sesay, A. 174, 175

284

White, S. 17
Whyte, J.H. 84, 92, 96, 143, 147
Williams, R. 4
Wilson, A.J. 50, 181
Wilson, Thomas Woodrow 31, 206, 220
see also Wilsonian postulate
Wilsonian postulate 68, 200
Wirth, L. 224 (n.2)
Wiseman, H. 177
Woodhouse, T. 78, 107, 113, 193
world society paradigm 19, 110
Worrall, S. 135
Wu, D.Y.H. 40

Ya'ari, E. 134
Young, C. 54
Yugoslavia
  draft on rights of minorities 218-19
  economic effects of conflict 92-3
  ethnocentrism in 82-4
  expulsion from 12-13
  hostility towards independent media in 83
  instability of 32-3
  non-alignment of 66
  oppression of ethnic minorities in 2, 61, 171-2, 211, 222

Yugoslavia (contd.)
  peace-keeping in 105, 122, 158, 168-72, 186, 187, 188, 198 (n.1), 234-5
  peace-making in 108-9, 122
  protection of ethnic minorities in 200, 211
  psychological distancing in 88, 99 (n.2)
  refugees from 12-13, 14
  separation of 2, 37, 39, 50, 82, 85, 228
  see also Bosnia and Hercegovina; Croatia; Macedonia; Montenegro; Serbia; Slovenia

Zambia 48
Zariski, R. 24
Zartman, I.W. 87, 107, 108, 114, 115, 121, 174
Zimbabwe
  hegemonic exchange in 48
  Lancaster House Agreement 115
  peace-making in 114
  state of emergency in 104
zonal functional system 232

286